THE COMPLETE IDIOT'S GUIDE® TO

Live Auctions

by the National Auctioneers Association

ALPHA

A member of Penguin Group (USA) Inc.

This book is dedicated to the many auctioneers who contributed information to this project and to those who helped build the live auction industry since its inception.

ALPHA BOOKS

Published by the Penguin Group

Penguin Group (USA) Inc., 375 Hudson Street, New York, New York 10014, USA

Penguin Group (Canada), 90 Eglinton Avenue East, Suite 700, Toronto, Ontario M4P 2Y3, Canada (a division of Pearson Penguin Canada Inc.)

Penguin Books Ltd., 80 Strand, London WC2R 0RL, England

Penguin Ireland, 25 St. Stephen's Green, Dublin 2, Ireland (a division of Penguin Books Ltd.)

Penguin Group (Australia), 250 Camberwell Road, Camberwell, Victoria 3124, Australia (a division of Pearson Australia Group Pty. Ltd.)

Penguin Books India Pvt. Ltd., 11 Community Centre, Panchsheel Park, New Delhi—110 017, India

Penguin Group (NZ), 67 Apollo Drive, Rosedale, North Shore, Auckland 1311, New Zealand (a division of Pearson New Zealand Ltd.)

Penguin Books (South Africa) (Pty.) Ltd., 24 Sturdee Avenue, Rosebank, Johannesburg 2196, South Africa

Penguin Books Ltd., Registered Offices: 80 Strand, London WC2R 0RL, England

Copyright © 2008 by National Auctioneers Association

International Standard Book Number: 978-1-59257-641-8
Library of Congress Catalog Card Number: 2007939739

10 09 08   8 7 6 5 4 3 2 1

Interpretation of the printing code: The rightmost number of the first series of numbers is the year of the book's printing; the rightmost number of the second series of numbers is the number of the book's printing. For example, a printing code of 08-1 shows that the first printing occurred in 2008.

Printed in the United States of America

Note: This publication contains the opinions and ideas of its author. It is intended to provide helpful and informative material on the subject matter covered. It is sold with the understanding that the author and publisher are not engaged in rendering professional services in the book. If the reader requires personal assistance or advice, a competent professional should be consulted.

The author and publisher specifically disclaim any responsibility for any liability, loss, or risk, personal or otherwise, which is incurred as a consequence, directly or indirectly, of the use and application of any of the contents of this book.

Most Alpha books are available at special quantity discounts for bulk purchases for sales promotions, premiums, fund-raising, or educational use. Special books, or book excerpts, can also be created to fit specific needs.

For details, write: Special Markets, Alpha Books, 375 Hudson Street, New York, NY 10014.

Publisher: *Marie Butler-Knight*
Editorial Director: *Mike Sanders*
Senior Managing Editor: *Billy Fields*
Senior Acquisitions Editor: *Paul Dinas*
Development Editor: *Nancy D. Lewis*
Senior Production Editor: *Janette Lynn*
Copy Editor: *Tricia Liebig*

Cartoonist: *Steve Barr*
Cover Designer: *Kurt Owens*
Book Designer: *Trina Wurst*
Indexer: *Johnna Vanhoose Dinse*
Layout: *Eric S. Miller*
Proofreader: *Mary Hunt*

Contents at a Glance

Contents

Appendixes

Introduction

Are you a frequent attendee and bidder at live auctions? Or interested in attending your first live auction?

Whatever category you fall into, you want to know how this process works and look like a pro. You can find your way through to success by trial and error, but why not come armed with knowledge?

That's where *The Complete Idiot's Guide to Live Auctions* comes in. It's a results-oriented, practical advice guidebook for anyone at live auctions.

Live auctions have been drawing crowds to this unusual form of selling since the idea first dawned on someone to hold up an item in front of a group and ask "How much will you pay for this?"

Ever since then, buyers and sellers have been learning the details of this method to get the most out of it that they can. And that's the point of this book: to help you as a buyer or seller be successful at a live auction.

More people today are hearing about, and attending, live auctions than ever before in history. This is partly due to a growing number of television shows that feature live auctions and appraising (estimating prices at live auctions or other methods of sale). These shows are not only entertaining audiences, but they are educating auction attendees and are drawing bigger crowds to local live auctions.

One of the most popular shows for years has been Public Television's *Antiques Roadshow*, where appraisers (many of whom are also auctioneers) analyze, describe, and provide a price valuation for items brought by average citizens. *Antiques Roadshow*, which began in England in the 1970s, migrated to the United States and then Canada. Many auctioneers credit this show with a surge in interest in collectibles and with people bringing items to auction.

Other popular shows include *Cash in the Attic*, which shows items from the attic taken through the auction process, and *Bargain Hunt*. Real estate-related shows include *Houses Under the Hammer* and *Flip That House*. There is also auto-auction television coverage on the Speed channel on many cable television systems. These shows are evidence that there is a growing public appetite for auctions, but the side benefits are that these shows are doing substantial education about the auction process. In *Cash in the Attic*, for instance, the viewer sees the process from start to finish, especially the valuation and bidding processes.

There has also been an increase in the local and national coverage of auctions on news programs. A three-minute segment on NBC's *The Today Show* morning program recently showed what is needed to become an auctioneer. The NBC reporter visited an auction school and interviewed auction contest champions. Another factor driving the increase in crowds to live auctions is the Internet site eBay.com, where people bid on items in a process similar to an auction. eBay gets people excited about the auction process and has drawn them to visit their local live auctions.

A Short History of Live Auctions

You can sound like a real pro at your next auction if you tell the auctioneer a bit of the following history. He or she will probably step back in amazement at your knowledge! Records handed down from ancient Greeks document auctions occurring as far back as 500 B.C. At that time, women were auctioned off as wives. And, in fact, it was considered illegal to allow a daughter to be "sold" outside the auction method.

A descending method was used for these auctions, starting with a high price and going lower until the first person to bid was the purchaser, as long as the minimum price set by the seller was met. The buyer could get a return of money if he and his new spouse did not get along well. Women with special beauty were subject to the most vigorous bidding and the prices paid were high. Owners of the less attractive women had to add monetary offers to make the sale.

In Rome, Italy, around the time of Christ, auctions were popular for family estates and to sell war plunder. Roman emperor and philosopher Marcus Aurelius sold family furniture at auctions for months, to satisfy debts. Roman soldiers sold war plunder at auctions. The licensed auctioneer, called the Magister Auctionarium, drove a spear into the ground to start the auction. Today we use an auction gavel.

American auctions date back to the Pilgrims' arrival on America's eastern shores in the 1600s and continued in popularity during colonization with the sale of crops, imports, clapboard, livestock, tools, tobacco, slaves, and even entire farms. Selling at auction was the fastest and most efficient means to convert assets into cash. Fur and tobacco were sold in volume in the early colonies. In the spring of each year, the auction method was used to sell raw rug pelts to the European merchants who arranged the transcontinental voyage to the Old World.

When the ships returned to the port in Europe, the pelts were auctioned to manufacturers, who would process them for the retail market. The early fur trade was chiefly responsible for the settlement and development of North America.

In the American Civil War years of the early 1860s, auctions were also used to sell war plunder. Many auction schools started in the early 1900s in America. The Jones' National School of Auctioneering and Oratory was believed to be the first. Although finding goods to sell was not a problem in those days, auctioneers faced other challenges. There was no amplification system for their voices—no microphones as we know them today. So they had trouble both being heard, and keeping their voices intact. Because travel was more difficult, and was mostly by horse and wagon, auctioneers enticed crowds by routinely offering lunch to those who came to the sale. Weather often dictated the time the auction started, as all were held outdoors.

The growth of the auction industry remained until the Great Depression of 1929. Some auctioneers traveled the country to liquidate the estates of farmers whose farms had failed because of drought and bank foreclosures. The decline of the auction method of marketing followed the poor economic climate and did not rebound until after World War II.

Auctioneering began to make great strides after World War II. The sale of goods and real estate was booming. There was a need in certain cases to move real estate and personal property faster than the private market would allow. Thus, the modern day auction business was born. Auctioneers were now businessmen who dressed in suits and ties. They began to nurture the business and raise the reputation of auctioneers. Besides the public, auctioneers began to have links to banks, attorneys, accountants, the court system, and government agencies.

During the 1990s, auctioneers were using computers, fax machines, cell phones, and other technology to make their businesses run faster and more smoothly. Some auctioneers began taking photographs of small auction items and projecting them onto big screens so the crowds could get a closer look at the merchandise. Auctions burst into cyberspace in the middle of the decade. The ever flourishing eBay was launched in 1995 and would go on to become an online leader in the bidding business. Many auctioneers today offer both live and online auctions to meet the needs of customers near and far. Technology allows buyers to participate in the sale without even being there.

How to Use This Book

This book is designed for easy understanding by the average person. You need not be a regular attendee of live auctions to get tips here, but there is much helpful information for the auction veteran, also. The chapters follow a logical order, describing the basics, and moving through the buying and selling processes. Feel free to skip ahead to a section that looks most interesting to you, and to keep this book for reference (take it with you to auctions!). The chapters are divided into four parts. They are:

In **Part 1, "What Is a Live Auction?,"** you'll read how live auctions are defined, why to go to auctions, the hunt for a good value, how live auctions differ from other sales, and an overview of the auction industry's categories. You'll also learn about the auctioneer and other auction staff, buyers and sellers. We'll also tell you about auction settings today, and about how to find auctions to attend.

In **Part 2, "Bidding and Buying Basics,"** we tell you how live auctions work, technology used at live auctions, how to bid, and most importantly, the bidding strategies. We'll also explain the Buyer's Premium and details of paying for your purchase.

In **Part 3, "Buying Successfully at Live Auctions,"** you'll find tips on how to succeed in each of the main categories of art, antiques, and collectibles; personal property and estates; real estate in all its categories; charity benefit auctions; automobiles; and farm and livestock.

Part 4, "Sellers' Success at Live Auctions," is for you if you ever want to sell an item or a houseful of items (or your house!). You'll learn about steps for contacting with the auctioneer, agreeing on terms and situations, the valuation of your property, and about selling in the right venue and closing the sale and getting your money.

Last but not least important, the appendixes include a glossary of auction terms; resources such as organizations, websites, and publications; and sample forms of bidder registration forms and a basic sales contract.

Sidebars

As you read the text, you'll notice the occasional sidebar. There are four types.

def•i•ni•tion

These short sidebars describe common expressions used in live auctions.

SOLD!

Practical tips are important and we discuss how to make the best out of live auctions in these sidebars.

From the Podium

How about some trivia and interesting facts about live auctions? You'll find them here.

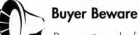

Buyer Beware

Be cautious before an auction. Special concerns and things to avoid during live auctions can be found here.

Acknowledgments

Thank you to the Book Review Committee members of the National Auctioneers Association for their work in reviewing this book prior to publication. Each of them is a veteran auctioneer and leader in their fields. They are Stephen Karbelk, CAI, AARE; Robert A. Doyle, CAI; and Wil Hahn, CAI; and the NAA Board of Directors. This book was compiled by Steve Baska, publications director of the National Auctioneers Association.

Trademarks

All terms mentioned in this book that are known to be or are suspected of being trademarks or service marks have been appropriately capitalized. Alpha Books and Penguin Group (USA) Inc. cannot attest to the accuracy of this information. Use of a term in this book should not be regarded as affecting the validity of any trademark or service mark.

Part 1

What Is a Live Auction?

Many of us have been to a live auction, but never really understood the many people and procedures that are at work. It looks simple, but there's a lot going on under the surface! Do you know what the auctioneer, ringmen, buyers, and sellers are all doing? If you learn that, you're a step ahead of the game in enjoying and being successful at live auctions. This part examines the roles of each of the players, the myths at work, the auction settings, and how to decide which live auction is right for you to attend.

Chapter 1

Live Auctions Defined

In This Chapter

- ◆ How to define live auctions
- ◆ Why go to live auctions?
- ◆ How live auctions differ from other sales
- ◆ What the auction industry encompasses

Chances are that most people on Earth have heard the word *auction*, and even the phrase *live auction*, because auctions occur in every corner of the globe and have thrived for thousands of years.

A live auction is an extremely simple concept: hold up an item for sale in front of a crowd, and see who will pay the highest price for it. It makes perfect sense!

A live auction is also the purest and simplest form of the auction. Defined a little more specifically, live auctions occur when people physically gather in one place to buy an item by bidding against each other until the highest offered price is reached. When no person offers a higher price than the last person, an auctioneer declares the item as sold to the highest bidder.

Why Attend Live Auctions?

There's an excitement about a live auction that makes it a special event that draws people again and again. And if we look closely, there are several factors at work in a live auction.

A crowd at a live auction.

First, there is a natural curiosity about what unique or interesting items are for sale at a live auction. Attendees wonder if they will find that certain item, maybe a type of furniture they've been looking for.

Second, there's the *big* curiosity about the price that will be obtained: will the item sell low or high? Every bidder probably wants to win at a low price, a bargain price. We feel so good, so successful when we feel we've bought an item at a price below what is usually paid for it. On the other side of the scale, every seller wants a high price for his item, as much as he can get when bidders compete.

From these opposite ends of the price spectrum comes the live auction, similar to an ancient arena sitting in the middle with a crowd around it, with the item for sale as the prize being battled for. Bidders and sellers play out their own strategies (described later in this book) and the final winner determines the fate of the auction item.

Third, live auctions are also a social event where neighbors often meet and many people make new friends. Live auctions also are a family event that enables families to spend time together in a shared interest. And regular auction attendees greet each other.

And less obvious, is the great educational opportunity at live auctions to learn about art, autos, furniture, and every type of property sold, by talking to other attendees, sellers, and auctioneers. You learn about values, construction of items, collection of practices, and so on.

When you walk into a live auction you can almost see the raised eyebrows and feeling of anticipation in the air, whether it is before or during the auction. People are looking, competing, winning at the goal of getting a small treasure. Live auctions are all the above and more.

How Live Auctions Differ from Other Sales

There are many different types of sales venues when you want to buy or sell something. Often people don't compare them when planning a purchase or sale; they just pick the method they are familiar with.

For example, here are a few of the different types of sales venues: retail stores usually operate by having a fixed price marked on the item; wholesale or discount stores also have fixed prices. Garage sales or swap meets may have fixed prices or a sign saying "Make Best Offer" on some items, indicating the seller is much more willing to negotiate a purchase price.

Houses and automobiles for sale have a listed asking price, but almost everyone knows it is common practice for the buyer to try to negotiate a lower price. So you can see there are differences in how sales venues approach price.

SOLD!

A big difference between an auction and other sales is that items at auction are sold as-is, meaning without warranties or any promises to fix defects.

A live auction is different from all these types in at least three major ways: first, and most obvious, is that there's a crowd of people standing present and interested in buying that item. Second, the price is determined by competitive bidding upward until there is no higher bid given; there is no negotiating the price downward.

Third, the item is sold as-is, meaning it is sold in its present condition with no promises of repair by the seller. Also consider that garage sales, swap meets, and these other types of sales are very time-consuming for the seller (including the prep time, the time spent sitting and waiting for customers to come, and so on).

Most of the marketing at these sales comes in the form of a cardboard sign stuck in the ground, and sometimes through a general ad that publicizes the event, but not usually each individual item. And when the sale is over, there are always a large number of items left. You may have had a garage sale or yard sale, only to end up with half the items you had for sale back in your house.

The procedure is more professional with an auction. The auctioneer and his or her staff take care in preparing items and estimating their fair market value. They then professionally market the sale so that people from throughout the county, state, or even the world will know about it. And they make it their job to create a competitive and entertaining atmosphere that attracts consumers to the sale. And most important, everything sells.

An auctioneer's hand gestures, eye contact with the crowd, and rhythmic chant, stirs buyers and brings the auction to life. Through auctions, sellers can obtain the highest possible price, dispose of all their property, and receive money for their goods all in one day. Buyers have the opportunity to shop for unique merchandise and pay the price they want in the spirit of competition in an open market. All these things separate auctions from other types of sales.

From Homes to Horse Auctions: An Overview

The live auction industry is comprised of many individual categories, from art and livestock auctions to luxury home and collector car auctions. A brief look here at the major categories will help you understand what the recent changes are, so when you attend these auctions you can act and speak with knowledge about what is going on.

The fastest-growing category was residential real estate auctions (homes, condominiums, other residences), with revenues that grew at a rate of 12.5 percent higher than 2005 figures. Overall, residential real estate generated $16 billion in sales for 2006.

From the Podium
Overall, the live auction industry is in a state of sustained overall growth, of growing revenues and number of auctions, with changes in many areas. The MORPACE International 2006 year-end statistical report showed that auction industry revenues grew overall by 7.1 percent in 2006 compared to 2005.

These are auctions where bidders gather inside a home or on the front lawn, for instance, with the auctioneer standing in front of them as bids are accepted. The home is usually sold in a few minutes. The growth in this category is due to several factors, including that more sellers are putting homes at auction because the traditional brokerage listing method was taking a very long time, and because more auctioneers are selling real estate and seeking clients, veteran auctioneers say.

Following closely behind that leading category, are commercial and industrial real estate with a 9.3 percent growth in 2006. This includes commercial buildings such as office buildings, gasoline stations, retail stores, and industrial buildings such as warehouses.

Business investors and entrepreneurs often buy their properties by auction, as well as by private listing. Investors like getting good values in a decisive fast sale format, which auctions provide. And sellers especially see that an auction on a certain date can help ensure a sale and reduce their costs from continuing to own a property they want to sell.

Also in the real estate sector, land and agricultural real estate auctions grew at 8.4 percent in 2006. These are auctions where bidders gather (sometimes in a hotel ballroom) and participate in an auction of many parcels of land, called a *multi-parcel auction*, and the bidder can choose which piece of land he or she wishes to buy. It's an effective way to break up and sell huge tracts of land. More vacant and agricultural land is coming to market as farm holdings are reduced and more of the U.S. population moves to cities from the country. This is a trend that will likely continue for some years, experts say.

Art, antiques, and collectibles auctions had nine percent growth in 2006. Partial credit goes to television shows featuring art and antique auctions. Consumers watching *Antiques Roadshow* and *Cash in the Attic* are cleaning out their attics and basements to bring things to auction that would not have come to attention in earlier years.

These auctions are typically in auction houses and occur everywhere from rural settings to the most upscale areas of New York City.

Charity auctions, also called fundraisers or benefit auctions, had revenues up 6.6 percent in 2006. This was due to more clients bringing more auctions to fruition with more auctioneers entering that niche. Clients include small groups such as churches and schools, and large groups such as nonprofit organizations as in the American Heart Association or the United Way.

> **From the Podium**
>
> According to a Harris Interactive Survey, consumers spend an average of twice as much at live auctions ($988) than at Internet auctions ($475).

More groups such as these are finding that a fundraising auction can raise more money than any other fundraising method, especially when a charity auction specialist auctioneer helps them with organizing and marketing of the event. Subcategories of charity auctions include wine auctions, where a wine auction specialist is hired for his or her knowledge of the product and event planning.

Automotive auction revenues experienced a 6.5 percent rise in 2006 as that category continues as the largest gross revenue producer in the entire industry. Auto auctions occur in auto auction houses where cars are driven through a lane in front of an auctioneer seated above the crowd. The bidding occurs more quickly than other forms of auctions, with the next vehicle driven in quickly to be sold.

One factor driving up revenue is the broadcasting of auto auctions live on the Internet, simultaneously with the onsite auction, sometimes drawing more auto dealers to bid than there are bidders that physically show up on the auction floor, and driving up prices as a result. But there are still many local auto auctions where the public turns out in large numbers onsite at the live auction to find a good value on all types of vehicles.

Among the low growth categories are commercial and industrial machinery and equipment at 1 percent. These are auctions of machines in industrial shops such as in a printing company, woodworking shop, or pipe-making shop.

Many of these large items are sold on the Internet today because of their high international demand, such as machinery equipment buyers located in developing countries. Also with low growth are livestock auctions at 1.4 percent in 2006. Livestock auctions have changed with lower volumes sold at auction than in the past.

SOLD!

To be a more effective bidder and buyer, look at auctions sometimes from the seller's perspective. If you can understand the seller's reason for selling (is he desperate for money?), it will help you set your bidding limit and strategy.

More cattle, for instance, are sold by direct contract arrangement to slaughter houses. Personal property auctions grew at 0.6 percent in 2006. This includes estate sales, where a deceased person's goods are sold after his death.

The two categories reflecting a decline in revenues were agricultural machinery, with a 0.7 percent decline, and intellectual property, with a 1.6 percent decline. Intellectual property includes patents, product designs, copyrights and other items of intellectual creation.

Farm machinery sales have declined as the number of farms in America has declined in recent years. More people are moving from the country in to cities. Fewer farms exist today than in the past, so there is less need for farm auctions. Some auctioneers who specialized in farm and agriculture items in the past are moving more heavily into real estate sales, as they adjust their businesses.

What This All Means to You

Most people reading this book will be bidders and buyers who enjoy attending live auctions, or want to start attending. Some of you bidders will also become sellers at some point.

It is important for you to know the reasons that people attend auctions, and the trends in the industry. This will help you be more successful in your bidding, buying, and selling.

For example, here are a few reasons that sellers bring their items to auctions. Knowing this will help you, the bidder, win your sought-after items:

◆ A speedy process, quick turnaround. Home sellers like that an auction is immediate. It happens during a set time and is completed during that time. It's quick and efficient. Knowing this, bidders can estimate how urgently a seller wants and needs to sell, and you can base your bidding accordingly.

◆ You set the time and place of your sale. Seller's love this idea, versus leaving an item in a store to sell or in a traditional real estate listing. Bidders like this idea too.

◆ Comprehensive marketing of your property. Part of conducting an auction is marketing it to the general public to get as many people there as possible. Auctioneers have comprehensive mailing lists they use to market their sales. They run advertisements, distribute fliers, and more. They are marketing specialists. A good marketing effort can easily bring 300 to 400 people to a live auction.

◆ Buyers come prepared to buy. Auction-goers come with money in their wallets and are prepared to go home with property. As a bidder, you'd better be prepared and have the money to purchase. For real estate auctions this is especially important because buyers must be pre-qualified to buy through a deposit of a certified or cashier's check.

◆ No negotiating price downward. Obviously sellers like it when prices go up, and bidders want prices to stay low, but there's a rush of excitement for bidders when prices climb. But you have to know how to control your emotions and your bidding.

◆ Auctions work in good and bad economic times. How can that be, you ask? Well, when the economy is bad, more people feel forced to sell at auction to move their home or car quickly, for example, to avoid carrying costs from piling up every month. But when the economy is good and many people are interested in buying an item such as a home, the seller knows this and thinks that an auction is a good way to pit the competing buyers against each other to achieve the highest price.

Sure, it seems a bit strange that one method of selling, as in auctions, would work well in both a good or bad economy, but it is true. When products sit on a storeroom shelf in slow periods, they are often taken to auction to sell them on a certain day and get the best price possible. And, if an item is a hot-seller, even better at auction!

What's the key? Auctions successfully sell items. Sellers may sometimes take less than they hoped, but the item is gone! And bidders are always drawn by the hope of a bargain.

Help from Television Shows

Live auctions are booming in popularity and attendance for several reasons.

There is a growing number of television shows featuring live auctions and appraising. These shows not only entertain, but they are educating auction attendees and are drawing bigger crowds to local live auctions.

One of the most popular shows for years has been Public Television's *Antiques Roadshow*, where appraisers (many of whom are also auctioneers) analyze, describe, and provide a *price valuation* (how much an item is likely to sell for at auction) for items brought by average citizens. *Antiques Roadshow*, which began in England in the 1970s, migrated to the United States and now Canada.

Many auctioneers credit this show with a surge in interest in collectibles and with people bringing items to auction. Other popular shows include *Cash in the Attic*, which shows items from the attic taken through the auction process, and *Bargain Hunt*.

Bidders get no small education watching these shows. If you see a live auction on TV and understand how people bid, it's a big boost toward making you comfortable in bidding at a local auction. These shows not only show the basics, but the host explains the process, often from the seller's point of view and how much money they made. But, you, as bidders, get an inside-view of this world of auctions.

Real estate-related auction shows include *Houses Under the Hammer* and *Flip That House.* They give an idea of price at auction, as well as the process. There is also auto-auction television coverage on the Speed channel on many cable television systems. Classic car auctions draw hundreds of thousands of viewers as cameras zoom in on the rare sports cars and others that Baby Boomers are buying to relive their thrill of their teen years. Once again, people see these TV shows and decide to come to their local auction.

Check your cable or satellite system guides for the time and channel where these shows appear. These shows are evidence that there is a growing public appetite for auctions, but the side benefits are that these shows are doing substantial education about the auction process.

A new 24-hour auction channel also started in fall 2007 called the Auction Network. It features live auctions of every category: cars, homes, horses, charity events, and so on. It also has basic how-to shows on bidding and selling, and features biographies on auctioneers, ringmen, and others involved in the auction process.

This network is also believed to be the first "interactive" auction TV channel. For example, bidders can go to the Auction Network website and run a search for an item they collect, such as autographed boxing gloves, and the search will give them the time and location of auctions featuring that item. They can then bid in real-time through the Auction Network site. This brings live auctions to a television-watching crowd, as well as a computer crowd.

> **From the Podium**
>
> Although not a live auction, eBay has drawn millions of new bidders and sellers to local live auctions.

Changes such as this are affecting live auctions more every year, and attendees see these changes reflected at their local live auctions. Sure, you can attend and bid at live auctions in the same way as in past decades, but if you don't pay attention to new technologies that interact with live auctions, you will be confused when they are discussed and utilized in the middle of a live auction.

If you're not informed, you'll wonder how and why Internet bidders are bidding against you in the live auction. You'll wonder why there are video cameras set up on the sides or middle of the room. Today's live auctions are not the same as your grandfather's auction. We'll discuss more of these changes in coming chapters.

eBay Increasing Auction Popularity

The online auction company eBay also has popularized the auction process to the entire world and drawn in millions of new bidders and sellers to local live auctions. As you meet people at live auctions, you will likely find that some of them came from this experience.

Why and how did this happen? eBay is a very convenient way for people to buy items from their home. That brought millions of people to its website. There they learned the concept and excitement of bidding. They then thought it would be fun to go to a local auction. Also, many of them decided local auctions would be a good place to find items they can resell on eBay, in hopes of making a profit there.

eBay is not a live auction held on a single day with a live crowd physically present bidding until a highest offer is reached. Rather, it is an auction by posted computer bids, across several days, with a set ending time when the last highest bid wins the item. There is no auctioneer calling for one more final bid to ensure that the highest bid has been received, therefore, eBay is not a pure auction.

That difference impacts you as a bidder and a seller, and shows how eBay differs from a live auction.

The Least You Need to Know

- A live auction is when people physically gather in one place to buy an item by bidding against each other until a highest offered price is reached.

- The desire for a bargain and desire to collect rare items are probably the top reasons people attend auctions.

- Auctions work well in good and bad economies, as odd as that seems!

- Auction revenues are growing each year. The industry revenues overall grew 7.1 percent in 2006, compared to 2005.

- Television shows featuring live auctions are some of the best ways to learn about auctions.

Chapter 2

Myths and Misconceptions

In This Chapter

- The three types of auctions
- Auctions are not just liquidations
- From super-simple to today's sophistication
- Some talk fast, some talk slowly

As with other long-established industries, live auctions are subject to their clients' long-held beliefs about the way this business operates. But some of those views are vastly oversimplified, outdated, and wrong. They fall under the category of myths and misconceptions.

So in this chapter, let's break myths about live auctions and replace wrong information with accurate information that will help you be a better buyer or seller at auctions.

The Item Always Sells to the High Bidder

While most items sell, sometimes they don't. The reason: there are different types of auctions, all which have conditions set by the seller ahead of time. It's his or her auction, of his property, and he sets the rules to some degree. One type of auction is the *absolute auction*, where the seller and auctioneer announce that the item will absolutely sell to the highest bidder, as long as there is at least one bid offered when the auctioneer opens the auction.

Another type is the *reserve auction*, where a minimum acceptable price is set by the seller. If the bids do not reach that price level (the reserve), the item is not sold, unless the seller chooses to reduce the reserve.

A third type of auction is *auction subject to seller confirmation*, in which the seller can accept or reject the high bid. This means when the high bid is reached, the auctioneer turns to the seller and asks if he wants to accept that bid. The seller will then say yes or no.

def•i•ni•tion

An **absolute auction** is an auction with no minimum price on the item. The item will sell regardless of price if one bid is made when the auctioneer opens the auction.

An **auction subject to seller confirmation** is an auction where the seller determines if the high bid is acceptable to him.

The type of auction procedure chosen by the seller is announced before the auction, and printed in the Terms and Conditions, so all bidders are aware and will not think the item will automatically sell to the high bidder. Here are a few more details on these types of auctions.

Absolute Auction

There is power in the term absolute auction, because many bidders know the term and automatically think they may get a valuable property at a low price, or at least a fair price. This seems the purest form of auction because everyone knows the item will be sold to the high bidder under true market conditions.

Bidders love this type of auction. Sellers have more at risk. But a professionally conducted absolute live auction normally brings a good price for the seller because the auctioneer has assembled qualified bidders who will bid the price up to market value.

But a low price is possible. For that reason, some prospective sellers seek ways to avoid a final price that is too low. This is where the other forms of auctions began.

Sometimes a seller will ask an auctioneer how to advertise an auction as absolute, but still establish a minimum price at the same time. The ethical auctioneer knows this is deceptive to the public, and illegal, and will not allow it. Sellers seeking games and schemes are a danger to everyone.

In an absolute auction, the auctioneer has a vested interest in ensuring that the auction moves forward, as his commission often depends on the completion of the sale. If an auctioneer has reason to believe immediately prior to a scheduled auction that few bidders will show up, the auctioneer will discuss that concern with the seller and tell of the option to cancel the sale. The auctioneer, as an agent of the seller, has the fiduciary responsibility to advise the seller of what to expect before every auction. Withdrawal of property must be done prior to the opening of the auction.

Reserve Auctions

When it comes to protecting an item from too low a price, an auction with reserve is a common way. Sellers set the minimum price.

In this auction, each auction lot offered will sell to the highest bidder only if the auctioneer accepts the amount of the highest bid and declares the lot sold. Whether the auctioneer accepts the highest bid is a question that is answered only after the auctioneer considers the amount of the reserve price. Sometimes the reserve price is disclosed by the auctioneer so the bidders know if a bid is made at or above the disclosed reserve, and that the item will sell.

Auction Subject to Seller Confirmation

In an auction subject to seller confirmation, the seller has not settled on a required minimum price before the bidding. He wants to leave it open because he may have special conditions to consider before auction day. This can be good for the high bidder because he may be able to convince a seller to take his high bid rather than reject a stated reserve.

But the lack of a pre-determined selling price before an auction can also be negative. This is because greed is a driving force in auctions. Sellers can never sell for too much, and buyers can never buy for too little. When a reserve price is not determined before an auction, the amount the seller will accept can become a moving target.

To overcome this concern, auctioneers need to have a good reason as to why the seller is motivated to sell and why the buyer should participate in the auction. Generally, items with reserve are more expensive, like cars or real estate, while lower priced items sell at absolute auctions.

Auctions As a Last Resort Method

Some people think an auction is the last method to try, after others have failed. This has been an especially common perception for the sale of real estate since people usually list their property with a broker when they have to sell.

People think that if a house didn't sell in a traditional real estate listing, the urgent seller has gone to the last option—an auction. This is not always true. Many sellers are turning first to auctions because it offers many advantages, namely a quick sale at a good price for a property in as-is condition.

For example, in February 2003 *The Wall Street Journal* ran a story on this trend in the business section with the headline "Auctions Are No Longer Only for the Desperate."

The story said "The real-estate auction has come up in the world. In the past, auctions were almost exclusively the last resort for desperate owners or banks eager to get a failed property off their hands. Now, an auction is one of the first options many owners think of to sell commercial properties."

The story said that sellers now include blue-chip companies and building owners "under no imminent financial pressure to sell." This also applies to homeowners who have seen the auction method draw and crowd and bring a comparable price to other methods, and sometimes even more if a bidding war erupts.

Why the change? People are testing new methods and new outlets faster than ever before. Why not try a well-advertised auction to generate excitement among home-buyers? Especially among commercial real estate, the target buyers are investors. If an owner knows the buyers will be an investor, the best way to achieve the highest price in the shortest time is to invite all of the investors to show up at one time to bid. Investors see this as an easy way to buy. Sellers like that it minimizes their carrying costs and accelerates the sale process. A seller does not have to be desperate to be motivated. Many sellers have reasonable price expectations and prefer the speed and excitement of the auction process.

It is true that foreclosed properties are still big business and carry the last resort image. But don't view all real estate auctions as a last resort. You probably don't view a classic car auction that way, so there's no reason today to do that with real estate.

Instead, attend an auction or two in your area to get a feel for how they are conducted and the prices that homes are being sold for.

Auctions As a Super-Simple Operation

Auctions seem really simple. You may think, "I just show up, bid, and then pay on the way out if I have the high bid."

Well, not quite right. There are a few more steps and details. Soon you'll see the auction as a modern business transaction, not just a country handshake.

SOLD!

Be sure to read the terms and conditions given to you when you register. If you bid, you are bound by these conditions.

Auctioneers want it to be simple for you, but also fair to all parties. As explained earlier in this chapter, the high bid doesn't always buy the item because there are different types of auctions. Here are a few more details about auctions:

◆ You have to register and get a bidder number when you arrive at the auction site. You can't just mingle into the crowd and raise your hand without a number.

◆ You should read the Terms and Conditions sheet handed to you at registration because you are bound by them if you bid. You can't try later to void the sale because you didn't know there were terms of the sale.

◆ Plan your bidding strategy and limits. Have you thought about this? The auctioneer will set specific bid increment amounts that bidders are asked to use. A wise auction attendee knows that auctions are not a super-simple affair and that a little preparation and attention to detail pays off.

Auctions Are the Same Today As Fifty Years Ago

Some live auctions, especially in small rural towns, look the same as they did 50 years ago. You see the crowd gathered around the auctioneer selling. And this particular auction may be operated much the same as 50 years ago, but don't think that applies to all auctions.

Technology has changed. Laws change. Business methods change. Auctions have moved forward.

One thing you might see that you never have in the past is a *reverse auction*. Instead of starting at a low price and working up to the highest bid, this auction is over with the very first bid. The auctioneer begins by asking for a very high bid amount, then a lower amount, then another lower amount, all the while waiting for the first person to bid, and that person will win. It is exciting to watch the anticipation on bidders' faces as they watch each other to try to guess who will jump in first to bid and win. If two people bid at the same time, then a regular auction format is held from that price and proceeding upward, not downward as the reverse auction started.

In a reverse auction, the bidder knows he has to bid as high as possible to beat all competition, so he or she may overbid the actual value of the property, to the glee of the seller. This style is said to build tremendous anticipation and strategizing before the auction for properties in high demand, and can result in higher revenues.

Technology is very different today at some auctions. A video auction is one in which photographs or moving video images of sale items on a big screen for the crowd to see during a live auction. Video auctions also allow the crowd to see small items, such as jewelry, much more clearly. And the auctioneer can sell more items faster.

And totally new from 50 years ago is the live onsite auction that is held simultaneously on the Internet to allow people to bid online when they cannot be there in person. These live Internet auctions, also called *webcasts* are being used for all kinds of auctions. More on webcasts in Chapter 7.

All Auctioneers Talk Fast

The fast-talking style that auctioneers use is called *the chant*, because it sounds like a chanting rhythm used in songs. Nobody knows exactly when it started, but it was likely an early response to an energetic auctioneer's desire to keep asking people to make bids.

The auctioneer does not want to have silences when trying to sell an item. He uses the chant to, first, keep asking for higher bids, and second, to create excitement and entertainment that keeps the audience's attention.

In this rhythmic rolling talk, the auctioneer uses filler words to fill the space and time in-between bids. Filler words are usually small words. An example of the chant with filler words is ...

"1 dollar bid, now 2, now 2, will ya gimme 2?"

"2 dollar bid, now 3, now 3, will ya gimme 3?"

"3 dollar bid, now 4, now 4, will ya gimme 4?"

The filler words are everything except the number. Filler words are used to remind the buyers of the last number bid and give buyers time to consider their next bid.

Auctioneers today agree that their primary objective is to have the bid numbers be clearly understood. The entertainment aspect of this sing-song style is far less important to the sale, but it is fun for most auctioneers.

Auctioneers learn how to perform the chant in auction school. They practice tongue twister phrases, filler words, and practice numbers until the chant is easy, like a second nature to them. They also enjoy participating in bid calling contests around the country to see who has the best chant style, presentation, clarity, interaction with ringmen, and effective *catching of the bids* that are given by the bidders.

Associated with the chant, it's important for attendees to also know that the auctioneer's job in selling an item from the podium is to, first, describe the item clearly to the crowd, telling things such as brand name and condition; second, to take the bids (usually with the chant); and third, to declare the item sold (or not!). So, the chant is the middle part of the process of selling each item.

Auctioneers say that the more people who like to listen to the chant, the more people will stay at the auction. Some auctioneers do not like to use words in the filler places, only numbers. By staying with numbers as fillers, these auctioneers are trying to drill in the price of the item being auctioned. This can be easier at a car auction, for example, bids come fast and furious, but the same method may not work at a real estate auction where the bids come in more slowly.

An auctioneer from Denver says that "The more you hit people with the numbers, the more they are thinking about bidding." A bidder may eventually bid to get the auctioneer to move to another number, he added.

Auctioneers talk fast to entertain, but their main goal is to be clearly understood.

With the chant, auctioneers are trying to keep bidders involved in the auction. And, the auctioneer uses physical techniques to control his voice.

"I like to keep my lungs filled with air. I like to sell from my diaphragm. I know that is what they teach in auction schools, and I agree with the philosophy," one auctioneer said. "I've heard of another technique that works. Don't breathe when you need to breathe. Breathe before you need to breathe. With this method, you'll be full and ready to go when you need the air."

Auctioneers also spend time working on their body movements, including pointing to bidders, nodding a "thank you" for a bid, standing or sitting, or walking amongst the crowd.

Differences in the Chant

The bid-taking, or bid calling style of auctioneers differs among the different types of auctions. For example, at fine art auctions and jewelry auctions most auctioneers speak slowly. They like the slow pace that gives bidders extra time to consider their next bid, and they like the quieter atmosphere where familiar dealers often attend.

However, the fast chant is typically done at estate sales, livestock sales, and regular consignment sales were the general public attends and enjoys the entertainment value and excitement of the chant. At car auctions, the chant is super-fast because the auctioneer is selling each car quickly. The attendees there are often dealers and regulars who understand the fast and unusual style.

Often, the more experienced the bidders are, the faster the auctioneer can chant and still enable the bidders to clearly understand him. If a bidder does not understand what bid number is being called for at any point, he can ask a ringman nearby.

So don't be surprised if you go to an auction and the auctioneer is not doing the fast-talking chant. He or she may not enjoy or feel skilled in that aspect, which is a small part of the auction business. It's a visible aspect that many enjoy, but the real focus is on being sure all bidders understand clearly what is being said.

Some auctioneers today also speak Spanish, or at least call some numbers in Spanish, to serve that audience. The auctioneer may do so slowly, or use an interpreter.

Auctioneers all face a common problem when calling a sale. They can damage or lose their voice. Fast-talking can increase this risk, so they may speak slowly. Auctioneers can minimize the risk by practicing good vocal technique, vocal hygiene, and taking better care of their overall health.

Bidding with the Chant

As a bidder, you should be bidding in synch with the chant. You should be listening closely and following the rising bids.

> **From the Podium**
>
> Auctioneers protect their vocal cords by not smoking, doing vocal exercises to strengthen the muscles, taking breaks during long auctions, and drinking warm teas that soothe the throat.

It's another myth that if you raise your hand at the wrong time to scratch your nose or your head, that the auctioneer will think you've bid and that you'll be stuck with paying for an item. The auctioneer and ringmen are trained professionals who know the difference between an itch and an intentional bid. They look for clear gestures, eye contact to confirm the bid, and support from the ringmen.

The auctioneer does not want any misunderstandings with bidders. To avoid having the auctioneer think you are making a bid, look away from the auctioneer. It's when you have firm eye contact, coupled with a bidding gesture, that your movements can be misinterpreted.

In real bidding, get in rhythm with the chant, and even anticipate the next bid amount so you'll be ready to bid. When the auctioneer says "I've got 10 dollars, do I hear 20?", you'll know if you want to bid 20. If you want to bid 15, tell your ringman or the auctioneer.

The auctioneer, often with the seller, decides at what price the bidding will start, and by what increment amounts he will keep the bids rising. The ringmen may also advise the auctioneer to adjust the amounts lower or higher by seeking what is happening among bidders.

Starting a high-priced item out at a below-value price can stimulate interest, but can backfire if the auctioneer does not keep bid increments high enough. One auctioneer recalled an auction he attended where a young auctioneer started the bidding for an art print at a low price and then asked for $10 increments. The auctioneer got more than 15 bids for the print, but it ended up selling for much below its value because the auctioneer didn't use the first couple of bids to get up to the print's true value.

"Many times people have come up to me after auctions and said that although they didn't buy a certain item, they did bid on it a couple times. They were participating," said auctioneer Paul C. Behr, CAI, of Denver, Colorado. "The reason they participated was because I started the bidding at a level where they could participate. That bidder will be ready to come to another auction because they feel they will be able to participate again."

Sometimes the auctioneer will come out and stand right among the crowd while he is chanting. This encourages bidders to act.

"At the start of an auction, I'll consciously move toward the crowd until I'm among them. I really think it makes a difference as far as whether people feel you're participating in the auction whether or not they feel you are one of them," the same auctioneer said. After a person has bid on an item, auctioneers and ringmen will return to that bidder until the bidder refuses to bid more.

From the Podium

Bidders want to know three main things: what is being sold; what the current bid is; and what the next bid is that the auctioneer wants.

Auctioneers should not underestimate the intelligence of their bidders. Many bidders today really know how much a particular item is worth. Some people research the values on the Internet well before the auction. And in many cases, so should you. It will help you bid with the chant and be successful. You only have a split-second to make a buying decision, and you must be prepared.

How do you decide on the increments you want to bid up by? You want to bid low, of course, but not embarrassingly low. Accept the auctioneers amounts if they are close to those you had in mind.

An auto auctioneer says he is frequently faced with buyers who want him to drop the bidding down by increments of $50, instead of the $100 he keeps asking for. So, he will take the $50 increase and then ask for $100 on top of that.

"The buyer thinks that a $50 increase breaks the auctioneer down," he said. "He thinks he's getting a whale of a bargain. But he's still there bidding $1,000 later. The only thing is he's done those hundreds in fifties and he's tickled to death. So I just let him go and be happy with it."

Auctioneers say an important key to reaching a target price is to keep the bidding increments at a level that will be conducive to getting the bids up to the value of the item. By keeping the bids at regular intervals the bidders know what to expect next, which keeps the bids coming in faster and at a constant pace. Some auctioneers jump all over the place with bid increments to keep the bidders guessing.

The Funny Filler Comment

Experienced auctioneers know that a funny or insightful comment made at the right moment not only can effectively encourage more bidding, but it helps the auctioneer connect personally with the audience, and provides entertainment.

Here is a list of "one-liner" funny comments used by auctioneers or ringmen.

- Isn't that sweet. He's checking with his daughter.
- Sir. If you don't bid on this item again, we are both going to regret it in the morning.
- Now, let's sell the one that works.
- Sir! If you *really* love her, you will buy it for her!
- You'd stand a better chance of getting it if you'd bid.
- Don't let a good buy go by.
- For your money, it's a honey.
- You'll be sorry when you get home and sober up.
- Look out, you are out!

- Remember, it wasn't raining when Noah built the Ark.

- Too many of you are thinking of something else.

- Don't hesitate or you'll miss what you came to buy.

- Above average in quality, below average in price.

- Thanks for the help, I just need a little more.

- The only mistake you'll make is to let it get away.

- Quiet enough to start a prayer meeting.

- It's the last step in the race that counts—one more bid may get it.

- If you have to ask him/her, you're whipped before you start.

- The chance of a lifetime that won't be the mistake of a lifetime.

- It's only money, you're gonna make plenty of it in your lifetime.

- Get in there and help yourself.

- It's what you came for!

- It will be an antique someday.

- Somebody hand me the dental pliers.

- Just go ask him/her to go and grab a Coke ... It'll only take a minute ... just long enough for you to get it.

- You better buy it. Why in 20 years or so it could be worth nothing!

- Friend, if you get that item for that price, then by golly you better go to church tomorrow! You can trust me.

- Your wife/husband really wants you to buy this!

- Ma'am, are you gonna let that big guy do that to you?

- Today's the day. We're not having an auction tomorrow!

- Life throws ya curves ... you learn to swerve

- If I say *pleeeeeease*, will ya take the other one, too?

- Don't let 'em beat ya for 50 cents!

◆ They know a deal.

◆ Take a chance ... Columbus did!

◆ You're going to be saying shoulda ... coulda ... woulda ... tomorrow, folks!!

◆ Where you gonna find another one?

◆ Keep on biddin'. I'll let you know if I think it's gettin' too high!

◆ Let your money buy you happiness, sir.

◆ Don't leave here with nonbuyer's remorse!

◆ Remember that today's the auction. Tomorrow it's back to retail!

◆ I hope tomorrow you are in need of one of these and you say you wish you would have bid on it.

◆ Remember folks, when you buy quality, you only cry once.

◆ Don't wake up cussin' tomorrow for what you didn't buy today.

◆ Ahhhh, a smart man always checks with the boss.

◆ Buy both (or all) and you will never get the wrong one.

The auctioneer may also do a funny crowd exercise, such as ask everyone to raise their hands at the same time. Then the auctioneer will say "Good. I just wanted to see if everyone's hands work!"

The Least You Need to Know

◆ There are three basic types of auctions: the absolute, the reserve, and the subject to seller confirmation.

◆ Always read the Terms and Conditions sheet handed to you at registration because you are bound by them if you bid.

◆ Bid in synch with the chant. You should be listening closely and following the rising bids.

◆ Filler words in the chant are used to remind the buyers of the last number bid and give buyers time to consider their next bid.

People at the Live Auction

In This Chapter

- Center of the action: auctioneers, ringmen
- The business staff supports it all
- There's a difference: bidders and buyers
- The seller holds the power

A live auction is a gathering place for several categories of people involved in this business. The more you know about them, and their roles, the more successful you can be as a buyer and seller.

In this chapter you'll learn about the auctioneers and their staff, including ringmen and clerks; as well as the bidders, buyers, sellers, other attendees. Each has a role to play, a goal they are seeking and strategies they use to get what they want. Let's begin with the auctioneer.

Auctioneers

The auctioneer has to fill many roles at the same time. To auction attendees, he appears to be the ringmaster, bid taker, announcer. To his staff, he is the boss who contracts with the seller and makes decisions about how the auction will proceed. To the seller, he is the person who sells items for the highest price possible.

A combination of training, skills, and determination are essential to the success of an auction business. The single most important role an auctioneer has, but an unseen one, is that of marketing expert. Auctioneers must advertise a client's property through the appropriate methods to reach a specific audience, including through print publications, direct mail, e-mail, and other venues.

Then he has the vital roles of organizing the auction structure and being the *bid caller* from the podium. But behind it all is the ability to market auctions and merchandise effectively, which comes from an intimate knowledge of the specific types of merchandise, their value, the demand for such merchandise, and the targeted market.

> **From the Podium**
>
> There are an estimated 30,000 auctioneers in the United States, with some of those being in the business part-time.

The majority of auction companies are independent ventures, although there are some larger regional and national auction houses. Building and maintaining an auction business can mean dozens of hours of preparation for every hour of the actual sale. Auctioneers often call on family members to help handle sale logistics and staff auctions.

In addition to long hours, an auctioneer's annual income depends on the effort and time devoted to the business. Beginning auctioneers get their start working as a part-time auctioneer and holding down another job. As with any business venture, the return in income is largely dependent on the amount of time and effort spent making a go of the business.

The auctioneer has authority and influence with each party in the auction transaction: bidders, buyers, sellers, attendees. For example, bidders and buyers must abide by the terms of the sale set forth by the auctioneer's company. The auctioneer, in turn, has a primary duty to the seller, but the auctioneer also has an ethical and legal responsibility to treat every party fairly. It's a balance.

Auctioneer Education

Many auctioneers got their start working as a clerk or bid caller for the family auction business. Some of these people now run businesses that have been in their family for several generations. Many auction companies continue to be family held endeavors, with extended family members helping organize and staff auctions

But, most auctioneers today attend an auction school. There are about 26 auction schools and programs, either independent institutions or programs that are affiliated with a community or 4-year college.

Schooling can last for a couple weeks or as long as a college semester. Students can expect to learn …

♦ the trademark auctioneer chant.

♦ how to market their services and sales.

♦ how to get started in the auction business and run the business.

A second option is to gain practical experience as an apprentice under an experienced auctioneer. Apprentice auctioneers assist in organizing and running sales, and learn many of the crucial day-to-day operations of running an auction business. In fact, some states require an apprenticeship before they will issue you an auction license.

> **From the Podium**
>
> The auctioneer's authority stems from state laws, court decisions and business regulations. These laws identify his role as an agent for the seller, his duties to keep funds in separate accounts, and other requirements.

The choice of education can depend on the licensing requirements for auctioneers in their state. Many states that require licensing for auctioneers only accept educational credit from specific auction schools or programs. Often licensing boards will waive the educational credits if an applicant served an apprenticeship under a licensed auctioneer. If an auctioneer also seeks to sell real estate, he may be required to hold a real estate license in addition to an auction license.

Required apprenticeships can range in length from conducting a few auctions under an auctioneer's guidance to one or more years.

After an auctioneer is established, they must also take continuing education classes each year to keep up on new laws and advancements in their profession. Also, more auctioneers are choosing to take *specialty designation* programs, meaning classes focused on one specialty, such as benefit auctions or estate auctions, so they can establish themselves as experts in one or more fields.

Another option for auction students is to get a Business Administration degree with a major in auctioneering that is offered through Tri-State University, of Angola, Indiana. Classes are offered online and on campus at the Angola North campus site.

Students work on the degree in three steps: first are general education classes, followed by a business core section that includes finance classes, and then 11 specific auction courses, including State Laws, Introduction to Auctioneering, Auction Law, Real Estate Auctions, Bankruptcy Auctions, Appraising, and others. Following coursework, students serve a working period of apprenticeship under an auctioneer.

Generalist or a Specialist?

Some auctioneers are generalists, meaning they auction all, or most, types of merchandise. They conduct estate sales, art, real estate, and others because there are many similarities in setting up and running an auction of different types of property.

This auctioneer will research the value of items brought to them by a seller and will hold a professional sale on nearly anything. If they do not feel comfortable with a type of merchandise, they will call in an expert appraiser to help determine value or they will obtain the assistance of another auctioneer that specializes in that niche field.

Other auctioneers are specialists in only one or a few categories of items. They like the narrow focus, the feeling of becoming increasingly skilled in one area, such as commercial real estate or firearms. They learn the applicable laws and become known across the country, drawing clients from a wide area.

More auctioneers today seem to be specializing. There is also an influx of middle-aged people becoming auctioneers as they start a second career at 40 or 50, and many say they always enjoyed auctions and harbored a secret desire to be an auctioneer. About 65 percent of auction school students are middle-age.

Auctioneer Obligations

The auctioneer's primary obligation is to be an agent for the seller, meaning to represent the seller in this business transaction called an auction. In that transaction, the auctioneer works to get the highest price possible for the seller's property, under the terms and procedures he has agreed on with the seller.

But the auctioneer also has obligations to treat every party fairly. One obligation is to disclose all terms and conditions of the auction to all parties. Another is to disclose things that bidders may not physically see or expect: such as when the auctioneer enters an *absentee bid* on behalf of a bidder who is not physically at the auction but has submitted a bid in advance.

Buyer Beware

When an auctioneer places an absentee bid himself, he is automatically in a role of potentially serving two clients. Some states prohibit this.

A key factor is that the auctioneer is obligated to be open and fair to all people involved in the auction.

Ethical auctioneers know to whom their duties are owed. They disclose all procedures, fees, and relationships of importance to all parties.

Contract Auctioneers

Although many auctioneers have their own company—and sometimes their own auction building—some choose to work for other companies on a contract basis, known as *contract auctioneers*. They take a more hands-off approach yet still reap the benefits of each auction they call.

In addition, when an auctioneer works on contract, he shows up a few hours before an auction that other people prepared and he

def•i•ni•tion

A **contract auctioneer** is an auctioneer who is hired by another auction company to do bid calling at one auction. He is generally an independent contractor working one project at a time.

takes the stage to call the bids from behind the podium. He or she is an expert at it. They know how to work with ringmen and the crowd to get the most money and provide great entertainment.

This auctioneer does not have the worries that come with running the whole show, securing the seller and keeping him happy. But then this auctioneer also may not have as much of a regular income, sick pay and retirement plan, or an insurance plan.

When a new auctioneer gets out of auction school she may not have a wide enough field of experience to keep her busy, or no desire to start her own firm, so being a contract worker can be appealing.

Some auction companies only do several large auctions a year, so it makes economic sense to contract out part of the auction duties to a contract auctioneer to minimize the overhead costs. A contract auctioneer can establish a regular income stream by working for these companies.

Ringmen

Ringmen are the men or women who stand in the crowd and relay the bids to the auctioneer. The terms ringman, bidspotter, bid assistant, and ring person all refer to the person taking the bids from the audience during an auction. They sometimes holler loud so the auctioneer can clearly hear them.

Ringmen also hold up items for viewing, and wear a special shirt or vest to identify them as an auction employee.

But a professional ringman does far more than spot bids for the auctioneer. They often establish a relationship with the bidders before an auction, asking which items the bidders are looking for. The ringman helps the bidders know when the item is coming up for sale, the ringman answers questions about the item, and he watches the bidder closely when the item is in the sale process.

Ringman Angie Meier catches a bid during NAA's 2007 International Ringman Competition, which she won.

Role of the Ringmen

The ringman's role or duty is to watch his section of the crowd. He is usually assigned a part of the crowd to get bids from. He walks back and forth some of the time, and may stand beside one bidder while that bidder is active.

Increasingly today, more ringmen do their job full-time, traveling among auctions across the country. They may do an auto auction one day, a livestock auction the next. The skills of the ringmen apply across the auction specialties. Some sellers get to know ringmen very well and request specific ones for that seller's auction.

Auctioneers also like to work with certain skilled ringmen, and may fly a ringman clear across the country to work an auction that day.

Being a ringman is a second-career for some men and women who enter this profession. Many of them make more money than they did in a previous career, and they enjoy the fun of auctions and the ability to set their own schedules.

All aspects of the auction industry are undergoing changes toward increased professionalism, including ringmen. In fact, their specialty is entering a new era of greater demand, education, and higher salaries.

Ringmen earn from $0 up to $10,000 for a single day's work. That $10,000 figure is based on a percentage of the gross revenue. The average pay range is $100 to $700 for ringmen at a wholesale car auction.

Also part of a ringman's duties is to know the "Who, What, When, Why, Where, and How" of performing at any type of auction:

- Who: A ringman will know who is bidding, who is likely to be a bidder or buyer, and who has the last bid, who has the runner-up bid.

- What: A ringman knows what the auctioneer currently has bid, what the auctioneer is asking for, what the prior bid was, what type of items or property their buyers or bidders are waiting to bid on, and what hot buttons to push. A ringman knows a great deal about what they are assisting to sell (product knowledge).

- When: A ringman knows immediately when their bidder is out, when to ask for another bid, when to go back to the runner-up bidder, when a bidder is done, and when the auctioneer is about to sell the item being offered.

- Why: A ringman knows why their buyer is at the auction, why their buyer or bidder wants a specific item or property, why the seller is selling, and why they've been hired to serve as a professional ringman and they look the part by dressing in professional clothing, which may include a vest with the logo of the auction company printed prominently on it.

- Where: A ringman knows where the current bid has come from, where the last bid came from, where the likely buyer or bidder is, and where their assigned section is. They also know how to stay in it.

- How: A ringman knows how to help generate more buyer participation, knows how to communicate with their auctioneer and other ringmen, how to assist their auctioneer when needed, how to negotiate with a buyer when necessary to generate more participation, and how to assist another ringman when needed.

A good ringman will also know how to develop a relationship and a good level of trust with their bidders.

Ringmen Education

Ringmen are educated at either a professional ringman's school, seminars at conferences around the country, or by working as an apprentice ringman with auctioneers; or a combination of all these avenues.

In ringman training, they are taught hand signals to communicate clearly with the auctioneer from a distance in a noisy room. This includes signals showing bid numbers and other information.

For example, a palms up hand gesture means someone is out of money. The letter O pointed at a person indicates he is the owner of the item, and the ringman will not accept bids from that person.

Ringmen also know the numbers and the increments, and how to ask the auctioneer with hand signals if he will cut the bid to a lower price.

Clerks and Support Staff

Auction companies employ many clerks and support staff that carry out much of the hard work of setting up and running the auction, while the auctioneer seems to be the star of the show.

Office people experienced in business management are employed in auctions today. Medium-size firms employ accounting staffers, a human resources manager, an advertising and marketing director, a computer technician, and sometimes a graphic designer to design brochures.

Larger auction firms employ their own lawyers and other highly specialized people that smaller firms hire outside when needed. In small firms, including many family-owned and run businesses, many family members work in varied office jobs to make the family firm successful.

It can also take a lot of people to set up an auction, especially an estate auction where the auction staff must go to a home with an accumulated lifetime of items. They must sort through dozens or hundreds of boxes, clean up furniture, and set up all items for auction. This is where full-time and part-time set-up staffers come into play.

These experienced workers know how to sort and display items in lots for an auction in ways that are attractive and logical for attendees to see when they come to an auction site. Sometimes the set-up staff will find hidden unexpected items in boxes, such as money, drugs, jewelry, or other valuables. The workers have to act ethically and within business guidelines set by their auction company.

Bidders

Bidders are people at the auction trying to buy an item by offering a price (a bid). They hold up their bidder number (printed on a card, or paddle) or simply raise their hand, or sometimes even nod their head (normally only when they have already been bidding and the communication is clear between the bidder-ringman-auctioneer). Nobody wants a bid to be mistakenly made by a bidder who is nodding for some other reason or is simply scratching his nose.

Who can bid at the auction? Attendees who are registered, even children if they are supervised by parents; people qualified by having put down a required down-payment in cases of real estate requirements; auctioneers and even sellers can bid in some states when their involvement is fully disclosed.

A bidder places a bid during a live auction.

Because an auction is an open sale, the rule with few exceptions is that anyone is qualified to become a bidder. A person qualified to become a bidder at an auction may also delegate another to act as an agent or representative in his or her behalf. If an agent does bid for another at an auction without disclosing his or her identity until after the auctioneer's hammer falls, either the principal or the agent may be held liable for the purchase price.

Serious Bidders

There are different types of bidders. There's the novice, which puts in a bid to learn how the process works, and doesn't really care if he wins the item. There's the tentative bidder, who offers a low price for something he or she wants a little, but not much.

Then there are serious bidders. They want the item badly and are willing to bid aggressively to get it. They have likely set a bidding strategy, including a starting bid, an incremental bid procedure (at what higher increments to keep bidding), a maximum bid, and when to exceed their maximum if new conditions appear.

These are savvy veterans. They look serious. They may act fast and confidently. They may ask questions of the auctioneer and may discourage other people from bidding by staring at them or even say something intimidating or antagonistic. Or they may decline to talk to other people. They are deep in the game, and fun to watch.

Puffing Bidders

Bidding at auctions by the seller or his agent is known as *puffing*, or inflating bids, and, unless disclosed, is a fraudulent practice. This is true even in auctions with a reserve because it creates the misleading impression that there is a greater demand for the goods than actually exists.

def•i•ni•tion

Puffing is when a seller, or someone working with him, places bids to run up the price on his property, creating an impression there is greater demand than really exists. He is puffing up the price.

However, this practice is permitted when the auctioneer makes it clear that the seller is reserving the right to bid. It is crucial for the auctioneer to make it very clear to bidders that the seller is reserving the right to bid.

If the auctioneer knowingly takes a bid on the seller's behalf, and notice has not been given to the crowd that the seller reserves the right to bid, the buyer may at the buyer's option void the sale or take the goods at the price of the last good faith bid prior to the completion of the sale.

Bidding by the auctioneer is also legal when disclosed and when approved by the seller. The concern is that, by bidding on the seller's goods, an auctioneer and his or her staff may be acting contrary to the best interests of the seller, to whom they owe a duty of loyalty and utmost good faith.

In reserve auctions, the auctioneer may open the auction at a price below the seller's reserve price just to get the auction started. But under no circumstances can an auctioneer bid for a seller in an absolute auction after bidding has exceeded the seller's reserve price. That is why it is the auctioneer's desire to get the reserve price as low as possible, so the buyers know the property will potentially sell at a reasonable price and the seller has reasonable expectations.

Bid Riggers

Bid rigging is also illegal, and is when agreements exist among buyers at auctions not to bid against each other for the purpose of purchasing goods at low prices. It can be a felony of federal antitrust laws and punishable by fines and imprisonment.

The U.S. Department of Justice prosecutes this action as antitrust violations, bid rigging, or price fixing.

Some common forms include bid suppression, where competitors agree to refrain from bidding or withdraw previous bids so designated bidders can win; complimentary bidding (also known as cover or courtesy bidding), where competitors agree to submit phony bids that won't qualify; bid rotation, where competitors take turns being the low bidder; and market division, where competitors agree to divide markets among themselves.

def•i•ni•tion

> **Bid rigging** is when buyers make agreements at auctions not to bid against each other for the purpose of purchasing goods at low prices.

Sometimes it's a group that elects one person to do all the buying, and then the group divides the items.

Buyers

A buyer is the successful bidder. He only becomes a buyer when the auction hammer falls and the item is declared sold.

There are novice buyers and veteran buyers. Auctioneers treat new buyers as new bidders.

"We're in a constant process of education for bidders and buyers," said an auctioneer. "It's not unusual for us to have an auction where the majority of people in attendance have never been to one before. I explain to the people who I am representing and what their interest is."

Buyers have obligations by law. Some buyers try to back out of a deal. They get buyer's remorse, and regret they bought the item. Maybe they paid too much. Maybe they didn't look at the back of the item and now see a scratch. There are very few situations where you can withdraw a bid after the item is declared sold. State and federal laws govern buyer and seller obligations.

Collectors

Collectors are some of the most frequent and experienced buyers. These are private individuals buying for their own collection of art, cars, or whatever the property may be. They are very savvy about the value of their items, the item history, the construction materials, resale value, and so on.

You may find yourself bidding against collectors. Often they like to talk to fellow bidders about their collections, especially if you ask them about their interests. They may be competing against you for an item, or they may not care for a certain item and be glad to advise you on the value and rarity of an item.

Dealers

Dealers are people buying items at auctions for resale to other customers. Many dealers have shops of their own from which they display and sell. There are antique dealers, art dealers, and so on.

Live auctions are a regular source of goods for dealers, who often go every week. As with collectors, they know the values and almost exactly what they can resell an item for.

Some live auctioneers depend heavily on dealers and sell large amounts to them. These people get to be good friends. Sometimes bidding comes down to one dealer and several individuals, and the dealer will bid higher.

Auctioneers often call dealers to tell them exactly what items are coming to auction.

Sellers

Sellers are the owners of the property who are offering their items for sale auction. These are the people who contract with the auctioneer. The seller tells the auctioneer what type of sale he wants (absolute or reserve, for instance), when and where it should be held, and other details.

The seller is the boss of the whole auction. The auctioneer is working for the seller and usually must follow the seller's directions.

The seller, also called the owner, may be seen standing near the podium or in front of the auction hall talking to the auctioneer or he may be sitting in the front row. The auctioneer and staff will be consulting often with the seller. Some savvy bidders may also ask the seller questions before or during the auction.

Motivated Sellers

The motivated seller has high motivation to sell. This may be a homeowner who is moving to another state and needs to sell his home. It may be a car owner who needs money to pay bills or for some other purchase.

Auctioneers will sometimes advertise that the auction features a motivated seller. Buyers see this as code language that a low price is very possible. But that is not always the case. You never know really how desperate a seller is, unless they have placed a minimum price on the property that is announced to bidders.

An auctioneer wants a motivated seller, but not a desperate seller because that opens the door to potential problems. Desperate sellers have been known to hide defects in property, lie about important aspects, and create other problems.

Veteran Sellers

If you've sold many times by auction, you know the ropes. Veteran sellers can make it easy on the buyers and auction staff by not being demanding and nervous about the process. They know the auction usually results in fair market value for their item.

But veterans also can try to work the system to their advantage in undesirable ways.

"We have to be very strong with sellers and warn them not to bring friends to the auction to drive up the prices," said a longtime auctioneer. "I'll get the legal contracts out and make sure sellers understand that we cannot permit anything like that.

Veteran sellers often also know the laws about what they can and cannot sell. But they still rely on the auctioneer for advice. For example, auction items that can't be sold include a mounted black rhino or seemingly old carved whale's tooth it could end up costing you $20,000 and up to one year in prison.

Although these items don't come up often in the United States, many other seemingly harmless animals do show up regularly enough to take note of the consequences if you were to inadvertently sell one at auction.

Auctioneers should know that certain animals are protected under several federal and state acts that prohibit the sale of live or trophy animals, whole or in part.

Attendees

There are three types of auction attendees: the first are the *auction enthusiasts*, a core of current live auction attendees. They comprise one-third of all current live auction attendees.

The second group is *auction regulars*. They are one-third of current attendees. They're interested in live auctions, but they are not spending as much as the enthusiasts. The third group is *auction potentials*. They don't attend live auctions now, but either have in the past or are likely to in the future. They consist primarily of lapsed live auction attendees and of active online auction consumers. They are well-educated about live auctions, but they are not attending now.

About 92 percent of the potentials have been to a live auction in the past, and they are interested in attending in the future.

> **From the Podium**
>
> Seventy-five percent of attendees bring the whole family when they attend an auction.

How to Interact with People at Auctions

As you learned in this chapter, there is a wide group of people that come together at an auction. It will help your success at auction if you know at least the basics of how they operate, their motivations, and their possible level of experience.

The more you interact with fellow bidders, sellers, auctioneers, and others, the more you will learn, and the more efficient you may become at buying or selling at auction. Auctions are a social atmosphere. People like to talk there. Don't hesitate to strike up a conversation and ask questions.

If a fellow attendee doesn't want to tell you why he is there, he likely thinks you may compete to buy a certain item he wants. Don't take it personally. Just move on. Keep on interacting, learning, bidding, buying, and enjoying.

The Least You Need to Know

- ◆ Auctioneer education includes a two-week auction school and/or a one-year apprenticeship (in some states), followed by continuing education required each year, as determined by state laws.

- ◆ The single most important role an auctioneer has is as a marketing expert, to bring in bidders.

- ◆ A professional ringman does far more than spot bids for the auctioneer. They often establish a relationship with the bidders before an auction, asking which items the bidders are looking for.

- ◆ Bidding at auctions by the seller or his agent is known as puffing, or inflating bids, and, unless disclosed, is a fraudulent practice.

- ◆ Sellers should have reasonable expectations of the price to be obtained at auction. Expect a fair price, not a very high price.

- ◆ There are three types of auction attendees: the auction enthusiast, the regular, and the potential.

Chapter 4

Auction Settings

In This Chapter

♦ Today's modern auction facility

♦ Herd 'em in to the auction barn

♦ Outside auctions are fun and necessary

♦ Special places for special events

The live auction setting is important to all parties involved. The type of building, the location in or near a town, and other factors can help determine whether people want to attend and the amount they want to bid, thereby determining the success or failure of the auction.

From the most upscale, expensive auction art gallery in New York City to the most humble barn where livestock is sold in rural areas, auctions are held inside and outside in nearly every location imaginable.

Who decides where the auction is held? In an auction where there is one seller, such as for an estate, it is a joint decision between the seller and the auctioneer, who gives his advice on the most successful location. An estate auction could be held at the site of the home where sale furniture and other items are currently sitting. Or the auctioneer may advise that all the estate items be moved to the auctioneer's building, which may be more comfortable for attendees and allow better item display.

In the case of a weekly consignment auction or auto auction regularly held in an auction house, with many sellers consigning their items, there's no question that the auction is held at the regular auction house.

This auction barn in Indiana is one of the largest auction facilities in the world.

Auction Houses

In the world of upscale art auctions, it is common to call an auction company an *auction house*. You'll hear people say "Sotheby's is the auction house that sold that item." They mean only the company. But people may also say they are going to Butterfield's auction house for an auction tonight, meaning they are going to the auction facility.

In this chapter, we refer to an auction house as the building where auctions are held. Not every auction company has an auction house. Some auctioneers do not want the costs and maintenance associated with owning or renting a building, and so only hold auctions in outside locations or other venues.

def•i•ni•tion

An **auction house** is a general term for an auction company, but is also used for the building where an auction is held. Rarely does it mean an actual house.

But what does a typical auction house include? Normally there is a large parking area with room to drop off and pick up items; a main auction room where items are displayed and sold; offices on the side for clerking; a concession area for food and beverages; restrooms; and sometimes a backend storage area.

A typical auction house may be in the 5,000 to 10,000 square-foot range. But some auctioneers have built or bought much larger buildings to provide greater services, based on the type of property they sell.

One such facility is in Wellington, Kansas, near Wichita, where auctioneer Larry Theurer, CAI, GPPA, bought a 28,000 square-foot building that once was home to a Wal-Mart. The building was empty for six or seven years, its windows covered with paint. He calls his facility an auction center.

"We believe we can do better for our clients by having them bring all their merchandise to one location—thus the words auction center. And those clients seem to appreciate it," he said. When he books an auction and asks where people would like the items to go for bid—onsite or at the facility—almost invariably, the response is "I want you to take it to your center to sell it."

By being near a major highway and being climate-controlled all year, his building draws attendees from a wide area.

It's no mistake that Theurer calls his facility an auction center instead of an auction barn. To him, there's a big difference between the two.

"We put that idea behind us a long time ago," he said. "What does barn denote to you? Just what it sounds like." Instead, he believes that by calling it an auction center, it attracts a different kind of clientele, "It's all in how you perceive it," he said. "I think auction center are words that attract a little better quality of merchandise."

Today his facility has an auction auditorium in which furniture is sold. There are separate areas for auctions and transactions in progress. There are conference and mailing rooms and an office area.

SOLD!

Many auction company managers routinely reject items of low quality that are unlikely to sell. Not everything a seller offers to an auctioneer is accepted for sale.

In the auction auditorium, furniture up for bid is arranged just so. "I'm a big believer that showmanship is a big part of salesmanship," he said. Furniture isn't set up in rows, but instead in groupings. It might take more time to set it up that way, but the result is that the pieces are viewed as they eventually will end up with other furniture.

And if you visit the auction center, don't expect to experience a marathon day with long auctions that keep people under the roof for hours and hours. Theurer doesn't think people can be kept at an auction more than four or five hours. After a while, they begin to wane. But if people start to get hungry during a visit to the Theurer auction center, they can stop for a quick bite to eat at its cafe. Visitors can take a bite out of the Gavel Sandwich if that sounds good. Or any of the other menu items with auction-themed names.

In all, the cafe seats 40 to 50 people and is an important part of the facility. It gives visitors the chance to get something to eat while they are already at an auction, but it also attracts people who want to look around. The cafe, Theurer said, "gets people out there."

"They come out to eat two or three times a week, just to see what's new in the center," he said. "There may not be anything that they want, but they're going to tell somebody else."

One of the challenges to operating an auction center is inventory control. Thousands of items can get stacked deep in the building before they are auctioned. A manager is in charge of controlling the inventory and keeping track of where the merchandise is and to whom it belongs.

Some auction houses or centers have a holding area where items are placed after being auctioned and before being picked up by the buyer. Some do not, opting instead to hand the item directly to the buyer at purchase.

Many small and large auction centers also try to control inventory by not accepting poor-quality items to sell. When a seller brings a big load of numerous items to drop off at an auction house, the inventory manager has the right to reject items he thinks will not sell, as long as that right is in the contract with the seller.

"We try to screen as much as possible," Theurer said. "We try to be up front and say we don't think it will sell, but we do sometimes have to take things and dump them." And though they won't do any major repairs on items, employees at the center will do things like clean and polish items. If they think major repairs need to be done, they suggest the seller takes care of them. Or they'll get someone to fix it and charge the cost back to the seller.

Seating, Standing, Moving Around

Want a nice seat at a live auction? There may be plush seating, hardwood folding chairs, or no seats at all. In many live auctions, the crowd moves from one area of the auction to another, following the auctioneer as he sells, and everyone stands in a circle around the auctioneer. There may be no chairs for the public, even though there should be for those needing rest or special assistance.

So take your own seating. Put a padded folding chair in the trunk of your vehicle. You may not need to bring it in to the auction house, but, then again, you may decide to! At least you'll be prepared.

Where is the best place to sit at an auction? In the first few rows—it ensures you a good view and that you will be seen easily when you are bidding. But, good ringmen will see you no matter where you are in the auction crowd, so sitting midway back in the crowd may be more your preference so you are not too close to the big video screens and you can see some of your competing bidders.

SOLD! _____

If you want to be sure to get a comfortable seat at some auctions, bring your own folding chair. Sometimes auction crowds stand, with no seating.

Sitting in the very back is sometimes chosen by people who just want to watch the auction, newcomers who do not plan to bid, or people who will be talking with others or on cell phones and do not want to be disruptive.

At a standing-only auction, where should you stand? The answer is where you can see and where you can be seen by the ringmen and auctioneer. Don't get stuck behind a tall person. But, pick a spot and try to stay there while you are actively bidding so the ringmen and auctioneer can see you clearly. When your item comes up for bid, if you can, go ahead and move to the very front of the crowd.

A tip about walking around during an auction: it can be distracting to everyone involved. There are bidders who are incessant auction disrupters. They walk back and forth, bidding from one side to another, shouting out questions, talking on cell phones, badgering about price. Don't be a disrupter.

Auction Barns

A barn is normally referred to as a place livestock is kept. So, it's no surprise that horses, cows, pigs, and other livestock are sold in barns across the world.

A typical auction barn for livestock has pens close to an auction ring. The animals are herded or led from the pens into the ring, where the auction is occurring. The auctioneer sits on a stand above the animals. The crowd sits in semi-circular seating around the ring, also above the animals so they can see the animals clearly.

But although some upscale auctioneers shun the term auction barn, others like its folksy sound as a place where they can sell antiques and other items, especially in the Midwest or rural areas. So, don't let the phrase fool you.

Outside Auctions

Auctions have been held outside probably since at least the Roman era, 2,500 years ago, and still are today. A cool, sunny day spent outside at auction is great fun. But any temperature extremes or bad weather suddenly make the indoor auction look a lot more practical.

When is best to attend an auction outside? Spring and fall, in most parts of the country. (If you're in San Diego, maybe anytime is fine!) That's when most auctioneers probably hold their highest number of auctions outside. But, the main reason for outdoor auctions is cost and logistics. If a seller has a lot of heavy equipment or a high volume of property, the cost to move it indoors may be too high. And, the auctioneer may believe the property will sell better in its "natural location." It is a marketing decision that balances the costs of benefits of the expected sales result.

Why would anyone prefer outdoor to indoor? Many reasons. Outdoor auctions have an informal feel that can be more fun than any indoor location. Auctioneers set up tents to cut the sunshine, and seating to provide comfort. People driving by may see the crowd and pull in on the spur-of-the moment.

The sale items may also be set up outside, such as rows of cars or farm machinery. It's like a car show where people walk from car to car to inspect them and see them sold.

Coping with Bad Weather

Attendees and the auction company should be ready to cope with bad weather. Most auction companies planning an outdoor auction watch the weather forecasts closely and will announce to the crowd their bad weather plan. In case of light rain, they are usually covered fine by tents on site. In case of hard rain with wind, they may move the auction indoors or delay the auction a short time to let the storm pass.

Prepare yourself by carrying an umbrella in your vehicle.

The Auction Topper and Mobile Office

When a live auction is outside, the auctioneer may stand in front of the crowd with the sale items in front of him. Or, he may sit in an auction topper truck while he calls for bids. He may also work alongside the auction clerking trailer, discussed later.

The auction topper is a shell that fits on the back of a pickup truck. The auctioneer can sit in this camper-style shell with an open window, from which he looks out over the crowd. This keeps the auctioneer out of the sun and wind, reducing wind noise into his microphone, and he can sit comfortably during a long auction.

The auction topper usually has the auction company name and contact information painted on the side, which also promotes the firm to attendees. Auction topper styles can range from very simple to elaborate and very expensive.

An auction clerking trailer like this serves as a mobile office at outside auctions.

Another outside auction vehicle is the mobile office, also called a cashier trailer or registration trailer. This is like a recreational vehicle, with space inside for attendees to register, restrooms, and space for auction clerks to work with computers, printers, and other office equipment. These mobile trailers have awnings that fold out to provide weather protection and other features. They typically range in size from 12 to 20 feet.

Hazards at Outdoor Auctions

Sounds like simple advice, but many people don't remember that you must be exceedingly careful at any outdoor auction setting, even more-so than indoors. Although auctioneers are careful in their auction set up, there are electrical wires, holes in the ground, and other hazards.

Estate auctions at the home of elderly people can be special hazards if not cleaned up well. An auctioneer in West Virginia tells of an 87-year-old man who held an estate auction to disperse his belongings before he died. Snakes were one of the hazards the auctioneer had to eliminate before auction.

"As we walked near the pile of railroad ties (weeks before the auction), the seller mentioned that we should not disturb his pet copperhead snakes. We observed two copperheads wrapped around a corn snake. When asked why he didn't kill them, the seller replied, 'There are several here and only one has bitten me,'" the auctioneer said.

"During the removal process, we encountered insects, rodents, snakes, and spiders that are not indigenous to West Virginia and possibly not the contiguous United States. We were also approached by a snake hunting club. They informed us that they would like to purchase all the snakes found on the premises. The next day, 24 men and women showed up for the hunt. They were able to capture nine of the copperheads and two blacksnakes. One of the blacksnakes was more than 6 feet long. The next day, we were informed that two of the copperheads had a total of 11 young."

At outdoor auctions, watch for hazards by examining the ground you walk on, the chairs you sit in (for weak structure), the parking area (for cars darting around unmarked areas), and weather dangers including heat stroke.

Of course, medical problems and broken bones happen indoors. Be aware of your surroundings, especially if children and the elderly are with you. Check for other flammables, such as gasoline, liquid propane tanks, or petroleum-based solvents. If an accident happens, the auction company will call for medical help and offer appropriate help themselves.

You can also help other attendees who are injured. Good Samaritan laws generally prohibit legal action against any person that renders emergency medical care or assistance to an injured person at the scene of an accident or emergency.

Hopefully you and the auction employees are ready to help with general first aid: things such as sprains, scrapes, cuts, burns, or mild chemical exposure. You, and they, should also have a First Aid kit. So, how well are you prepared for emergencies and first aid situations? And are you watching for such oddities as snakes? Be trained, prepared, and ready to act.

Another oddity, but rare possible hazard at estate sales, are feuding family members who can't agree on how the sale of a deceased parent's property is to be conducted. An Arizona auctioneer said she had an auction where "two armed guards were present to prevent the six family members from attacking each other. The auctioneer survived a very contentious auction day and luckily no legal action resulted."

In extreme cases such as this, sometimes an auctioneer will try to talk the family out of having an auction. People usually have an over-inflated idea of what their items are worth and this is even more so the case when people have an emotional attachment to the items being auctioned. Often the estate will just not bring enough money to justify an onsite auction because of the high level of setup to properly prepare the estate for sale.

It is very difficult for heirs or elderly people to give up the possessions of a lifetime. Attendees can see these emotions erupt occasionally at an estate auction. One family member may want to sell a box of highly collectable beaded dresses from the 1920s, while another does not. An argument erupts on the auction site, and makes the auction setting unpleasant for a short time.

Special Settings and Previews

Live auctions are often held in places other than the auctioneer's building, the home where an estate auction is held, or a regular outdoor site of a farm, etc. Let's talk about a few of these, and the previews that are allowed on these sites.

Such sites include commercial businesses, including retail stores, especially where a business is closing. If a bridal shop, for example, is going out of business, you may go to an auction there, in the store, as the inventory is held up or auctioned in racks. This eliminates the need to transport sale items.

Residential real estate auctions are often held at the home, sometimes in the front yard of the home and sometimes inside the home. Neither site is necessarily better, unless the crowd is too large to fit in a small room.

Sometimes an auctioneer will sell several homes in one day, traveling by car from one home to the next, selling each on its site. The attendees may follow in a caravan to each site, bidding on each home.

Another special setting is the storage unit auction, where crowds gather at the door of a rented storage unit that has been abandoned or unpaid by its renter. The auctioneer opens up the door of a rented storage unit, after the auctioneer has been hired by the rental company manager, and the crowd inspects items inside and then bids, hoping for great values on abandoned items.

Previews of sale items occur in different ways for different settings. A preview tour of a home for auction may be allowed by appointment days before the auction, or the auctioneer may open up the home for one hour before the auction. Check with the auctioneer. Smaller estate auction items and storage unit auctions, for example, typically have no advance previews before auction day, but only on the auction day.

def•i•ni•tion

A **multi-ring auction** is one auction location where people are gathered in several rings, adjacent to each other, as auctioneers sell simultaneously in each ring.

A preview is your chance to examine the items well, because they are sold in as-is condition, so take advantage of a preview.

Multi-ring auctions also present a special setting, and they can be inside or outside, sometimes at fairgrounds. A multi-ring auction is one auction setting with multiple auctions occurring at the same time, typically in adjacent rings where small crowds gather in front of each auctioneer.

For example, one auctioneer may be selling antique furniture, while another is selling artwork and household goods. While this is occurring in one building, outside there may be a hay bale auction occurring, and next door in the barn there may be a live-stock auction going. Many rings of action!

One such auction is by auctioneer Ken Frecker, CES, in New Haven, Indiana. He hires three to seven auctioneers working separate rings that operate simultaneously. Each man has his own public address system. They're aided by ring people when needed at the front line, and an organized backstage crew of clerks, cashiers, and car parking attendants.

This multi-ring auction shows the small crowd gathered around one of the many rings operating at the same time.

A large auction facility in Missouri.

Another multi-ring auction he conducts is at the Hillsdale, Michigan fairgrounds and includes a flea market area, which adds to the unusual setting.

"When we took over the business in 1993, there were about five vendors. Now in the summer we get 150 to 200," he said about the flea market vendors.

At these multi-ring auctions, often the seller sets up his own display of the items. Naturally, he will try to get the auctioneer to sell something that normally an auction manager may reject as low quality.

One auctioneer said "Sometimes you have a seller who has no idea that a worn out inner tube that will fit nothing is worth nothing. They're holding it up during the auction, trying to get you to sell it as the auctioneer."

Auctioneers handle this by charging sellers a dumping fee if their items can't be sold. This makes sellers choosier about what they bring in.

> **From the Podium**
>
> Auction companies are trying many methods today to draw more young people to auctions, including having a comfortable setting and sale items that young people desire.

These multi-ring auctions have a country flavor, an old-fashioned sale bazaar atmosphere that many people like. Multi-ring auctions serve as important community marketplaces, drawing together huge numbers of buyers and sellers. They are also an excellent training ground for new auctioneers.

If you attend a multi-ring auction, you may want to bring a friend to help you cover all the property coming up for auction in the different locations, so you don't miss bidding on items that you desire.

The Least You Need to Know

- The term auction house can refer to an auction company, or the building where an auction is held. Rarely does it mean an actual house.

- An auction topper is a shell that fits on the back of a pickup truck. The auctioneer can sit in this camper-style shell with an open window, from which he looks out over the crowd.

- Take your own chair to a live auction, even if you end up leaving it in your car—you never know what the seating arrangements will be like.

- Multi-ring auctions are a special setting that live auction fans enjoy for their great variety of items and entertainment.

Chapter **5**

Finding Auctions and Deciding to Attend

In This Chapter

- From newspapers to road signs
- All in one place: the auctioneer's website
- Go prepared, from chair to checkbook
- Auction duration: a few minutes to twelve hours

So, you're ready to go to a live auction to find certain items or just to look and enjoy the excitement of the event. How do you find live auctions and decide if it is a good one for you to attend?

Finding live auctions is mainly through advertising formats reaching you, and you reaching out to the auctioneer or his website for information.

Still highly popular and effective are ads in newspapers and trade magazines. Direct mail from auction companies is also an advertisement that finds its way to you. There are outdoor signs. There are TV and radio ads. Perhaps the fastest way is using the Internet to find your local auction companies' websites, which list their upcoming auction dates and site. Let's look at these varied methods.

Advertisements

Many newspapers have special sections, often called the *auction block*—usually in their classified ads section—which advertises live auctions. Look especially in the Wednesday, Friday, and weekend editions as they advertise upcoming weekend auctions.

The ads describe details of one upcoming auction: an estate auction, home auction, and so on. They tell about sale items and sometimes show photos. A new trend in auction advertising, because newspaper ads are increasingly expensive, is that the auctioneer runs a small ad that mostly directs the reader to visit the auctioneer's website for more details.

In the past, auctioneers ran big ads with more photos and lists of sale items, but today those things are posted on websites.

Many auction attendees also search for ads in their trade magazines, meaning specialty publications such as those for antiques, tractors, and other products. Auctioneers place ads there to target collectors specifically. If you want antiques, you should be subscribing to antiques magazines and looking for ads in the back of those magazines.

Road signs, yard signs, and billboards are another way to find auctions. Signs go up in front of homes for auction weeks before the sale saying "Real estate auction or "Estate auction " and give the date and contact information for more details. Stop and write down the contact information and then call for more information, or visit the auctioneer's website.

SOLD!

Local cable TV ads are increasingly used to market live auctions, especially real estate, to reach the exact types of potential buyers desired.

TV and radio ads are also used more today than ever before to advertise live auctions. Cable television ads have become less expensive recently and are used by a growing number of auctioneers to hit target markets.

"I run ads on cable TV for the County Tax Delinquent Property auctions that we do and get good response," said a New York state auctioneer.

An Arkansas auctioneer uses cable ads for six auctions in a typical year. He runs a 30-second commercial 2,300 times during three weeks. "Every time the spot runs we get phone calls and you can always tell when a commercial has run because we watch the hit counter on our website," he said. The advertising targets professionals; doctors and attorneys that watch programming such as CNN and ESPN, among others.

TV ads often start out with a scene of an auctioneer doing the chant at a live auction in front of a crowd, which grabs the attention of the viewer, especially the auction lovers. A voice-over announcer then describes the upcoming auction and gives the website address for more information. It's often easier to remember a simple website address than a long phone number, so that approach is taken as more people have computer access.

Auction direct mail is advertising that comes directly to a list of auction attendees that the auctioneer has compiled or purchased. Use it to your advantage; don't just throw it away without looking at what the auction items for sale are.

A good mailing list of qualified buyers is the key. Auction direct mailings are aimed to be consistent and regular. They are written in such a way that they try to demand a response from you.

Radio ads are also used for live auctions, but radio is perhaps the most highly targeted media. A rap music station has a specific young audience, whereas a news station or classical music station has an older audience. You'll notice the different types of live auctions ads on each station.

"A radio representative may come in and say they have listeners within the ages of 25 to 55 with an average yearly income of $125,000. That sounds like someone who would buy real estate right? But it could be a youth-oriented audience whose lifestyle tends more toward expensive cars than nice homes," one auctioneer said.

Typically auction firms run their radio ads about a week before the sale. For real estate they make good use of radio's broad coverage in a specific geographical location.

A live remote broadcast the day before an auction is also used to get people to attend an auction preview. A live remote broadcast from the preview location has the ability to catch those people listening to the radio in their cars and within driving distance of the area. Because it's broadcast as an event, there's less intimidation for auction novices, and more attraction as something to see and browse. Auctioneers highlight plenty of incentives to get visitors to return for the actual auction, such as bargains, unique items, local celebrities, and charity benefits.

Mine the Gold in Auctioneer Websites

Your local auction companies' websites likely have a calendar of upcoming live auctions right on the first page of the website. The company wants to make it easy for you to find the auction date, location, item catalog, and other details, so they put them in a visible spot on the homepage of the website.

When you see a live auction on the schedule you may want to attend, click on the photo or underlined link for more information. Also be sure to sign up with your local auctioneer to get regular e-mailed notices of upcoming auctions. There is usually a button on the auctioneers website that says "Sign up for e-mail notices," or similar wording. Some auctioneers send thousands of these notification e-mails each week to huge lists of attendees.

An auctioneer's website has sections listing upcoming auctions.

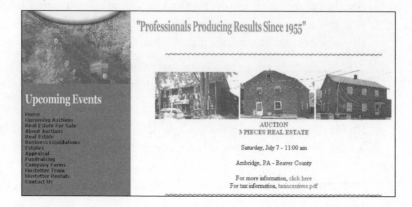

Websites help establish an auctioneer's credibility. While you are on the website, look around in all sections of it. You'll learn more and become a better bidder and buyer. There are photos of past auctions, info on the company's history, and success stories.

Another way to find the types of live auctions you want is to search on the Internet for them. Go to a search engine website, such as www.google.com, and enter something such as "estate auctions, California" and it will bring up many links to websites with estate auctions in California, or any other state you want. You'll have to wade through some websites not of interest to you, but many will be.

Some companies or auction-related organizations also have an easy and very specific search function to find live auctions near you. One is at the National Auctioneers Association website, www.auctioneers.org. At the top of the homepage is a Find an Auction button. You can enter the type of auction you seek, the date and location area, and hit Enter and it will bring up a list for you.

Deciding to Attend

You want to make a good decision about whether to attend a certain auction. What factors make you decide in favor or against?

Sale item is the top factor on the list. Does the auction have a certain exact item that you want? Or, does it have a range of items, maybe antique dressers and other furniture that you think you may want but need to see in person? Let's face it: you decide to attend an auction to buy something of interest to you.

Secondly, how badly do you want the item or items, versus the distance you must travel to attend that particular auction. If you want a certain rare painting very much, but the live auction is a six-hour drive, you'll go anyway. The distance is a minor obstacle for you.

If you are only interested in a few items, contact the auction company in advance to find out if you can submit absentee bids, which are written bid proposals prior to auction day. Typical absentee bids terms are: the bids be in writing, payment is guaranteed if you are the high bidder, and you must identify your opening bid and maximum bid. The auctioneer will then bid on your behalf in the manner consistent with the bidding increments set for the auction. These could be $50, for example. The auctioneer will not automatically sell the item for your maximum bid. Thirdly, expectation of a *bargain* is a big deciding factor for many people. Because some people still equate an auction with a last-resort method of sale (often a forced sale) they think they are more likely to get a big bargain—buying an item at a price far below its real value.

In fact, the bigger the bargain the buyer perceives he got, the happier he or she is. That's part of the psychology behind retail stores advertising a "75 percent off sale." Wow, you think, "I'm paying far less than this is really worth! What a good deal for me!"

But, keep in mind, this is not a garage sale, where prices are often intentionally cut to be as low as possible to sell something. The auctioneer works to prevent any buyer from paying far less than an item is truly worth. He wants you, the bidder, to get a good value, but he wants the seller to get as much as possible by bringing in competing buyers to establish the *fair market value*, on that day. Don't expect (or demand) to get a bargain. Expect to get a fair price.

def•i•ni•tion

Fair market value is the most probable price which an item, including real estate, should bring in a competitive and open market under all conditions requisite to a fair sale.

So, at some time you may hear the auctioneer say something about fair market value. Let's tell you what that is exactly.

Fair market value is not only The most probable price" which an item should bring at auction, but the buyer and seller each must each be acting prudently and knowledgeably, and assuming the price is not affected by undue stimulus.

These definitions have several important components that you should know and recognize at auction, including that

◆ the buyer and seller are typically motivated.

◆ both parties are well informed or well advised, and acting in what they consider their own best interests.

◆ a reasonable time is allowed for exposure in the open market.

◆ payment is made in terms of cash in U. S. dollars or in terms of financial arrangements comparable thereto

◆ the price represents the normal consideration for the property sold unaffected by special or creative financing or sales concessions granted by anyone associated with the sale (USPAP 2003 Edition, p. 224). The *Uniform Standards of Professional Appraisal Practice* (USPAP) are generally accepted standards for professional appraisal practice in North America. USPAP standards are set by The Appraisal Foundation for all types of appraisal services. Standards are included for real estate, personal property, business and mass appraisal.

Notice that this definition states that market value is the *most probable* price that a property *should* bring. It is important to recognize that market value is an estimate of value, not a statement of fact.

If an auction price is equivalent to market value, then these conditions, terms, and relationships of the auction must match those in the definition.

Social Event, Entertainment, and Education

You may decide just to go to a live auction as a social event. You may decide that you're not as interested in buying as you are in taking the family for a fun day of being at an auction, meeting friends there, educating your children about auctions and items, and so on. All are good reasons to decide to attend.

Here's an example: auctions are a way of life in central Pennsylvania, a major part of the social fabric. The unique blend of cultures there include the Amish, the Pennsylvania Dutch, and those of English background, and they all enjoy auctions as a social gathering and for commerce.

The town of Gordonville, Pennsylvania, population 100, holds an annual mud sale (so-called because the mammoth consignment sales are held during spring's traditional rainy season). This sale attracts more than 17,000 people from Pennsylvania and 24 other states. More than 5,000 bid numbers are given out during the course of the day.

A mud sale auction in Pennsylvania.

The narrow streets are lined with cars and horse-drawn buggies; both filled with anxious auction-goers. The automobiles and carriages are forced to park in the muddy side roads and fields. The horses are walked to a nearby barn to keep warm, only the chassis are left outside to the elements.

"A lot of people come with the intention of spending money," says Ralph Shank, the mud auction's general chairman. "They have a good time, even if they end up buying things they don't need."

The one-day marathon auction, which is spread across seven acres, features more than 20 auctions at the same time. Shank says 75 registered auctioneers donate their time and talents for the day, in exchange for free food and fellowship.

"We treat them good," he says. "They have a warm place to relax and plenty of coffee and good old-fashioned Pennsylvania Dutch food." Quilts and other soft goods, most made by the electricity- and car-shunning Amish, are big favorites at the sales, as are antiques, crafts, furniture, and collectibles. Other auctioneers call the bidding for horses, buggies, farm implements, straw/hay, household items, produce, and food.

Gordonville is just one of several mud sales held in picture-postcard-like Lancaster County for the benefit of the local fire companies. Other spring mud sales are held in nearby Gap, Bart Township, and historic Strasburg, scene of the movie *Witness*, starring Harrison Ford.

If people go there only looking for a bargain, they might leave empty-handed and disappointed. The large crowd of out-of-state bidders, drawn by the high-quality Amish goods and the friendly, almost carnival-like atmosphere, easily pushes up the prices. But, when you have the opportunity to buy unique items at auction like this, it is often worth it.

Another deciding factor: the terms and conditions and fees may affect whether you want to attend the auction. If you don't want to buy something in as-is condition, and that is the firm condition under which items are sold, then you may not want to attend that particular auction. Check the payment methods also. It's unlikely, but you may find the auction firm does not accept the only payment methods you are able to offer, so why attend that auction?

Some auction houses also require a deposit as soon as your bid is accepted. What can you do if you are bidding on several lots in a row? Leave a check with the auction house before the bidding starts to cover any bids you may make. Full payment is also due immediately after the estate auction. If you don't buy anything, your check will be returned.

Another thing to be aware of is the fact you may be required to remove your purchases immediately or within a certain time period such as within 24 to 48 hours. Be sure to check the house policy and have your transportation set up. This may affect your desire to attend that particular auction, versus another one on the same day with a different policy.

Does it cost to attend the auction? That may be a deciding factor, also. Most auctions have no attendance fee, but some benefit auctions may have a fee to attend dinner with the live auction starting midway through dinner. These charity auctions and fundraisers are becoming more numerous and professionally run in communities all across America. You may already have noticed this change if you attend fundraisers for your local churches, schools, civic groups, nonprofit organizations, or other groups.

Style and reputation of the auctioneer may also influence your decision to attend. In some cases, you may not like the personality style of the auctioneer or feel he or she does not have a good reputation, and therefore decide not to attend. In most cases, give the auctioneer the benefit of the doubt. You are usually at an auction to buy an item, not to socialize with the auctioneer.

A final tip about deciding to attend a live auction: remember that you also can attend many live auctions via computer , while staying home, and placing your bids by computer. You can also attend by sending someone in your place to bid for you. But for the most effective and fun way, go in person.

Catalogs Help You Decide

Item catalogs are a big help in deciding whether to attend an auction. Many auction firms publish photographic catalogs with descriptions and estimated values for each lot. A lot may refer to a single item or to a group of items auctioned together. The catalogs also include the dates and times for the previews and auctions. While this is most common for high-dollar items, it is also be used for unusual collections of mid-ranged priced items like collector dolls and other items. Online versions of catalogs are available on the auction firm's website generally three to four weeks prior to the auction. You may purchase a catalog or sign up for a one-year subscription and have a copy automatically delivered, along with the prices realized from the last sale. You may also sign up to be on the firm's mailing list to get exclusive information on your select areas of collecting via e-mail and alert you when the catalog is placed online.

Some catalogs are scholarly and beautifully illustrated, and many experience a second life as important art-world reference tools. Descriptions in fine catalogs include information about provenance (ownership history), size, condition, the artist or specific work if available, and value estimates.

Estimates in the catalogs are provided as an approximate guide to current market value, and should not be interpreted as a representation or prediction of actual selling prices. This estimate, expressed in a low/high range of dollar amounts, is reached after a specialist compares prices realized for similar items in recent auctions and other sales venues. Other factors that guide the setting of estimates include the condition, rarity, provenance, and market potential of the item. They are determined well in advance of a sale and are subject to revision.

Previews

Auction previews are your chance to inspect each item before the auction. Pick up the item, run your hand over it, look for any faults and be sure you can accept them. Look for faults in the finish and structure. Condition reports for some sale items may be available upon request. Look for loose or missing table legs, a vehicle that doesn't start, or glassware that has chips or cracks. Although these may be acceptable to you, it may affect the amount you want to bid, so look before you bid.

def•i•ni•tion

An **auction preview** is an open house time when the public is invited to inspect property for sale at auction, prior to the sale.

The times of the preview can be obtained from the auction company's website, or advertisement, or by calling the company. At the previews, staff is available to answer your questions and guide you through the auction process.

What to Take to an Auction

Take an official identification card, which may be requested when you register and at payment time. An ID card can include a driver's license, with your full name, age, photo, and address; or can be a nondriver's ID card which are commonly given in New York and some other states and serve the same identification purpose but do not provide driving privileges.

Take some form of payment: cash, check, credit cards, debit cards, or so on. Check with the auction company before the auction to see what types of payment they accept.

A typical weekly consignment auction at an auction house accepts cash, local check, Visa and Mastercard, and other credit cards. But, at their onsite auctions, away from their building, they may accept only cash and local checks, not wishing to deal with the costs of processing credit cards. Check with the specific company.

Bring a large enough vehicle to transport your item, if possible. If you can't, some auction houses will let you pick up within 24 hours, giving you time to rent a vehicle or arrange other pickup.

Bring things to secure and protect your item for transport, including soft blankets, ropes, or tie-down cords.

Bring personal items. A pen to write in the catalog to note sale prices, a folding chair (in case the auction does not have a comfortable one—you can always leave it in your car), an umbrella in case the auction is outside without a tent, any medication you need during the day (you don't want to have to leave just as your item is coming up for bid), and any other items you need to be comfortable on a day trip.

Bring a good attitude to a live auction. Bring your patience and an expectation to have a good time. Don't be a bidding bully, a snob to other bidders, or a disrupter. Some people come to an auction to disrupt, even stop the auction for some reason. They shout and even tell lies.

Disrupters can be removed by auction staff or by police from an auction. Here's an example, so you'll know what can happen (but usually does not!).

An auctioneer in Virginia said "While doing my pre-auction announcements on a condo unit, a real estate agent (and resident of the complex) interrupted and stated to my registered bidders that, even if they were the successful bidder, they may not be able to live in the unit unless approved by the board as stated in the house rules. She then stated to all present that we (the auction company and the owner of the condo) had no right to auction the unit. At this point, two of the six bidders walked out."

"This disrupter also printed in her condo monthly newsletter that the auction company had agreed not to sell the unit for less than $500,000. It was untrue. The seller's reserve price was below that and never made any such agreement."

So, if you have a disagreement, keep it out of the live auction. Talk to the auctioneers in private. Be a good auction attendee.

How Much Time Live Auctions Take

In the distant past it was widely accepted that people wanted to spend all day at a live auction. Lunch was sometimes served by the auction company to the crowd. By today's standards, that was a slower time.

Today, auctioneers try to complete an estate auction (that used to take all day) in three to four hours.

SOLD!

It is perfectly acceptable, even preferable, to tell the auction-eer that you request a certain item be moved up in the lot order so you can bid on it sooner.

"Many people today want to drop in to get an item and then leave," says an estate auctioneer in Washington D.C., "so I try to be done in four hours."

To help you spend even less time, auctioneers will announce a timeframe for the sale of each section of items. For example, at 1 P.M. he will start selling furniture, at 2 P.M. jewelry, and so on.

But, it is also perfectly acceptable, even preferable, to tell the auctioneer that you request a certain item be moved up in the lot order so you can bid on it sooner. He may agree, if the request is reasonable and is acceptable to the seller.

He may want to wait if a different time has been advertised or if another bidder for that item is expected to arrive after the time you want to bid. It's a balancing act by the auctioneer, but he wants to help you if he can. You may also want to call days ahead of time and make that request.

Another tip to really save you time: offer to buy the item before the auction. The seller may take your offer. Some items, including homes, are sold before the auction, which is then cancelled in time to notify prospective attendees. Although auctioneers want to carry through with the auction, they will advise the seller on the best course of action when a good offer obtained in advance. If the seller is under financial pressure and a pre-auction offer includes a quick payment, the seller may choose the "certain money." It is the seller's decision.

Some live auctions still take all day. Estate auctions, or auto sales or other auctions can still take eight or ten hours if there is a huge amount of material to sell. This is fun, too.

The Least You Need to Know

- To find live auctions, look for the auction block section of your local newspaper.

- Use your local auctioneers' websites to see the upcoming list of live auctions, and to sign up for e-mailed notices of auctions.

- Check with the auction company before the live auction to see what types of payment they accept.

- Tell the auctioneer that you request a certain item be moved up in the lot order so you can bid on it sooner.

Part 2

Bidding and Buying Basics

Almost everyone knows the idea of placing a slightly higher bid to win an item at auction, but there are actually three basic bidding strategies you can use to buy at auction. And when you are deciding how much to bid, you should also know whether a buyer's premium and other fees apply and will affect your final payment. In this part, you'll find out those details and also get a quick overview about how a live auction works, from registering when you enter to paying as you leave. But be sure to dig in to the chapter on bidding strategies!

Chapter 6

How Live Auctions Work: Basic Steps

In This Chapter

- ◆ Your first stop: the registration table
- ◆ These are the conditions you agree to
- ◆ Examine closely and buy carefully
- ◆ Payment sheet tallies all the charges

Let's do a brief run-through of what goes on at live auctions, from your arrival at the site to the time you take your item home.

We'll pretend in this chapter that you've just arrived at the auction site. We'll walk through the day and even describe what goes on behind the scenes (that attendees don't usually see).

Some of these topics will be covered in more depth in later chapters, but here are the basics to help every novice and to give a few reminders to the auction veterans. The information here applies to virtually every type of live auction.

When you arrive at the auction, you'll usually see a big sign in front of the building that identifies clearly where parking is allowed and where the entrance door to the auction center is located. (If there is not, tell the auction staff they should post those!)

Look for a parking spot that will get you in and out without getting boxed in where people will be loading furniture or other items bought at the auction. The auction staff should keep loading areas clearly marked, but take the initiative to guard your own access and your own vehicle from being bumped or boxed in.

Parking at outdoor auctions can also be in a field, so watch for mud, holes, and other problems for your car (and for walking!). You do not normally need a parking permit, unless you are at a swanky auction in a fancy area of town.

Enter the auction at the door indicated and look first for the registration table, counter, or window area. There should be a sign indicating the registration area.

A registration table like this at auction may have several people working by hand or at computers.

Register at the Door or Pre-Register

What is registration? It's where attendees give their name, address, and other information to the auction company so they can provide you with a bidder number and have your information on hand in case you buy something and come through the checkout area later to make a payment.

Most important, it's also where you sign the registration document that explains to you the conditions of the auction. Your signature means you agree to abide by the conditions of the sale.

At most auctions today you cannot bid unless you are registered and have a bidder number. Auctioneers and sellers do not want a disorganized event where people are bidding who are not registered and who may leave after placing a high bid, but before paying.

Being registered gives the bidder at least a minimal feeling of commitment to act responsibly in the process. If the registered bidder disappears after making a high bid, he or she can usually be tracked down through his registration address.

Pre-registration is also something you may need for some types of auctions, such as city property auctions or real estate auctions. A city government offering surplus property, or other sellers offering valuable property, may require you to post a down payment before you can bid. This can be done with the pre-registration.

To pre-register, go to the auction company website (or the city's website, for example) and download a pre-registration form, fill it out, and fax it back. Then when you arrive at the auction, go to the pre-registration line to get a bidder number.

Pre-registration is also beneficial for you, the attendee, by getting this small chore completed before auction day. And it helps the auction company and seller to more closely estimate the number of bidders coming to the auction.

A registration form is typically a one-page sheet, front and back. The front side of the sheet has blanks for you to fill in your name, address, phone number, e-mail address, driver's license number, and a place to make a check mark beside the form of payment you will be using (cash, company check, personal check, and so on).

Below that, the form states a very important section: the terms of the auction. You are asked to sign and, by doing so, are committed to those conditions.

Terms and Conditions on the Registration Form

Here's an example of several common conditions on the registration form:

◆ Provide accurate personal information on registration forms (don't lie!).

◆ In a dispute between bidders, the auctioneer settles the dispute or can put the item up for auction again to resolve the dispute.

◆ Each item is sold as-is, meaning no implied promise to correct defects. All sales are final.

◆ Purchaser assumes complete responsibility upon auctioneer saying "SOLD!"

◆ In case of legal action arising from this auction, the case will be governed by laws of this state.

◆ I agree that there are sufficient funds in my account to pay for the purchase of this item at auction.

Each auction company may have some different conditions. Read them carefully and if you don't agree, don't sign and don't bid. But know that most auction companies include standard business terms and are trying to serve you, the bidder; they are not trying to take advantage of you.

Registration for real estate auctions has something extra: a Property Information Package (PIP). This contains property photos, descriptions, terms of the sale and financing information, along with all pertinent documents, in hard copy (or it is also downloadable online in Adobe Acrobat or .pdf format).

Real estate auctioneers encourage bidders to register one to two hours before the auction. By doing so, you will have more time to consult with onsite staff who are prepared to assist you with your last minute questions regarding the property and the auction process.

Your Bidder Number

As soon as you are registered, the clerk will give you a bidder number that is printed on a hard-paper paddle, sheet of paper, or some other form. This is the item you hold up when you make a bid. If you place the highest bid, the auctioneer will see your number and say "Sold to bidder number 102" (for example). A clerk watching the action will write down that bidder 102 purchased that item, and will expect to see you for payment later.

Your bidder number (or paddle) may have the bidder number printed on both sides, or just one side (and the auction company logo on the other side). Be sure to notice that, and hold the numbered side toward the auctioneer when you bid.

You may also wish to return the bidder paddle at the checkout table when you leave. If you lose your bidder paddle during an auction, tell the staff immediately and get a new paddle.

Grab That Auction Catalog

When you register, the clerk will offer you an auction catalog, which will list the items for sale. The catalog may be as simple as a printed list (no photos) of items in order, or it may be a full-color, glossy, thick publication with photos, descriptions, estimated values, and other details.

Hang on to your catalog. Use it to follow along through the sale. Take your pen and mark off the items sold so you can easily keep track. Many people also write the prices beside each item after they are sold. They do this for future reference in case they want to compare prices to a similar item at a future auction.

An auction catalog such as this is your guide to the order and details of items that come up for auction.

Examine the Lots

The hour before an auction is one of your best times to examine items, also called *lots*. There may not have been a separate time for a formal auction preview of the property prior to this auction day, or maybe you could not attend that preview.

So these minutes before the auction starts can be a time to examine the items closely. Most times the auction staff encourages you to do that and will assist you and answer your questions.

def•i•ni•tion

Every auction item receives a number, which is referred to as an auction **lot**. Also, several small items, such as hand tools, can be grouped together and sold as one lot.

From the Podium

In this pre-auction period, take a minute to meet other attendees. Most of them are happy to talk and enjoy the social atmosphere.

Many auction companies publicize the exact examination time on their website, along with a brief description of how the auction will progress. Here's an example: "Public live auction item viewing will begin at 3:00 P.M. Viewing will end at 5:45 P.M. The live auction will start at 6:00 P.M. The live auction will occur with two tables (40 items), then a brief 10-minute break will occur. After another two tables (40 more items) another 10-minute break will be taken, and so on."

In some auctions, such as storage unit auctions, the examination is like a treasure hunt. The auctioneer opens the storage unit and pulls out boxes, but in most states the units must be sold in bulk (all items together), and no one is allowed to touch anything because the delinquent renter can pay his debt up to the start of the auction. But sometimes buyers find great values, from jewelry to rare motorcycles that have been abandoned by the owner for some reason. The attendees have only a few minutes to examine the items and determine what their high bid will be.

Tips for how to examine items:

♦ Look closely at the entire item. Has it been repainted? Visualize what you could do to change the look of the item.

♦ Check for cracks, loose legs, and other structural problems. Ask yourself how you could fix those and whether you should fix those (if you plan to resell a rare item, often its best to leave it in the condition found instead of changing it).

♦ Call someone for more information. At auctions you often see people on cell phones asking a spouse or expert for guidance. You hear the attendee say "I've found a great oak dresser. The finish is good and it has one cracked leg. How much should I bid?" You'll probably have time to make such a call before the auction, or at least before the item comes up. Keep your voice low to be considerate of other people around you.

♦ Remember the as-is condition of sale. The seller will not promise to fix any defects. One of the appeals of an auction is that you buy the item with any defects you see.

Examine furniture closely.

In the examination period, there may be some items you may touch only while an auction staffer is watching you, to ensure the item is not stolen (small jewelry). And you may be prohibited from touching some items, such as rare paintings, where a touch may damage the product.

The seller has the right to determine how items can be examined. You do not have a right, as bidder, to demand to touch an item. You are not the owner yet.

Behind the scenes tip: before every auction, the auctioneer and staff are watching and sizing up the bidders. They are looking for likely high bidders, possible thieves, potential groups of fraudulent bidders working together as a coordinated ring, and so on.

"We look at the audience to determine age, experience, and buying experience and consider their motive for being there," one auctioneer said. "Why are these people here? Are they here to buy for professional reasons or are they here for entertainment? Are they here for social reasons?"

Announcements and a Mock Auction

Next, the auctioneer takes the podium and makes welcoming comments and announcements.

One announcement may be changes to the lot order. Some items may be moved up sooner or back later in the schedule for some reason. The auctioneer will usually tell why.

Some items may have been sold prior to the auction. As mentioned before in this book, that practice is permitted, but the auctioneer always tries to alert bidders prior to auction day.

There may also be items added to the auction. The auction staff may hand out an addendum sheet (addition) to the catalog. The auctioneer will announce that, also. He may also announce any additional conditions of the auction that were not printed on the registration form.

After all comments, the auctioneer may say he will take a minute to hold a one-minute *mock auction* to show attendees how bidding works. This is helpful for first-time bidders and breaks the ice a bit before the actual selling begins.

The auctioneer will do a mock sale of one item. Someone will hold up an item, and ringmen often will act as bidders making bids. They may play out a couple scenarios of bidders hotly competing, or bids coming in very slowly. Then the auctioneer pounds the gavel and says "SOLD!"

def•i•ni•tion

A **mock auction** is a practice example of selling an item so attendees can see how the process of bidding and acceptance works in the live auction.

A mock auction can be more complicated, and necessary, in a multi-parcel real estate auction. In this live auction, auctioneers sell multiple tracts of land and keep track of bids on boards as groups of parcels are put together. The mock auction shows the bidders how the process works before they really start the auction.

Bidding and Buying

Finally the auction is ready to begin. Take your seat, it's showtime! Most auctioneers move quickly into the first item. The crowd is excited to begin. Be ready to bid!

Open your catalog and see the first item. A ringman may hold it up in the air for the crowd to see, or it may simply appear on a large video screen.

The auctioneer will first briefly describe the item. "This is a Dell Laptop computer, brand new, with a 15-inch screen and …" This description is to confirm the item matches what is in the catalog, and to get you interested. Look at what a neat item this is!

Then the auctioneer will tell at what bid amount he wants to start the bid. He may first say "Let's start this at $900. Who will give $900?"

Now the auction has really begun. The auctioneer is asking for bids. Bidders will respond and start the bidding where they desire, which may or may not be $900. In the next chapter we'll get in to bidding strategies and psychology. Bidding can be as simple or complicated as you want for yourself.

Let's say somebody thinks that Dell computer is a good buy at $900, so he bids. He holds up his bidder card. The auctioneer asks for $950 because he wants to get more money. But there are no bidders at $950. He backs down to ask for $925. No bidders. The auctioneer yells "SOLD!" and it's over just that fast.

If the item did not have a reserve price, or if the reserve price was met, that item is sold. The bidder instantly became the buyer (and new owner) when the auctioneer yelled "SOLD!" The buyer is now in possession of the item.

Talk about wearing many hats! Did you notice the bidder instantly became buyer, owner, and possessor? What does that all mean to him?

Here are a few things it means: he's now obligated to pay that exact amount bid. He's made a legal contract by placing the bid and winning. He is the owner, so all rights and responsibilities transfer to him. If the item is dropped and breaks, he's still obligated to pay (so he should grab that laptop and hold it!, but only after it is paid for). And, as possessor, he's obligated to arrange to take that item home, usually within 24 hours, but some auction companies require you to take the item away on the day of the auction unless other arrangements are made. Behind the scenes tip: all the auction staff knows these basics. A novice buyer may not! The auction staff (and even other bidders) will try to tell the new buyer these things for the buyer's own protection and to avoid complications for other attendees.

After the item is sold, a ringman may hand the item directly to the buyer or, if it's a large item, it will stay put for later pickup.

Now the auction moves on to the next item and the process begins anew with a fresh set of possibilities. Any kind of bidding can occur! That's the excitement of the live auction.

Buyer Beware

Put your item in a safe place immediately after you've won your bid, if possible. Don't let other attendees handle your item. It they break it, you've got a dispute with them, not the auction company or the seller.

On the next item, you may also hear new things said. The auctioneer may say "We've got a $1,000 bid from the Internet," or "We have a pre-auction bid of $1,000 that comes in to play at this time." Those kinds of comments may take you totally by surprise if you're only thinking bids come from bidders standing on the floor. We'll discuss what those mean in the next chapter, but the point here is to pay close attention to what the auctioneer is saying, and be educated as to what these comments mean (that's why you're reading this book!).

As the auction carries on, you may want to leave your seat to go to the concession stand or the restroom. No problem at all, but don't leave your bidder card or paddle unattended where someone else can take it. Live auctions are usually an informal setting, and nobody will take your seat if you put a coat or something on it to make it appear reserved.

But watch that you don't miss an item coming up that you want to bid on. It happens and is highly frustrating! You might get caught up in a phone conversation outside and stay too long away from the auction floor. Stay focused!

Also as the auction continues on, you may see a new auctioneer take the podium. This is normal. Auctioneers need to rest their voices, so an assistant or partner may take over for a short or long period.

You may have to listen closely to get your hearing adjusted to understand the new auctioneer's chant. But the auctioneer's goal is to be very easy to understand and to carry on in all ways from the previous auctioneer.

Checkout Payment and Pickup

At many live auctions, you do not need to wait until the auction is over to pay and take your item home. Just head to the checkout window or table, make your payment, and out you go.

A buyer paying before he leaves.

Auctioneers know that many people today want to leave after they have bought their item, so they set their business practices to accommodate that. But this depends on each auction house.

What all is included in your payment? Here are the elements: These are normally all included in the payment sheet handed to you for the clerk for your inspection when you go to the clerking table or office to pay.

♦ Your final bid amount (the amount you bid and was accepted as the final winning bid by the auctioneer)

♦ A buyer's premium (buyers at many live auctions are required to pay an additional percentage fee to the auction house based on the final price of the bid. This may help pay the auctioneer's fee, advertising, and other costs).

♦ Any shipping and handling fees

♦ Sales taxes

Quick checkout options: some auctions have a fast checkout service. You can give the clerks a blank signed check made out to the auction company, or let the company imprint your credit card, and then the form. Your bidder card will be marked as "paid in full." The company will keep these signed checks and credit card forms on file during the auction. If you do not make any purchases, your voided check or credit card form will be shredded or returned to you by mail.

An invoice detailing your purchases will be mailed to you one week after the event. Consult your accountant on any tax matters. The auction house will let you know if any sales taxes are due on your purchase.

A final tip at checkout: if you were interested in items that did not sell because the reserve was not met or some other reason, give the auction clerk or auctioneer your business card with the lot number of the item and the maximum price you would spend for the item printed on the back of the card. They can present your card to the seller, who may change his or her mind, and contact you.

Buyer Beware

Check the total amount you are charged for your item at checkout. Do the math yourself to be sure a clerk did not make a mistake.

The pick up and takeaway of your items is also similar to checkout in that most auction companies want you to be able to take your item immediately. But if you have a large item or many items that require coordination or assistance from the staff, you may need to wait until the auction is over.

Some live auction firms have a notice similar to this: "No purchases may be removed until the conclusion of the auction. Following conclusion of the auction, merchandise purchased must be removed from the premises within the time limits announced by the auctioneer at the sale. Any merchandise not removed within that time limit shall be deemed to have been abandoned by the purchaser and ownership thereof reverts to the seller. Any deposit or other payment made by the purchaser to the auction shall be retained by the auctioneer as liquidated damages for the failure of the purchaser to comply with the purchase agreement."

Some people, seemingly eager to make a purchase, will leave an item for days or weeks at an auction facility. That's rude, and risky.

Picking up big items takes some planning and equipment. Try to come to the auction with suitable transportation and equipment, such as loading dollies, ropes, and blankets, so you can leave with your purchases. If you have to go home and borrow or rent a truck, it costs time and money.

Be sure to ask the auction company about pickup time requirements, and let them know when you plan to come back. Their staff will often help you load your item.

Some auction companies also arrange to have a moving company on site for hire to transport your items if you hire them. This is common with machine equipment auctions that have to be carefully disconnected and professionally transported. If you know ahead of time you'll need this service, find out the cost so you can figure it in to your bidding amounts.

The Least You Need to Know

- Pre-registering can save you time. Go to the auction company website to download a pre-registration form, then fill it out and fax it back.

- Nobody can bid without being registered.

- Expect the final checkout price to include your final bid plus a buyer's premium fee, sales taxes and shipping fee.

- If you don't take your item home in a certain timeframe, ownership may revert to the seller.

Technology at Live Auctions Today

In This Chapter

◆ Video auctions improve lot visibility

◆ Live audio from the auction!

◆ Auctioneer's website is an info goldmine

◆ Computers revolutionize auction clerking

Technology has changed the look and operation of many live auctions dramatically in the last few years as auctioneers use new innovations. More bidders are asking to see new technology in use at auctions, so auctioneers are responding.

In this chapter, we look at the main types of technology that you'll find at live auctions and how they can help and, sometimes, hinder you.

Big Video Screens at Auction

Perhaps the most visible example of new technology at live auctions is the big video screens at the front of auctions. There is often one large screen on each side of the stage.

def•i•ni•tion

A **video auction** is an auction where photographs or moving video images of sale items are shown on a big screen for the crowd to see during a traditional live auction.

A *video auction* is where photographs or moving video images of auction items are shown on a big screen for the crowd to see during a traditional auction. This offers many advantages.

One advantage is it gets everyone out of the weather, when they may normally be standing outside to see estate items or farm sale items. Instead of walking in the snow and freezing weather to stand beside a sale item, you stand inside where it's warm and take bids as you see items on a screen.

Video auctions also allow the crowd to see small items, such as jewelry, more clearly. And the auctioneer can sell more items faster.

Big screens such as this one at live auctions help bidders see the object currently being sold by the auctioneer.

"You can sell 120 to 150 items in an hour because the bidders see the item on the screen with a lot number in the photo, and then they just pull out their catalog and read the details. It's a lot of work up front, but it makes the auction go fast," said an auctioneer from Washington State.

Sometimes the auctioneer will set up large televisions at the front, middle, and rear of the crowd. Or, they may use a projection screen system with one huge screen.

"I've got a screen that is 10 feet wide by 8 feet tall. I have a DLP projection system with 1,500 lumens (a brightness measure). It's very bright. It costs about $5,000," said the auctioneer from Washington.

The auctioneer runs this system with a computer and software. Some use presentation software such as PowerPoint, PowerShow, or IviewMulti-Media.

The photos of sale items are typically shot the day of the auction with a digital camera. And, the sale item shows up onscreen with a lot number in the photo that corresponds to the lot number in the printed catalog, so the attendee can follow along with the catalog.

Moving video presentations on big screens are used to show real estate, livestock, and other property. A video of a home or building can be something simple, such as a person walking through each room with a camcorder, or can be a professionally produced virtual 360-degree tour as is commonly created for home sale today. Moving videos are also becoming more common for livestock so the bidder can see the horse, cow, or other animal moving in a healthy way and to enable a visual examination of its physical appearance.

Even better than just moving images, is when the auction company puts music to the video of an item.

"It shows off your property great. There's something about putting music to pictures that's effective," said an auctioneer. "Putting items on a big screen in front of the crowd speeds up the auction, makes everything look better, and gives you credibility. I did a farm equipment auction recently when we had 56 mile per hour wind. Instead of standing outside to see the equipment, the crowd was inside with the big screen (a projector puts the image on a 10- by 12-foot screen). We did not lose those bidders who would have left because of the weather. The seller said to me afterward that the screen probably earned him $100,000. And he's right."

Another use for big video screens is to display the current bids. Bidder poster boards have done this in the past, and are still used at many auctions, but the usage of video screens is increasing. This occurs especially at upscale auctions in Europe, where bids are shown in many currencies. Multiple parcel land auctions also use screens or poster boards to display multiple bids in this method of auction.

Also, a note about small screens: at many auto auctions, auction monitors (such as TV screens) are used to allow customers to track the status of vehicles running through the auction lanes, as well as to post information about titles, arbitration, and post sales inspections. Messages for auction participants can also be displayed on these monitors.

This large screen at a charity auction makes it easy for attendees all over the room to see small items being sold at the front of the hall.

Live Internet Broadcasts of Auctions

Live auctions, where a crowd gathers in the local auction building or other site, have always been the core of the auction industry. But a new aspect has also been emerging at live auctions.

def•i•ni•tion

A **webcast** is a live auction that is simultaneously broadcast over the Internet, allowing bids to be made via computer.

In some cases the onsite auction is also being simultaneously broadcast live over the Internet, in a *webcast*, so that people around the world can see, hear, and bid at the auction as if they were standing right there in the crowd. This helps bidders who cannot physically be at the auction that day and helps the seller by bringing more bidders to the auction.

You may have already seen this phenomenon. At a broadcast auction, there will typically be a video camera set on a tripod in the middle of the auction hall, capturing a wide view of the podium and the items held up for auction. This is so the people viewing on the Internet can see the events occurring. Also auction staffers operating computers are at the front or sides of the auction floor, taking the live bids coming from bidders on their own computers.

This live broadcast helps buyers who would prefer to be at the onsite auction, but they must be out of town on a business or pleasure trip, or they may be sick and cannot leave home. In those cases, you can go to an Internet website (chosen by the auction company) to see and hear the auction live, and bid on chosen items. When a bid such as that is received at the auction, the auctioneer says to the crowd, for example, "We have an Internet bid at $100."

This method of taking Internet bids live is similar to the procedure that has occurred for many years of taking bids by telephone, and even of taking pre-auction bids by bidders who leave their highest bid for the auctioneer to apply to their chosen item. Although an auction may seem, to a first-timer, that only people on the floor are bidding, actually all these types of bids are coming in.

Internet live bidding is not like an eBay auction or other format. It is simply like watching an auction live on your television, but also being able to join in the action. It is truly interactive.

As the auction industry and its customers continue to use more technology, these live broadcasts will become more prevalent across the country. This is now in its early growth stages. An auctioneer and seller must weigh whether the cost of providing this service will likely bring in more bidders, so they only conduct a live broadcast for items of wide appeal beyond the expected crowd on the floor.

Items of wide appeal include art collections; any rare collectibles that people seek worldwide including music albums or vintage toys; industrial machinery; real estate that investors and vacation home buyers desire; and so on.

You may wonder how many Internet bidders participate in a live auction, versus bidders at the auction site. The numbers can vary widely according to the type of items selling, and other factors, but a typical amount seems to be 25 percent. Here is a comment from an auctioneer in Indiana.

"I had a sale in Kansas City where 41 percent of the items sold went to the Internet bidders, and I had 250 people sitting in the crowd and about 180 people online," he said. "We got bids a lot higher than we normally would have."

The same auctioneer said some bidders on the auction floor are sometimes skeptical about the unseen Internet bidders.

"I've had people at auctions who were skeptical. Some say 'You're not really getting bids on there (the Internet)! You're just using it to run up the bids.' And I say 'Sir, come right over here to the computer and watch it.' And they see it and say 'That's pretty neat.'"

In an online auction, bidders have to register to get a screen name and password. When an item comes up for sale, online participants type in a bid amount and click the Submit Bid icon.

For bids on expensive items, some auctioneers require credit card information submitted online, just as onsite bidders are required to verify they have the financial ability to make the purchase.

A Florida auctioneer said, "I ask for credit card information to screen the serious bidders from the merely curious. In real estate auctions, where it is illegal to use credit cards, I ask for a 10 percent deposit check, which is not cashed unless that bidder wins."

SOLD!

To be sure you can bid without a time delay through a computer during a live auction, make sure you have a fast Internet connection service and a fast computer. Problems in either of those areas can make your bid too late to be accepted in a live auction.

In the first few years that live webcasts were conducted, there were problems with synchronizing all parties because of time delays and software glitches. For example, when the auctioneer asked for bids, it took a few seconds for his voice to be heard by people at home on their computers, and then, by the time they made a bid and it was received back on the auction floor, the delays slowed down the auction. But, the items were sold.

However, such problems have largely been overcome. The delay now is typically less than one second, experts say. Auctioneers use fast software, fast computers, and fast Internet connections. If bidders at home find a problem, usually it is on their end of the process, with their computer.

Although more bidders are tuning in to live auctions from home or their laptops as they travel, it takes time for the public to get used to this idea.

"It's going to take a gradual buildup of consumer confidence just as it took a gradual buildup of people buying on eBay," an auctioneer said.

To run an online auction, auctioneers either hire a company to provide one of their employees to run the computer and software, or the auctioneer buys the software and gets training to run the Internet auction themselves.

To learn about how auctions sound, register for a webcast auction and just listen. You do not have to bid.

Live Cameras at Auto Auctions

The live broadcast is especially popular in auto auctions. In the wholesale auto auction industry more than 80 percent of all wholesale auctions use some form of live broadcast, also called a *live streaming auction*. In some of these auctions 70 percent of vehicles are sold to online bidders. That's a high figure, with the normal being about 15 percent.

But auto dealers have embraced this technology because, in the past, they would have to leave their business for hours or days to attend several different auctions. Live Internet auctions now allow them to buy inventory without ever leaving the office, so they can avoid the expense of travel.

Streaming technologies have allowed the dealer to be placed right in the auction lane where cars are driven in front of the auctioneer and then driven off after sale. The dealer gets a bird's eye view from a camera located in the lane and he can hear all the action as live audio connected directly to the auctioneer's microphone is coming through his computer speakers. The auctioneer, on the other hand, knows who is logged in, what their credit limits are, how long they have been in the sale, as well as a variety of other reports all available to the auctioneer in real-time.

The bidder knows how much money he has left, how much money he has spent, and how many vehicles he has bought. Auto auction attendees look at web quality and delay.

The better technologies deliver a very high-quality audio sound and a TV-quality video signal. Fifteen frames per second or higher is the measuring stick. As long as the delay is less than a second for audio and video it appears to be almost transparent and puts the bidder right on the auction floor. If the delay falls below the one-second mark, it may cause confusion at the auction house, as bids may come in too late to be counted.

When a Live Broadcast Crashes

On October 21, 2006 a company that provides live Internet broadcasts had about 30 auctions broadcasting when, at about 10:20 A.M., that service went dead from a glitch in its computer servers. Until about 5 P.M. that day no bids entered were placed with the auction houses conducting those auctions, shutting out all the bidders trying to "attend" the live auction from home or wherever they were on their computers.

Those bidders found themselves out of luck. But the bidders on the floor at the sites of those 30 auctions kept on bidding because the auctions kept going. The lesson here is: trouble happens. If you want to be absolutely sure you can bid, go to the live auction site.

One of those auctioneers affected in that 2006 crash was conducting an auction of movie props and costumes in North Hollywood, California. The Internet crash cost him about $1 million, he estimated, and made many customers mad. The problem was compounded at this sale because most of the bidders were on the Internet; few had come to the live auction site.

"We had about 780 bidders signed up for the sale. There was only a few that showed up as live bidders, so we really were at the mercy of the Internet bidding," he said. "I got only about 35 percent of the sales for (that day) completed."

Internet live-bidding technology works nearly flawlessly 99.9 percent of the time today, experts say, but there are always going to be times when technology fails.

Here's another tip if you can't be at the live auction site, but are bidding by computer: leave an advance bid anyway. Be prepared for the worst-case scenario the Internet going down. Send a bid in advance to the auctioneer for the item you want, stating this is to be your highest bid. This procedure can provide a backup so in the case of an Internet failure, you are still in the running for your item.

Buyer Beware

Bidding via computer at a live auction can be brought to an instant end if the hosting website crashes. This has happened. If you want to completely avoid this possibility, attend the live auction in person.

It's also good for you, the bidder, to know about a new breed of auctioneer: the professional online auctioneer. He may never have worked a live onsite auction. He runs a live auction only on the Internet. The client asks only for the method to move the entire inventory at the highest possible price, so sometimes an Internet-only auction is chosen.

Nowhere can this be better illustrated than in the art and antiquities world. With such a small segment of the population participating in these high ticket auctions, the Internet is bringing together interested buyers into one sale and the staid auction houses that are not embracing the online technology are being replaced by the startups and smaller progressive auction houses that are conducting online-enabled or online-exclusive auctions.

Bidders and auctioneers are calling the live broadcast of live auctions the great equalizer, because it can help make a small auction reach a worldwide audience and get the same attention and success that a big company can. Suddenly, the small auction company can get a sale price equal to a big company because it has tapped the same bidders.

Marketing of Live Auctions Via Technology

Auctioneers have to draw you, the bidder, for a live auction to be successful. They do that with the latest technology.

One method is by e-mail. The auction company asks for your e-mail address when you register at an auction, and they ask for it when you visit their website. If you provide it, you are then on their e-mail marketing list. You will likely get e-mails announcing when an upcoming auction will be held. Some companies have sophisticated e-mail systems that enable you to identify the type of item you are interested in, and then you will get e-mail only for auctions with that type of item.

That e-mail blast may also suggest that you look at the online auction catalog, which shows the items for sale, with a description of the item. These online catalogs are becoming highly popular with bidders.

SOLD! _____

Regular auction attendees are signing up in increasing numbers to get e-mail notices of upcoming live auctions.

Another method you may receive an invitation to a live auction is by fax. Auctioneers do targeted fax promotions to likely bidders, in compliance with laws regulating fax marketing.

A Tennessee auctioneer who sold a Super 8 motel did a fax broadcast to 3,000 motel lobbies, which brought in many interested bidders, and the final buyer.

The auctioneer said: "Much of the auction's success was due to a simultaneous fax broadcast to 3,000 motel lobbies. This broadcast went out instantaneously and immediately unleashed a tsunami of reaction that netted us about 100 serious inquiries on a multimillion dollar property in two days," he said.

Targeted cable television ads are also being used today across the country to reach bidders in specific cities, counties, and regions. Cable television networks serve small areas and are more specialized today, so you may see ads enticing you to come to a live auction in your area.

Prices are normally less for local cable networks than for a national affiliate network, so auctioneers are buying packages of advertising and are filming commercials.

Radio continues to be a popular technology for live auction advertising, and some auctioneers also have talk radio shows in some cities where they discuss auction topics and take calls from listeners. You can learn a lot about the procedures of buying and selling by listening to these shows and the insider tips shared there.

Pre-Sale Catalogs

If you get a promotional e-mail inviting you to a live auction, it will also likely include a suggestion that you view the auction's pre-sale catalog on the auctioneer's website. Catalogs contain the photos and descriptions of the items for sale. Because all purchasing decisions in a live streaming auction are made relatively quickly, a catalog containing as much information about the items as-is possible helps the bidders.

In the auto industry, to provide a comfort level for users, it takes a minimum of six images to assist in the selling process of a certified pre-owned vehicle and it can take up to 12 images for a used vehicle, experts say. In most cases a very detailed condition report is generated by the auction house. This condition report goes as far as measuring remaining tread on the tires. In these types of sales it is not uncommon for the online bidder to have a better and more detailed view of the vehicle than if he was actually at the auction.

The Auction Website

As a live auction attendee, your success will be increased by using the website of the auction company that is conducting the live auction.

SOLD!

The homepage of an auction company's website almost always has a list of the upcoming live auctions, and a pre-auction catalog to view. Don't miss these vital sources of information.

Visit the website as a preparation for your visit to the live auction. In addition to viewing the auction catalog with photos and descriptions of items, you may be able to print off the catalog. Also look for the terms and conditions of the live auction, so you can consider these ahead of time.

Many auction websites also give tips on successful buying at their auctions, and explain steps in the process. This includes real estate auctions. They will explain about viewing the property, title insurance, closing the deal after winning at auction, and taking possession of the property.

Many of the questions you have about an auction or procedure may already be answered on the website. Also be sure to see the section that says "services," where the auction company explains its services in detail.

To keep up with the live auctions in your area, with that company, also be sure to sign up for e-mail notification by clicking the Get Auction Updates button or similar wording.

Auction companies try to make their websites visually appealing, but not overly flashy for the target customer. If you are seeing overwhelming or confusing information, tell the auctioneer about it. He or she wants to know.

As with other businesspeople, auctioneers are trying to use their websites to draw customers and to convert interested people into solid buyers and repeat visitors. The trend is more email notices, less direct mail and less newspaper advertising.

Computerized Clerking

Before computers were commonplace for business practices, live auctions were run by clerks keeping all records by handwritten notes. Today, computers do the jobs. Clerks enter the bidders' contact information, purchase amounts, and other details into computers. This saves time and reduces errors.

Now bidders can bid immediately after registering and can checkout immediately after bidding. Clerking systems allow the auction company to identify top bidders, reconcile receipts, and display the bids, buyer's premium, sales tax, and consignor commissions. Control reports assist employees in keeping track of the items up for bid as well as reserve amounts, high and low estimates, and absentee and phone bids.

Computers and printers today are also used to make bidder cards, receipts, the auction catalog with photos of sale items, and an auction summary for the seller.

Cashiering checkout at auctions was once the weakest link in the process, making customers stand in line after the auction before they could pay and leave. But, now technology allows buyers to "swipe" their credit card through a specially designed smart terminal when entering the auction site. Similar to checking into a hotel, the process is familiar and readily accepted by guests.

The mobile computer, at left, enables computerized clerking to occur while the auction is in progress.

During the auction their bid activity is entered into auction management software or tracked manually. At the end of the event, the successful bidders can bypass the traditional cashiering tables and go directly to the item pickup points where they collect their items and go home. If the buyer is using a swipe terminal, the device will automatically synchronize the amount due with the credit card on file in the terminal. Post event processing is as simple as connecting the terminal to a telephone line and uploading the transactions in a one-step process.

You may also see at live auctions a handheld version of this technology with a barcode reader built-in. The staffer scans the handheld device over a sale item to help with inventory management. For example, auctioneers lay out all the items they are about to sell in a warehouse. They then pick up the handheld device and scan the barcode for each item in the order that the items will be sold. After they have completed reading all barcodes in the order of sale, the auction is now lotted and they can then print catalogs, or upload web catalogs. Also with a barcode reader, data can be quickly read from a buyer's driver's license. This information is then recorded with the bidder number.

New technologies have made auctions more efficient for everyone who attends. Whether you are a buyer or seller, try to embrace the new things you see and use them to your advantage. The big screens, the Internet and other tech devices are here to stay and will only continue to improve your live auction experience.

The Least You Need to Know

◆ Big screen video auctions allow crowds to see small items more clearly while they are being sold.

◆ Live broadcast auctions help bidders by allowing them to bid via computer as if they are standing at the auction site.

◆ Use the auctioneer's website to prepare for the live auction by viewing the auction catalog and reading the terms and conditions of the auction.

◆ New technology allows buyers to swipe their credit card through a specially designed smart terminal when entering the auction site.

Chapter 8

All About Bidding

In This Chapter

- ◆ Different kinds of live bids
- ◆ The "big three" bidding strategies
- ◆ Where to aim your bid: auctioneer or ringman?
- ◆ How much should I bid?

Bidding at live auctions can be as simple or complex as you, the bidder, wish to make it. You've got choices, and power! The purpose of bidding, of course, is to place the highest purchase offer on the item at auction. Auctions are said to be the only game where you have to come in last to win!

There are several bidding strategies that have been developed by auction attendees during the years that can help you get your item at the lowest price possible on that day. That is the core of this chapter. But, first let's mention a few things about opening bids and the varied types of live bids that you will see at auction, so you know what is occurring on the auction floor.

Suggested Opening Bid vs. Reserve Price

In Chapter 5 we mentioned how the bidding on an item begins. The auctioneer will first briefly describe the item, and then tell what bid amount he wants to start the bidding at. He may first say "Let's start this at $900. Who will give $900?"

This is a *suggested opening bid*, not a firm requirement, unless otherwise explained by the auctioneer. Bidders are free to respond and start the bidding where they desire, which may be less than $900.

The opening bid requested by the auctioneer is determined by several factors. He wants to get the highest possible price for the seller by coaxing competition among the bidders. Market value of the item is one factor determining the starting bid. The auctioneer will try to start the price not far below the market value. He knows savvy bidders will have researched the value and expect the item may go for the current market price.

The opening bid may also be determined by a *reserve price*, which is a minimum acceptable amount (determined by the seller) that has been set on the item. The auctioneer may try to open at the reserve price, or only slightly below it.

The reserve price level may be disclosed to the audience before the sale, which helps the bidders by providing more information, or the exact price may not be disclosed, because the seller hopes competitive bidding without knowledge of the reserve will drive prices above his reserve.

A suggested opening bid may even be advertised for the auction item. For instance, you may see a suggested opening bid of $350,000 for a property that has an anticipated sales price of $500,000. By suggesting this opening bid, it lets the buyers know where the auctioneer would like to start the bidding, but in no way implies the property will be sold to the highest bidder above that price because the price is only suggested. A buyer does not have to read through the fine print in the Terms and Conditions sheet to know what is meant by the suggested opening bid. This bid amount gives buyers pricing guidance. These techniques work especially well with unique properties that are difficult to value. By simply having the clarifying word "suggested" along with "opening bid," the message to the consumer in the auction advertisement is that the opening bid amount is not the guaranteed sales price or even the minimum bid, but just the auctioneer's suggested starting price.

However, some sellers want to advertise an opening bid so low that it is unrealistic. This is a baiting tactic to draw people to the auction. For example, if a property is worth $95,000, but you read an auction advertisement that says "Opening Bid:

$1,000," the advertisement implies to the potential buyer that the seller may sell the property at or more than $1,000.

To the general public, the term opening bid equates to a minimum acceptable bid, when the reality is that the advertised opening bid is not the minimum acceptable bid, but just some really low number advertised to entice buyers to show up at the auction by giving the false impression that there is a chance the property could sell at the advertised low opening bid price.

Buyer Beware

Sometimes a super-low suggested opening bid will be advertised before an auction as a baiting tactic to draw people to an auction. But, the seller knows he will not accept anywhere near that low price.

The defense of this tactic is that the written Terms and Conditions sheet of the auction state that the seller reserves the right to reject the high bid.

Types of Live Bids

So now you understand what is going on with the requested opening bid and the role of a reserve price.

Next, the *live crowd bids* begin. Live crowd bids are those placed by people physically on the auction floor with the auctioneer. The bidders raise their bidder number, for example.

Bidders hold up their bidder numbers.

Advance bids, also called absentee bids, also begin to be in place as the live bidding starts. An advance bid is one placed with the auction company in advance, before the auction, usually by someone who cannot be physically at the auction.

These bids are recorded, sorted, printed, and appear on the auction manager's clerking screen instantaneously when the item is brought up to the auction block. The auctioneer will tell the audience he has an advance bid for a certain amount. An advance bid is given with a maximum price, but the auctioneer will apply the bid by increments, so the advance bidder can win the item without reaching his or her maximum, if possible.

Also competing with the live crowd bid are the live telephone bids coming in over the telephone. The auction's phone clerks tell the bidder what the current price is, and the caller places bids. The caller may also be listening on the Internet. The auctioneer will announce that he has a live phone bid for a specific amount.

Live Internet bids may also be competing with your live crowd bids. People sitting at home or other locations are listening live to the auction and are submitting bids by pushing a Submit Bid button on the website.

SOLD!

Sometimes midweek auctions are attended by fewer people, which can create less pressure to drive bids upward.

The auctioneer will announce "We have an Internet bid of $950," for example, indicating that the Internet bidder has placed the high bid.

All these types of bids are either live or are competing with your live bids.

Quantity You Are Bidding On

One other very important thing you need to know is the quantity of items you are bidding on. If there are six identical computers up for auction under one lot number, you can be confused and think you are only buying one computer when, in fact, you are bidding one price for each of the computers. Pay attention to the auctioneer's instructions about bidding:

 ◆ Single item bid: You bid for one item; a single coin for example.

 ◆ Single lot bid: This is one lot, but can be more than one piece of property. An example is that there may be 20 rare magazines in one lot. Your single lot bid may be $100 for all the magazines in that bundle, so you pay $100 (plus any buyer's premium and applicable tax).

- Multiple quantity price bid: This bid will be multiplied by the quantity in the lot to determine the total bid price. An example is if there are 50 coins for sale, and the winning price is $100; the winner gets all 50 coins for $100 *each*, or $5,000. This is also called "Times the Money" bidding by the auctioneer.

- Bidder's choice of quantity bid (also called the pick of the lot, or "high bidder's choice"): The high bidder has the option to choose the quantity desired, from one up to the entire quantity offered. The quantity desired will be multiplied by the successful high bid. This process can repeat until the entire quantity is sold or the auctioneer moves to the next lot.

So, listen carefully! When groups of items or similar items are offered the auctioneer will specify the terms prior to the sale. Watch out for sets of chairs, glasses, dishes, and so on. Quite often items are sold by the piece, meaning your bid is multiplied!

The House Rules of Bidding

Auction houses often have their own rules for bidding at each auction and sometimes for special items. The main rule is you must be registered and have a bidder number.

A secondary rule is often the increments by which you can bid. For example, you may be only able to increase your bid by $1 or $25 amounts, not by a penny, which would seem silly and a waste of everyone's time.

Another rule may be that only pre-qualified bidders, with financing in place, can bid on certain real estate. This protects the seller and everyone in the process. Read about rules for bidding on the auctioneer's website, and ask the crew on the day of the auction.

Auctioneers will either announce these rules or refer you to the Terms and Conditions sheet of the sale. There are not many rules really, because auctioneers want to keep the process simple.

Bidding Strategies

This section covers the major bidding strategies you will find at live auctions: lowball bidding, halfballing, and maximum bidding.

Lowball bidding is the practice of increasing the bid by the smallest amount possible to put you in place as the current high bidder. If someone has bid $10, you may bid $11 to lowball it, instead of $15, if this is an increment allowed by the auctioneer. This lowball practice is simple and logical for the bidder seeking to save money. A lowballer is reactive: he waits to see what another bidder will do, then reacts by placing another lowball bid.

Halfballing is placing a higher bid, about halfway to the maximum price you've determined earlier that you will go. The idea is to startle the other bidders, who may be lowballing, and for you to take a comfortable lead that may win the item or at least hold it for some time. For example, if the bid is $10 and you have a $100 maximum for yourself, you bid $50, sending the signal to other buyers that you are there to buy it.

Halfballing is also called jump bidding because you jump over the next expected lowball bids. Halfballing begins to get into the psychology of reading other bidders. If there's a fellow bidder that you know is also a frequent halfballer, similar to you, the strategy may not work well on that item.

SOLD!

Be assertive. Most bidders use only the lowball strategy on most items. But, to be more effective, try a different method when you think it will work better.

Maximum bidding is placing your highest bid. The idea is just to get it out there early and hope it will scare away other bidders from an item you really want and don't mind paying more for. You can place your max bid as soon as the bidding opens, or you can wait a short while, but veteran bidders know not to wait very long as bidding fever can overtake some bidders and make your max bid less fearful to them.

When your max bid is placed, the auctioneer will not act startled. He will simply say "We have $1,000 for this item. Do I hear $1,250?" He wants to keep the bids climbing. But other bidders will be taken aback and be quickly rethinking their strategy, asking themselves "Do I really want to go that high?" In those moments, the auctioneer is moving forward and you are closer to winning the item.

Read Your Competition: Bidding Psychology

Experienced bidders learn to read people, just as poker players are known to do. You may want to guess what your competitors are likely to do, so you can adjust your bidding strategy.

For example, if you're in a lowballing war with one other bidder, continually raising by a tiny amount, you may want to guess whether to jump to a halfball bid or a maximum bid to try to end the bidding quickly.

Pay close attention to the other bidders' habits, appearance, and strategies. Many people commonly think that the way a person is dressed (expensive suit versus shabby old clothes) gives a clue to their wealth and their bidding ability. You may figure you can outbid a shabbily dressed person by staying in a lowball pattern, but don't always count on it!

If possible, it is more effective to see your competitor's bidding patterns on another auction item or items. Did he back down when somebody jumped way over his bid? (If so, give it a try.) Did he stay in a lowball pattern to the very end of another item?

Some bidders try to quietly intimidate other bidders by standing close to them, or bidding quickly and aggressively. Some may act hesitantly, bluffing as in a poker game. Some bidders like a challenge and will choose to square off with you. They may eyeball you, even talk at you to distract you, but you should never distract or be aggressive with another bidder. If the auctioneer believes there is such tampering going on, he may stop the auction, hurting all in attendance.

SOLD!

To learn more about bidding strategies and bidding psychology, search the Internet for articles on those topics.

One special note: bidding at charity auctions is a different animal. Although some bidders there want to buy at a low price, others are willing to spend more money because it is a donation to a cause they support. Often bidding friends at a charity event will badger each other, making jabbing comments in a good-natured way. This does not truly fall in the realm of regular competitive bidding.

Bidding in live auctions is a bit like a boxing match or a card game. You develop your style, you have a plan for each event, you read your opponents, and you battle to see who will fold and who will win.

The best bidding system of all is to be friends with the auctioneer and ringmen. They are the ones to sell you the item. Some buyers try to be difficult in an effort to look like a shrewd buyer. This does not work. If the auctioneer believes you are being difficult during bidding, he and the seller may believe you'll be difficult when it comes to payment and closing of the transaction. It always pays to be friends with the auction staff.

Bidding Fever and Buyer's Remorse

Bidding fever occurs when your emotions take over and you get caught up in the bidding and can't stand to lose an item. Also called a bidding war, this erupts when two bidders, or more, are locked in battle. Bids are rising quickly, often beyond the market value of an item.

Bidding fever usually appears near the end of the bidding. Sellers want you to develop bidding fever, and some unscrupulous sellers may employ fake bidders (shills) to drive up the bidding prices to try to push you into a bidding frenzy. Don't take the bait. Set your plan and maximum price, and stick to it.

When is it okay to go beyond your maximum? Is it ever okay to give in to bidding fever? Yes. You may get to the auction and find that an item is in better condition than you expected, and therefore, worth more than the maximum you had planned to bid. Or you may find that the only other item of that kind in the world sold one hour before this auction for a higher price than you ever expected, so you'll have to adjust your idea of what its market value is.

Buyer Beware

Runaway emotions, ego, and lack of self-control lead to bidding fever. Stick to your bidding plan.

But be aware that bidding frenzy can lead to buyer's remorse—don't be sorry when you get home that you paid so much, even though you are glad to have won the item! If you can't afford the item at the prices involved in a bidding frenzy, drop out. Let it go. Tell yourself you'll find a similar version of this item at some other auction or another venue.

Shill Bidders

Shill bidders are those who are bidding only to raise the bids so the seller can get a higher price. They have no intention of buying. They may be a friend or employee of the seller.

Keep in mind that sellers or their representatives can bid on their own items when this practice is fully disclosed to the crowd. But when not disclosed, it is often illegal, unethical, and hurts the auction business.

How can you spot a shill? They often make the high bid early in the auction. They try to draw attention to the auction and then stop bidding as the auction nears completion. Also they step in late in an auction to rescue an item from a final low bid so that the seller can resell it later.

If you suspect someone, such as a buddy of the seller, is merely increasing the bids, report it to the auctioneer. Shills tend to bid on everything their friend sells, revealing that they have no interest in any one category or set of categories. In general, shills will bid high only when they are fairly sure they will be outbid.

Cancelling Your Bid

In general, after you've made an informed bid, you cannot retract it. It is a contractual offer to buy the item at your offered price. It says so quite often in the Terms and Conditions sheet that auction companies have you sign on your registration form. But, don't panic.

In daily practice, when can you withdraw or cancel a bid? If you made an honest mistake, such as heard a wrong number called by the auctioneer, tell the ringman or auctioneer that as fast as possible and explain why. They will likely cancel your bid on the spot. But don't wait and try to claim that excuse later.

You can also try to cancel your bid later if some form of deception occurred in regard to the item or the way it was sold. If the item was advertised and described in one way, for example as a computer with certain internal parts, and you later find those parts are different than described, you may have a basis for canceling your bid.

Bidding with the Ringman and Auctioneer

To bid effectively, you have to be seen clearly submitting your bid. Either the ringman or the auctioneer should be able to see your bidder number in the air.

Sit where you can be seen easily. Hold the number high and facing the ringman or auctioneer. Meet the ringman covering your section before the auction, if possible. Tell him which item you are interested in, and he will watch you closer when that item comes up for sale.

The ringman may step in closer to you and may ask you to bid certain amounts, or give you other advice. At the same time, the auctioneer is watching you and the other active bidders, while chanting the numbers he wants and that he has received.

One Colorado auctioneer said this about bidders: "The more you hit people with the numbers (in the chant), the more they are thinking about bidding."

Auctioneers are also using certain bid increments to get bidders to reach a target price that the auctioneer and seller want.

SOLD!

If you don't hear the bid numbers clearly spoken by the auctioneer, ask the nearest ringman to repeat them to you. Don't guess and proceed bidding anyway!

"The first two or three increments are the most important," he said. "That's where you get up to value. I'm not as concerned as to where I start as to where I'm at."

Starting a high-priced item out at a price much lower than its value can stimulate interest, but it can backfire if the auctioneer does not keep the bid increments high enough.

For example, if an auctioneer gets 15 bids for an item, that should be sufficient to sell it at a target price. But if the bids start too low on an expensive painting, and go up by only $10 per bid, after 15 bids the item will still be far below its market value and target price.

Buyer Beware

Don't let a ringman or anyone else convince you to bid more than you think is right for you.

Ringmen and auctioneers also know that sometimes the only thing it takes for you to bid is for them to ask you.

"People are just waiting to be asked," another auctioneer said. "Look at people's eyes and faces. Body language speaks louder then words."

Your eyes, facial expression, and body language can tell the ringman you are open to bidding. If you are turned away and looking away from them, you are not interested.

Can you bid by a mere nod of your head? Yes, but only if you are already locked in to communication with the ringman or auctioneer, probably only after you've already bid at least once. They will not take a bid from someone they think is only nodding to someone else in the crowd. They don't want to make that kind of mistake.

But if the ringman is standing next to you, asking you to bid, it is fine to nod your answer for a yes or no.

A good ringperson may also ask you, before the auction, what your opening bid on the item may be. It's fine to tell him or her. But don't try to lowball them too much. A good ringperson will not likely report a very low offer to the auctioneer if he knows the target price is much higher.

A veteran ringman said "Starting bids can make an auction go a lot smoother and a lot quicker. But, you have to be careful as a ringperson not to belittle the item in everybody's eyes just to get the bid. You don't want the auctioneer saying it's worth $15,000 and the ringperson suggesting it's only worth $2,000."

Instead the ringman will use hand signals to tell the auctioneer that $2,000 is bid, but the ringman will not shout out $2,000.

What will the ringman say to the bidder to bring them to a point of decision? Here are a few phrases:

"Do you want in? Now is the time."

"It's still a good buy at this price."

"What's a little extra when you know the money is going for such a good cause?" (charity auction)

"Let's not let the other bidder beat us out on this item."

Auctioneers and ringmen are constantly studying the bidders and adjusting their styles to your actions.

Auctioneers like to entice bidders by "hanging the number" out in front of the crowd, meaning they like to keep repeating the last bid or the next requested bid several times as the anticipation builds for bidders to act on that number. It's like dangling a hook in a stocked pond and waiting for the fish to strike!

Some bidders don't like the pressure a ringman can put on a bidder to make a bid. A ringman may stand right next to you asking repeatedly for another bid. If you are through bidding, just tell the ringman "I'm out." That is the signal to him that you will bid no more on that item. You are freeing him to focus on other bidders.

How Much Should I Bid?

What are guidelines to determine how much to bid on an item? First, do some research to find the current market value, meaning what price the same or similar items are selling for today. The Internet makes this easier today than in the past.

Look at the price for that item on eBay or do an Internet search for other methods appraising. The easiest way to avoid over-bidding is to do your research well before the auction.

 SOLD!

Research the item's value well and base your bid around that. Use the Internet to find what similar items are selling for.

In special cases of expensive items, you may want the opinion of a professional appraiser, but for ordinary items most people act as their own appraiser. Also ask collectors or antique dealers what they think the value of the item should be (you may want to call such an expert in an area of the country far away from you, in case you are concerned they will attend the nearby auction and bid against you).

When you find the value of similar items, then, before the auction, inspect the goods and see if there are any additional factors, such as wear and tear, that may make you need to lower the value. Also take into account the value appreciation that the goods you are bidding on may undergo in the coming years, especially if it is a rare item.

Then consider your budget and how much you want the item. Set a comfortable price range for yourself and resolve to stick to it. Start out bidding not too far below what you believe to be the current value of the item, and then work your way to that value and above it by a margin you deem is appropriate.

Who Is Allowed to Bid?

Can anybody bid at auction? Because an auction is an open public sale, the rule with few exceptions is that anyone is qualified to become a bidder. You do have to follow some rules, such as be registered and have a bidder number, and in some cases of real estate or other high-priced items, you may have to be pre-qualified to ensure you have the financial ability to pay.

Aside from specific cases such as that, anyone can bid. There are no age restrictions. Auctioneers have the discretion to accept bids from children, but the auctioneer will be looking to see that the child is acting under the guidance of a parent or guardian.

In some cases, the auctioneer also has the right to refuse a bid from persons he believes are not seriously placing a valid bid ("I bid one penny"), persons who don't understand what is occurring (a mentally ill person), or who do not have the intention to pay (such as a previous buyer who repeatedly did not pay for items).

A person qualified to become a bidder at an auction may also delegate another person to act as a representative in his or her behalf, but they should disclose that.

As mentioned, the seller of the property can only bid on his own item if it is expressly announced that he or she reserves that privilege. If the auctioneer knowingly receives a bid on the seller's behalf, or the seller makes such a bid, and notice was not given, the buyer can void the sale or take the goods at the price of the last good faith bid prior to the completion of the sale.

There are also situations where the auctioneer and his or her employees wish to bid on items. This is legal in some states, but the general rule is that an auctioneer can only purchase property with the consent of the seller. In some states, an auctioneer may not bid on property at his or her sale regardless of owner consent.

The Least You Need to Know

♦ The suggested opening bid is not a requirement, but should be used to base your bidding on.

♦ There are three basic bidding strategies: lowball bidding, halfballing, and maximum bidding.

♦ Be absolutely sure of the quantity of items you are buying when you place a bid. It may be one, or many!

♦ You can place your bid by gesturing either directly to the auctioneer or the ringman near you. The choice is yours. But don't wait too long, or your bid may be missed.

♦ There are no age requirements to bid, but check with your auction house for other rules.

Buyer's Premium and Other Fees

In This Chapter

- ◆ Buyer's premium pays the auctioneer
- ◆ When many buyers pay, the seller doesn't have to
- ◆ Arguments for and against this fee
- ◆ Taxes and other fees on your bill

The buyer's premium is a hot topic for bidders and auctioneers at live auctions these days. Some people like it and say it is a fair fee; others hate it and refuse to use it. This chapter covers the pros and cons and gives you a better understanding of all the fees involved in live auctions.

What Is a Buyer's Premium?

A buyer's premium is a fee the buyer must pay, on top of the final sale price of the item, to help cover operating expenses of the auction, typically as compensation to the auctioneer.

The buyer's premium is normally a small percentage of the winning bid, such as 10 percent. So if the final winning bid is $100 for an item, a 10 percent fee would be another $10, to equal a total amount due of $110 (plus any additional taxes or fees).

Compare this to charges typical at automobile dealerships for title fees, dealership add-ons, and similar things. When negotiating the bottom-line price with a dealer, most of the time these fees are not ever mentioned, yet they appear on the final bill of sale. Most dealers refuse to remove these charges as it is their form of a buyer's premium.

The purpose of the buyer's premium is to shift the burden for payment of the auctioneer's commission (his fee) from the seller to the buyers at auction. It's an alternative to the traditional commission method by which an auctioneer earns his money. The auctioneer can either partially or fully be compensated by the *buyer's premium*.

def•i•ni•tion

The **buyer's premium** is a fee the buyer must pay, on top of the final sale price of the item, to help cover expenses of the auction, such as compensation to the auctioneer.

Buyer's fees generally range from 3 percent to 20, depending on the type of auction, the area of the country the auction is in, and the preference of the auctioneer and seller, who both agree on all fees in their contract.

For example, some real estate auctions have a three percent premium. Ten percent is a frequently used amount for many types of auctions. But for example, one general auction firm in New York State doing estate auctions charges a 13.5 percent standard buyer's premium at its live auctions, with a 3.5 percent discount for cash and check payments. And at that firm, the buyer's premium for people bidding over the Internet is 20 percent.

Another example: Christie's auction house, the International seller of art and other upscale items, has been charging 20 percent for items up to $500,000, but the fee drops to 12 percent for items of more than $500,000. Rival auction house Sotheby's has been charging 15 percent on all purchases.

Although we show you a few exact percentages here, auctioneers are prohibited from discussing among themselves specific fees or percentages to strictly adhere to the Sherman Anti-Trust Act. This federal law is aimed at preventing businesses from fixing prices at the same level in their area or industry, which would deprive customers from finding lower prices.

During the years, substituting the seller's commission with a buyer's premium, or combining the two, has grown into an accepted operating procedure for the auction industry, especially in metropolitan areas. Of course, that doesn't mean it's used universally.

Some auctioneers say it won't pass muster with buyers in rural areas, especially, where many buyers are resistant to change and resist new fees more vigorously than urban bidders. But for most everywhere else in the nation, auctioneers are using the buyer's premium to solve a number of business issues such as the rising cost of advertising, fuel, insurance, taxes, rent and payroll.

Does the buyer's premium reduce bidder participation? One auctioneer who always uses a buyer's premium said "I cannot see any difference in the bidding participation, except in the small items less than $10. There seems to be more complaints from the buyers of items $50 and less than from the high-ticket buyers, such as real estate customers."

Frequent buyers and media observers of auctions say many buyers remain agitated at the buyer's premium, but those auctions stay popular because they offer good value for products.

Bidders can compensate for the buyer's premium by simply bidding 10 percent less.

Why Is It Charged to the Buyer?

By making the buyer pay more, the seller does not have to pay for advertising, clean-up, survey fees for a real estate auction, and any other costs, because the seller may already be paying a fee to the auctioneer for his services (depending on how those two parties have agreed to structure the fees of the auction).

And the auctioneer does not have to pay for these expenses either. By shifting this fee to the many buyers in a consignment auction, for example, the cost is spread among many people, lessening the impact on any one buyer.

Buyers have adjusted quickly in areas where the buyer's premium has been implemented. Auctioneers announce it and advertise it in brochures and newspaper ads, and place a sign at the registration desk on the auction site.

Don't try to claim you did not know about the buyer's premium because most auctioneers will make an audio tape of their opening announcements at live auction, and can go back to a taped statement on record, along with where it is published in the terms and conditions of the auction.

Buyer Beware

In your bidding plans, figure in how much the buyer's premium will cost you so you are not surprised at payment time. Beware of forgetting this important aspect.

Financial institutions, lawyers, and executives seem to adapt to the buyer's premium best. After all, these businesses have used some form of add-on expense for years. For example, when we talk about a loan, most of the time, there is an origination fee added, and when we talk about preparation of documents, there is a legal fee added on.

Marginal and over-financed property owners will go with buyer's premium auctions with greater acceptance than if a commission was coming out of the proceeds rather than added on.

Where the Buyer's Premium Began

It began in England. Christie's Auction House of England brought the buyer's premium to the United States when Christie's opened its doors in New York City in the mid-1970s. You may recognize the names Christie's and Sotheby's as the biggest art auction houses in the world.

Few auctioneers felt the impact of the new idea of a buyer's premium in the 1970s as much as Richard A. Rosner, a senior vice president and buyer at Tepper Galleries, New York's oldest privately owned auction house. Initially, the firm chose to not implement a buyer's premium, but the market forced them to reconsider.

"We thought resisting was a competitive advantage but it turned against us," said Rosner. "Our competitors had the edge because they were getting more goods from sellers. Christie's had chopped their seller's commissions from 20 percent down to 10 percent, while making it up with the buyer's premium."

The other New York auctioneers followed suit, as Rosnar watched his company fall behind.

Tepper recovered its momentum when management adopted the buyer's premium and could once again compete for sellers on an even playing field. In addition, Rosner found that the premium helped in acquiring estate merchandise from sellers looking to cash-out quickly.

"My gallery and others in New York like to buy estates outright," explains Rosner. "Our buyer's premium gives us an edge because we will sometimes pay [higher] to acquire the merchandise. But we know we will get it back and more with the buyer's premium."

Even with widespread success stories, some auctioneers steadfastly resist the buyer's premium. The most often heard complaint is that it goes against tradition. Such was the case with family owned Tri-State Auction and Realty, in Kingston, Tennessee. John C. Kimbel started the company in the late 1970s, and brought in his son, John Jr, CAI, and daughter Sandra.

John Kimbel Sr. had successfully vetoed his family's requests to adopt the premium all the way into the late 1990s. Then came the loss of a major auction because the seller chose a competitor that offered the premium. The experience gave the family all the ammunition they needed to turn Dad around.

"My Dad loves it now," says Sandra. "We do onsite auctions mostly for logging equipment and sawmills. It has really helped us because sellers have an idea of what kind of commission they want to pay, yet they don't realize that the cost of doing an auction has escalated tremendously over the years."

Advertising Is a Driving Reason

Most auctioneers spend much of their auction budget for advertising. The Tri-State company does about 35 auctions per year and typically mails 15,000 to 25,000 brochures to promote an auction. Some sellers are willing to pay a reduced commission and an advertising fee, but others aren't so cooperative, and that's where the buyer's premium makes all the difference to lure a seller.

"The larger banks and finance companies do not want to pay any commission at all, though they will pay an advertising fee," says Sandra. "But if you're not willing to do that they'll find somebody that is."

Another auctioneer said that "If the property isn't bringing in the price the owner wants, you have the premium to work with and you can give some of it back to the seller," he explains.

Who Gets This Money?

The buyer's premium is usually paid to the auctioneer as a method to replace the traditional commission method, in which the seller pays the auctioneer a percentage of the total auction proceeds. The buyer's premium has been in use about 40 years.

SOLD!
Sellers can get the buyer's premium as a reimbursement for advertising costs.

Another use for the buyer's premium is as a form of reimbursement to the seller for paying up-front for advertising costs.

Mario Piatelli, an auctioneer for more than 40 years, auctions real estate in Beverly Hills, California, and makes his sellers pay advertising costs in advance. After the sale, he uses some of the proceeds from the premium to credit the advance back toward the seller's escrow fees.

"When I started advertising with the *Los Angeles Times* it was $7.50 an inch and now it's more than $400 an inch," says Piatelli. "You can spend $25,000 as if it was nothing. I travel all over the country and I see that most everybody charges a buyer's premium. These days you have to."

Piatelli also said that his method screens out sellers that may not be serious, or harbor unreasonable expectations as to the property's market value. Because the seller will lose the advertising money should they back out of the sale, they have a vested interest in accepting the highest bid.

The buyer's premium is also effective for charity auctions. Charity auctioneer JoEllen Taylor, of Kissimee, Florida, says the buyer's premium helps her business because she can tell charity clients that bidders pay auction expenses and her fee, enabling 100 percent of the *hammer price* obtained at auction to go to the charity.

def•i•ni•tion

The **hammer price** is the price established by the last bidder and acknowledged by the auctioneer before dropping the hammer or gavel.

"I tell clients that the bidders provide for our services, allowing not only our auction event service but also for fundraising consultation for up to 10 months in advance of the event," she said.

Taylor says the buyer's premium is fully published and explained to the bidders on the night of the event and in advance by including it on all written materials such as the catalog, bid card, and checkout signage. "I also personally announce over the microphone prior to beginning the sale all the auction details, including the buyer's premium," she said.

She provides a written notice to clients that says, "The buyer's premium has been common in the auction world since instituted by Christie's Auction House in 1975, however this is a relatively new concept when applied to benefit auctions. The buyer's premium method of auctioneer compensation is exceptionally forthright and honest, and is most beneficial to charitable organizations for several reasons: these include that the organization receives 100 percent of your total dollars bid at auction, not just 'a portion of the proceeds', and our auctioneering services cost nothing for the organization."

Not Limited to Upscale Sales

Many auctioneers are finding the premium works well for them. And those sellers aren't limited to upscale antiques and big ticket items, reports Wade and Paula Clark, of Wade Clark Auctions, Port St. Joe, Florida. In fact, at their weekly general merchandise auctions, the Clarks charge a buyer's premium and a seller's commission.

"We show the sellers our consignment form which states our seller's commission and our buyer's premium," said Paula. "Even though you announce it and have signs, when people are bidding they don't think about it." Adds Wade, "People ask why we charge the buyer's premium and I say it's to keep the lights on and stay in business."

In 1996, Wade studied the Florida auction industry and found that 65 percent of all the auctions in the state were charging a buyer's premium. "When we opened in '96, we noticed that our competition in the larger cities made a big deal about the fact that they didn't charge the premium," recalls Wade. "The ones that did not go out of business are now charging it, and I'm sure 90 to 95 percent of all auctions in Florida now do the same."

> **From the Podium**
>
> Some government agencies refuse to hire an auctioneer that charges a buyer's premium. The agencies believe it drives away some bidders, so they only hire companies that do not use this fee.

Along with keeping the lights on, the buyer's premium helps auctioneers keep up with rising insurance rates, according to Billy Long, CAI, of Billy Long Auctioneers, Inc., in Springfield, Missouri. "I've been using the buyer's premium since 1989 ... I think as time goes by we will use it more and more because our general liability insurance has gone up tremendously. Of course, overhead in general has gone up too."

The amount of the buyer's premium can fluctuate significantly when selling a high priced item such as real estate. In fact, the premium can make a difference between an auctioneer making a profit and taking a loss.

> **From the Podium**
>
> When many in the auction industry stood opposed to buyer's premiums years ago, there was a pioneer of the real estate auction business located in Miami. Jim Gall, CAI, sold his first real estate auction with a 10 percent buyer's premium in 1983 when others told him there was no way it would work. As his company grew, many of the "big guys" of the auction industry told him and others that buyer's premiums would never work, but they did. He conducted successful auctions in more than 30 different states where the buyer's premium was introduced into the marketplace and used effectively. Although some said bidders would never pay an extra 10 percent, they did.

Complaints Haven't Stopped It

Use of a buyer's premium is simply one of the terms and conditions of sale selected by the auctioneer and approved by the seller. Bidders can gripe about it as a penalty, but can't refuse to pay it.

Auctioneers are trying to get the highest dollar possible to the seller, not the lowest price for the bidder. If a buyer's premium accomplishes that, the auctioneer will use it.

Most major auction houses continue its use today which speaks volumes about its effectiveness for sellers and buyers at auctions. If it didn't work, it would have been discontinued long ago.

Do bidders sit there and calculate the amount of their bid, less a 10 percent premium? Some do, but veteran auctioneers say that the "calculator crowd" never purchases anyway. Generally they are the ones who come to pay only a fraction of fair value.

The difference to a seller's bottom line at the time of settlement is usually much improved as the amount that would have been paid as a commission has been collected from the other side of the table. Most sellers who have ever sold using a buyer's premium go back to it again and again.

Pros and Cons of Buyer's Premium

Bidders and buyers may be interested to hear the pro and con arguments about buyer's premium from auctioneers on each side of this issue. So, here is such a discussion.

Pro Buyer's Premium

The case in favor of using buyer's premium is presented by Aaron McKee, an auctioneer in Manhattan, Kansas, who handles estates, farms, business liquidations, and charity auctions.

What is the basic argument in favor of the buyer's premium?

It puts more dollars in our seller's pockets and that's who I represent. If I am representing the seller and I believe that using the buyer's premium gets them more money, it's my fiduciary responsibility to set the terms of the auction so that it maximizes the return for the seller.

What do you say to those who hold the opposite view?

It's fair, and as far as the buyer is concerned, it is one of the terms we have set up for the auction. They have the freedom to adjust their bidding or to decline. As for auctioneers, I think those that don't like it are probably upset when they are bidding for auctions against other auctioneers that offer a buyer's premium.

Also it is harder for the older, more established auction companies to charge a buyer's premium if their buyers are used to a routine and have expectations. So it's probably an advantage for those auctioneers to say it's not a good thing because they want to defend what they do.

What do you think is the premium's impact on auctions?

Some buyers factor it in because they have preset buying levels. So if a person thinks of a maximum bid of $100 for something, most of the time they are disciplined enough to say, "I will go to $91 if there is a 10 percent premium." There is also a faction of people that are not that way and they drive the total bid up. That's why there are buyers that don't like the buyer's premium because they understand that it does end up increasing the total price.

What would it take to change your mind about the buyer's premium?

If I thought it was getting the seller less money. If the bottom line decreases because of the buyer's premium, then that will be the time to stop charging it.

Why do you think the use of the buyer's premium is growing in so many areas?

I think it has proven itself as a way to increase the total number of dollars that an auction brings in.

Do bidders understand the premium and remember it when bidding?

I do believe that it does affect their buying somewhat. I don't think it's completely out of their mind, but I'm not sure that they are able to completely overcome resistance if they have a desire to buy the merchandise.

Is the buyer's premium here to stay?

It seems so to me. But it's a hard question. I have thought about it and if there becomes a real public outcry that it is not a good thing and it brings in less dollars for the seller it should be ended immediately.

Con Buyer's Premium

The case against using buyer's premium is given by auctioneer Lyn Liechty, of Adrian, Michigan, who does not use a buyer's premium because he feels it does not represent a "sense of fair play" for the buyer. He does charity auctions, estate, household, antique, and real estate auctions.

What is your basic argument opposing the buyer's premium?

Our responsibility lies with the seller, but we owe our buyers honesty and a sense of fair play and truthfulness, I don't see any of those qualities inherent in a buyer's premium.

What do you say to those who hold the opposite view?

You can make an argument for the buyer's premium on upscale real estate or in the city where it's a real jewelry auction or fine arts and things of that nature. That's a different type of atmosphere and a different clientele. But when you have people that are struggling to make a living and you ask them to pay an additional 10 percent on a toaster, I find it rather offensive and self-defeating. I don't think those auctioneers are listening to the buyers.

What do you think the buyer's premium impact is on auctions?

I want auctions to be the best possible experience for the buyer so they won't want to buy things any other way. But the buyer's premium tarnishes the process and that's a problem. Buyers have to think of a lot of things already, especially if it's something important such as a house. To have to factor in something such as a buyer's premium and remember it makes it less than a simple process.

What would it take to change your mind on the buyer's premium?

Nothing. Sometimes when I draw people from the city they ask me if I have a buyer's premium and the reaction is one of relief when they find out they don't have to deal with it.

Why do you think the use of buyer's premium is growing in many areas?

I don't know if that is really true. I don't have any statistics but I think that at least 50 percent of the auctioneers nationwide don't use the buyer's premium and they are making money, so I just don't buy that argument. There are an awful lot of auctioneers out there that don't even belong to the National Auctioneers Association so you don't really have a clue what those folks are doing.

Do bidders understand buyer's premium and remember it when bidding?

I have been to plenty of auctions using the buyer's premium and you can see the people trying to do the math.

Do you think buyer's premium is here to stay or will it eventually go away?

Yes, it is here to stay, but that doesn't mean it's an improvement.

Other Fees Added

Along with the buyer's premium, buyers must pay a collection of applicable sales taxes. In some areas, local sales tax rates can be as much as 6 to 12 percent. So, for example, you take the bid, plus a 15 percent buyer's premium, which equals the total price. Then you add taxes on that, such as a 7 percent sales tax rate, and any other taxes and fees to arrive at your total bill. You may see a city tax, state tax, and a county tax on your bill. There is no legitimate way to avoid sales taxes, which some people may consider just as detrimental to bidders as a buyer's premium. If someone wants to argue buyer's premium" sales taxes would also be a legitimate subject. If you are tax-exempt, like a dealer buying for resale, be sure to bring your tax-exempt certificate with you to the auction. Notify the clerk when you register so there is no mixing on your final bill.

SOLD!

To avoid "final bill shock" from buyer's premium plus taxes and fees, ask the auction clerk in advance for an example bill for an item similar to one you may buy.

If you want your purchase shipped from the auction firm, they may provide that service for a fee, also.

For some products, such as a vehicle, there may also be permitting fees, dealer preparation, and other fees.

Here is an example of fees added on a used vehicle purchase in Adams County in Denver, Colorado.

Car $750
Buyer's premium $125
Dealer prep and handling $40
State tax $26.54
RTD tax $10.98

Adams county tax $6.86
Permit $7.50
Total $966.88

The Least You Need to Know

◆ The buyer's premium is a way to shift the burden of the auctioneer's fee from the seller to the buyer, or many buyers in an auction.

◆ Buyer's premiums range from 3 to 20 percent, and some Internet auctions are at 22.5 percent.

◆ Don't try to claim you did not know about the buyer's premium because most auctioneers will make an audio tape of their opening announcements at live auctions.

◆ You may see city tax, state tax, and county tax on your bill. There is no legitimate way to avoid sales taxes.

Chapter 10

Paying for Your Purchase

In This Chapter

◆ Full payment is due at checkout

◆ Credit cards and personal checks welcome!

◆ What's all that on my bill?

◆ No second thoughts after payment

Paying for your purchase at live auction is usually a simple transaction, but it helps to know all the elements of paying (and your final bill!) and the options you have in payment. Complications can arise, including when a buyer changes his or her mind after making the high bid or even days after paying. Let's look at each of these issues.

When Payment Is Due

At most auctions (except for real estate or some other high dollar auctions), full payment is due at least by the end of the auction, when you go to the clerking desk (or clerking office/business office) to pay. Some auction companies do not want buyers paying and taking items home while the auction is still occurring because it can be difficult for clerks to keep close track of people coming in and going out of the auction site while the auction is still in progress.

However, other auction firms allow (and even encourage) buyers to pay and take their items home soon after they have placed the successful bid and the gavel has fallen on that item. Check with the auction company on its policy before the auction, or at least when you register.

An auction cleerk takes payment after an auction.

Can I Pay Using "Layaway" (Pay Later)?

Some auction companies do offer a partial payment plan, with credit extended to allow you to make ongoing payments toward the full amount. Check the website of your auction company. And even if they do not currently offer a layaway plan, you can propose that they offer this service to you. Negotiate with them. The most they can do is say no. But negotiate ahead of time, not when you are standing at the clerking desk ready to pay for your item.

> **From the Podium**
>
> For a smooth payment procedure, check with the auction firm for what payment forms it accepts.

Because you have not yet paid for the item in full, you will likely not be able to take it home.

Here is an example of the *extended payment plan* offered by Heritage Auction Gallery, of Houston, Texas, as posted on its website. Note that it has a down payment and other requirements:

Extended Payment Plan for Signature and Online Session Auctions
Minimum invoice total is $2,500. Minimum down payment is 20 percent. You may take up to six (6) months to pay the balance (monthly payments of at least 1/6th of invoice total). Interest is calculated at only 1 percent per month (12

percent annually) on the unpaid balance, and must be kept current. There is no penalty for paying off early.

Nondealers only with pre-approved credit application. All traditional sales policies still apply. Due to the nature of the business and market volatility, there is no return privilege after you have confirmed your sale, and penalties can be incurred on cancelled orders.

To participate in this program, follow these steps:

1. Get pre-approved by filling out a credit application.

2. Bid normally and win some lots.

Heritage will maintain possession of all the lots until paid in full. Therefore, you must notify us of your intent to use our Extended Payment Plan on or before the day of the auction. All pre-shipped material must be returned to Heritage for the plan to be in effect. When you get your electronic invoice, select "other" from the payment options.

Payment of Real Estate at Auction

Final payment for real estate at auction is normally not due until closing of all transactions, about 30 days from the end of the auction. The winning bidder at a real estate auction has likely already placed a deposit of money (an earnest money deposit) with the auctioneer to establish the bidder as serious and having financial ability. The deposit, held in a separate escrow account, holds the purchase for the buyer until all legal documents are prepared to transfer ownership.

Often auction companies require that this be a nonrefundable down payment (for the winning bidder) as part of the terms set forth by the seller and advertised prior to the auction. Rarely does a property not close as scheduled.

But what happens then? A cancellation form releasing the down payment (*mutual release*) is a form that is generally signed by both parties when a purchase will not close as anticipated.

When a bidder makes a down payment for the sale of real estate, the auctioneer usually holds onto the proceeds as an escrow agent. When a real estate sale does not close, both parties usually end up demanding payment of the funds held in escrow. The auctioneer does not want to be in a position where he or she must decide to whom to give the money. The mutual release requires the buyer and seller to agree on the disposition of the down payment so the auctioneer knows how to distribute the proceeds, says attorney Kurt Bachman, a specialist in auction law.

Where Real Estate Deposit Is Held

The real estate buyer paying for a property should also know that auctioneers who are also licensed real estate brokers have a unique situation when handling the proceeds from a real estate auction. Generally, the law imposes a requirement on both auctioneers and real estate brokers to maintain trust accounts or escrow accounts in which they deposit funds being held for others. Selling real estate at auction creates a unique question with respect to which trust account the auctioneer, who is also a licensed real estate principal, should deposit the earnest money.

> **From the Podium**
>
> If you want someone else to pick up your item, some auction companies require that you sign a *third party release* enabling a representative to pick up your purchase.

State laws often guide where this money is to be held. For example, Indiana law expressly provides that principal real estate brokers' trust accounts shall contain all earnest money deposits, funds held for closing escrows, sale proceeds not yet disbursed, and all other funds belonging to others. The specific statutory language concerning earnest money in the context of a real estate transfer indicates that the responsibility for holding and accounting for earnest money proceeds is on the licensed real estate principal.

Payment Methods

Most auction firms accept cash, credit cards (Visa, MasterCard, American Express, and Discover Card), bank orders, cashier's checks, or other certified funds. Many auction firms will accept personal and business checks, but they typically require the buyer to sign a Demand Note that personally guarantees the check. Remember, passing a bad check is a crime.

Before the auction, check the website of the auction firm conducting the auction to see what methods they accept, or ask on the way in to the auction.

An easy way to pay is to be sure your credit card is already on file with the clerks of the auction firm. Also when paying, be sure to have handy a valid form of identification, such as a driver's license or other identification card.

Some firms also accept a bank wire of funds for fastest payment by long-distance buyers. Art auction firm Heritage Galleries describes on its website that "For fastest delivery upon receipt of funds, you should pay with a bank wire, cashiers check or bank money order, or have previously arranged credit with Heritage. Payments via personal or corporate checks may be held 5 days or more for the funds to clear prior to shipping. Payments with credit cards (Visa and MasterCard only, up to $10,000 from nondealers at our discretion) must be shipped to the billing address on the credit card for all new customers (some restrictions apply). If the address we have for you doesn't match the credit card address, the shipment will be held and you will be notified. Payments can be made by PayPal (up to $10,000 from nondealers at our discretion)."

If you are a regular customer, also note that you should have settled your account balance from any previous purchases, in case money is still owed, before making a new purchase.

What's in the Final Bill

Your final bill will include the purchase price (your high bid), a buyer' premium (if applicable), sales taxes where applicable, a shipping fee (if you want the item shipped), and possible other fees.

A buyer's premium is a fee the buyer must pay, on top of the final sale price of the item, to help cover operating expenses of the auction, such as the auctioneer's commission. The buyer's premium is normally a small percentage of the winning bid, such as 10 percent. So, if the final winning bid is $100 for an item, a 10 percent fee would be another $10, equaling a total amount due of $110 (plus any additional taxes or fees).

> **Buyer Beware**
>
> Review your final bill closely to see if there are any mathematical mistakes or any charges you disagree with. Carry your own small calculator and track all of your successful bids in the auction catalog.

Sometimes there is a collection of applicable sales taxes. In some areas, local sales tax rates can be as much as 6 percent to 12 percent. You may see a city tax, state tax, and a county tax on your bill. For some products, such as vehicles, there may also be permitting fees, dealer preparation, and other fees.

The clerk preparing your final bill should give you an itemized final bill and receipt showing you have paid in full. Keep your copy in case any questions arise later.

Credit Card Surcharges

Some auction firms, as with other businesses, charge a 3 or 5 percent fee if the customer uses a credit card to pay. So it costs you more to use a credit card.

The reason many firms charge a fee if the customer uses a credit card is because the auctioneer is usually charged that very same fee by the credit card issuer. He or she is simply passing that cost on to the card user in exchange for offering the convenience of credit card payment. Most merchants outside the auction industry often absorb this usage fee and the consumer does not know about it.

Although the law in each state differs, it is generally permissible for an auctioneer to charge a 3 percent premium for acceptance of payment by credit card. The buyer can avoid this fee by simply using a different payment method. The fee should be clearly disclosed to potential buyers in all promotional materials and at the auction sale.

Many auctioneers simply charge a higher buyer's premium and then reduce the price paid for cash or good check. An example is a 15 percent buyer's premium reduced to 12 percent for cash or per-approved personal checks.

This fee is also generally referred to as a *convenience charge*. Also, it is up to the seller if he wants his auction to accept credit cards. If the seller authorizes it, it is part of the contract between seller and auctioneer.

Some states have regulations that prohibit auctioneers from passing credit card fees on to the buyer.

Shipping Charges

Some auction firms will ship to you for a set fee, such as $3.50 per lot for shipping and handling, plus exact shipping charges. For larger items such as pallet lots or vehicles, you need to arrange for your own shipping of these items. The firm may also include private carrier insurance.

Shipping varies according to the item type, quantity, and value (for insurance purposes). Certain packages may cost more to ship and insure and you may be contacted if there are additional costs after receipt of shipment. All charges are based on shipping within the continental United States, and shipments to other areas will likely incur a higher charge.

Buyer's Remorse

Buyer's remorse comes in to play when talking about payment. The condition occurs when a buyer regrets his or her purchase, from reasons that may include price or condition of the item, and sometimes leading to a dispute with the seller or auctioneer.

But this brings up the question: when is a purchase legally completed? If the sale is legally done, it makes a world of difference to the actions that a remorseful buyer can take.

The terms and conditions statement at live auctions that each bidder signs clearly states that the bidder will not retract his bid or stop payment. If he or she does this, this is called legal *breach of contract*, says attorney Bachman.

def•i•ni•tion

Buyer's remorse is when a buyer regrets his or her purchase, from a possible variety of reasons, and sometimes leads to a dispute with the seller.

When the auction hammer falls, that signals the consummation of a contract between the seller and the successful bidder. Unless there is some fraud or misrepresentation, a valid contract exists at the completion of the auction. A district attorney will not intervene to file criminal charges, but a civil breech has occurred. It is really the seller who has a legal right of action against the buyer, because the auctioneer is representing the seller.

Generally, a buyer or seller may demand that the transaction be fulfilled, which is called specific performance. A typical action when a buyer refuses to pay is for the seller to notify the buyer in writing that he must complete the transaction or he will be sued for breach of contract. If he still does not pay, the property can be sold to the highest bidder at another auction. The breaching buyer would then be liable for the difference between his bid and the successful new bid at the later auction, plus any costs incurred in conducting the second sale as a result of the buyer's breach.

So if you are thinking of just not paying, and that there may be no consequences, think again!

Sometimes buyers will have a disagreement with the way the auction is conducted, such as whether a reserve price was revealed to the bidders. But bidders should not assume they know the laws that apply to auction procedures.

In general, if the seller wishes to fix a minimum price below which the property will not be sold, or to reserve for himself or herself the right to bid in person or through another, an express announcement to that effect must be made so that no one is misled. After the property has been sold, the seller may waive the terms of the auction sale by not insisting upon compliance by the buyer.

When Is the Item Legally Sold?

A sale at auction, as with every other sale, must have the assent, either express or implied, of both the seller and buyer. Where the seller reserves the right to refuse any bid, a binding sale is completed only when the seller accepts the bid. That means that you may have placed the highest bid and still not have bought the item, unless the seller agrees to release it.

Also, where the seller reserves the right to reject any and all bids received, that right may be exercised even after the auctioneer has accepted a bid, and this rule applies to the auction of public as well as private property. So the answer to "When is a sale consummated?" is "When the seller accepts the bid."

After a bid has been accepted, the parties have the same relationship as a promissor and promissee in a standard contract of sale. So generally, the seller has no right to accept a higher bid, nor may the buyer withdraw his bid.

Personal Property Physically Present

Where a sale of personal property is required to be made by "public auction," the general rule is that the property must be physically present at the sale and so exposed to view that people attending the sale can inspect it to determine its value.

There are exceptions, including that the thing to be sold is too bulky to be brought within the view of the bidders; and where inspection may be useless, as with a sale of bonds or stock shares. But, auctioneers should conform to the principle that most personal property should be present at the place of the sale.

Can a Minor Legally Buy at Auction?

Can there be a problem at paying time if a child buys something at a live auction?

Many times auction firms allow children to buy at auction, if overseen by a parent or other adult. An Idaho auctioneer said "Over the years we have had young kids attend auctions and buy things on their own. Normally we watch the parents to ascertain that it's okay with them. So far, we haven't had any problems, but in our sue-happy society, I can envision someone below the legal age buying something, taking it home and using it and breaking it and then coming back to the auction wanting their money back."

The answer to this is that in most states, a minor becomes competent to contract at the age of 18. In fact, if a minor buys something, that contract is voidable at the option of the child. If a 16-year-old child purchases a vehicle, then wrecks it, he or she could void the contract and seek to recover his or her money. The purpose of this rule is to protect minors from foolishly squandering their wealth through contracts made with crafty adults who would take advantage of them in the marketplace.

So children can buy at auction, but the auction firm is not required to sell to them and may wish to avoid problems by not selling higher priced items to minors. But, if the auctioneer clearly sells the item to a minor, the clerk should accept the minor's payment.

SOLD!

Children younger than 18 can buy items at auction, but the auction firm is not legally required to sell to them.

The Law Also Protects Bidders

Bidders should also be aware that the law, and auction practices, protects them. You may have a legitimate reason for having buyer's remorse, and legitimate recourse. Here are a few areas to consider:

False representation: The seller or auctioneer cannot say or imply something false about the auction, including making any warranty. They can't say "What am I bidding for, this Waterford crystal vase?" if it is not a Waterford. You as a bidder would likely rely on that description and make your bids based on that.

Puffing an item: The seller and auctioneer also can't say things such as "All this car needs is a new spark plug and she will be as good as new." If they do, the item better be fixable. If not, a judge will likely give the buyer his money back.

Audio taping and video taping: Live auctions by professional auctioneers are usually taped to provide a record of everyone's actions, in case there is a dispute later. You can ask to view these tapes if you have a dispute. They may prove or disprove your recollection of what happened during bidding.

Auction day announcements: If the auctioneer changes the terms and conditions on auction day, and you relied on those details, you may have recourse. Auction day announcements always take legal precedence over prior advertisements. Auctioneers can generally correct any errors or advise the audience of any issues that have come up. So never be late arriving at an auction since new conditions are only announced at the beginning of the auction.

Buyer's Remorse Options After Paying

Buyers with remorse should be aware that stopping payment on a check can constitute theft.

The Uniform Commercial Code (UCC) permits an individual to stop payment on his or her check. The individual requesting a stop-payment order must generally identify the check by providing the check number, so the bank will not pay the check.

An oral stop-payment order will generally expire after 14 days. If the stop-payment order is issued in writing or an oral stop-payment order is confirmed in writing it is effective for six months and may be renewed.

An individual must generally have a valid legal cause to stop the check. He or she should generally issue a replacement check. If someone fails to pay for items purchased at an auction, the auctioneer may file a police report for theft. The auctioneer may also be able to sue for the amount of the check, treble damages, and attorney fees.

Another example issue, after payment in real estate purchases, is whether the buyer must sign the purchaser's contract (done after the auction) for the auction bid to be an enforceable contract.

An auctioneer in Tennessee encountered a real estate buyer that refused to sign the purchase agreement right after an auction, and said that the Statute of Frauds says you must have a signed contract for it to be enforceable.

The answer is that the Statute of Frauds generally requires: (1) a written memorandum (2) that embodies the terms of the contract, (3) an adequate description of the real estate, and (4) the signature of the buyer and seller (some states may only require the name being entered while most require the signature). The Statute of Frauds is intended to protect buyers and sellers from fraudulent or deceitful conduct by either party.

But an important factor at auctions is the terms and conditions statement signed by the bidder. They agree to certain conditions on this document. The terms of the registration can permit the auctioneer to bind the buyer after the sale or may (on its own) be sufficient to satisfy the Statute of Frauds. Other terms of the sale may also be satisfactory. For example, where the auctioneer's catalog listed as a condition of sale that "the record of sale kept by the auctioneer and bookkeeper must be taken by the buyer as absolute and final in all disputes," a bidder at the sale, by virtue of his or her participation, agrees to accept the auctioneer's memorandum as satisfying the Statute of Frauds.

Each transaction is unique and the law in each state will determine what is required to comply with the Statute of Frauds.

The Least You Need to Know

♦ Payment can be done during or after the auction, depending on the policy of the auction firm conducting the live auction.

♦ Some auction companies offer a partial payment plan, with credit extended to allow you to make ongoing payments toward the full amount.

♦ A final bill includes the purchase price (your high bid), a buyer' premium (if applicable), sales taxes where applicable, shipping fee (if you want the item shipped), and possible applicable fees.

♦ The law provides protection from false representation from sellers or auctioneers.

Part 3

Buying Successfully at Live Auctions

Being a successful buyer takes different skills depending on the kind of auction you will attend. You can imagine that buying art is different from buying real estate at live auction, so there are chapters in this part about how to buy successfully at each of the major types of live auctions: art, estates, real estate, charities, autos, farm, and livestock. Yes, there are basic buyer skills, such as bidding, that you can use in the different categories, but to get that "extra edge," read the sections about the auction categories that interest you most.

I'D JUST LIKE TO REMIND THE GENTLEMAN IN THE BACK THAT IT'S NOT CONSIDERED APPROPRIATE TO YELL "IN YOUR FACE!" WHEN YOU PLACE A WINNING BID.

BARR

Chapter 11

Buying Art and Antiques

In This Chapter

◆ Decide which art you want to collect

◆ Antiques are much more than furniture

◆ Be ready for bidding surprises!

◆ Do your research

Art and antiques are two separate categories, but are often referred to in one phrase and practiced as one specialty by many auction houses today, from the most well-known firms (Sotheby's and Christie's) to small local auction houses. Sometimes it is called "Estate antiques and fine art," or similar phrases.

The opportunity to find a hidden treasure at auction is perhaps larger in these categories than any other. Or you may find a nice little item, resell it for a few dollars more, and then see it come up later at auction for thousands more. That's what happened to Isador M. Chait, of Los Angeles, who later became an appraiser and auctioneer of Asian art and antiques.

Chait was at a local swap meet when an American Indian mask caught his eye, and he paid $50 for it. Later an art dealer bought it from him for several hundred dollars. Then, within months Chait saw the same mask on the front cover of a Sotheby's catalog. From that lesson in art value, Chait went on to open a store in Los Angeles dealing in art.

Buying Art

What is art? It is all items of artistic expression, including paintings, sculptures, weavings, drawings, and works in many other mediums. It can be original work or a reproduction (a copy, but still valuable and of high quality). Fine art is anything hand-crafted, says veteran art auctioneer James Jackson, of Cedar Falls, Iowa.

Interest in fine arts and antiques is strong these days, he says. "In the general population, people understand it as only paintings. In the industry, though, people who are informed understand that fine art encompasses a wide field."

Auction buyers are especially interested in oriental rugs, lighting, nineteenth century music boxes, and Asian contemporary art. "When the stock market is soft, people want to invest in a tangible investment," he said.

Auctioneer Jack Christy conducts an arts and antique auction.

Buyer Beware

Art at auction can look like original art, but may actually be reproductions. Do careful research and hire an appraiser when in doubt.

Let's say you want to begin buying fine art at live auction. How do you begin? First, decide which type of art you want to collect. Pick something that you will often view and enjoy, something you really like. Experts advise against picking only items for investments, hoping they will rise in value. You will be less likely to spend time really learning about this type of art, and hence will be a less effective buyer. Instead, if you look at pink glass or western art, and would like to display those in your home, focus on one of those as your specialty for collecting.

Next, find your local and regional auction houses that offer this type of art, and get your name on their e-mail list to be notified whenever these pieces come up for live auction. Also begin reading books and researching on the Internet about your category. Become an expert with knowledge and skills that will help you be a successful collector, proud of the pieces you choose and the fair prices you pay!

Be willing to travel out of state to find good pieces of art, also. For example, Chait, the art auctioneer from Los Angeles, sends out videos of auction items to interested bidders who live outside California and many of them visit his auctions, or they fax or call in their bids.

Who are bidders at art auctions? They include average interested individuals, but also professionals such as art dealers, decorators, expert private collectors, and museum personnel.

Can you bid effectively against the professionals to get good artwork? Absolutely yes! They may often not be seeking the same pieces that you are. There is such a wide variety of art at auction that you can likely amass a good collection of pieces of your particular interest at reasonable prices. If you lose a piece at one auction to a dealer with more money to spend, another piece will come along soon. Do your research, bide your time, and enjoy the auction and the collecting processes.

However, the first step to collecting is to research whether an item is an original, the authenticated ownership history of an item when needed, and the value.

Researching: Original or Copy?

The first thing to do in researching a piece is to determine if it is an original or a reproduction, as best possible.

The word *provenance* is used often in art and antique worlds, meaning discovery of who actually created the piece and who owned it from the time of creation to the present day.

def•i•ni•tion

Provenance is the origin or source from which something comes, and the history of owners of an item.

Viewers of the TV show *Antiques Roadshow* are familiar with this concept because that's the main purpose of the quick appraisals done on the show: determine where a piece was made and give an estimate of its value if sold at live auction today.

You can determine these things in three ways: by relying on the auction company's experts; by your own research (heavily using the Internet); or you can hire a professional. If you are collecting art prints (a copy of an original painting) of small or moderate prices, for example, you can easily do your own research. You've already accepted that you are not buying an original piece by an artist, but you can determine current market value by searching recent sale prices on auction firm websites, online auction websites, art price service websites, and so on.

You can also arrange to meet the auction firm's expert at the auction house to view the art and to ask questions. Often this is more productive after you have done your own research, so your questions on details can be answered.

However, if you are seeking original artworks for high amounts of money, it is well worth the price to employ a professional appraiser knowledgeable in that specialized field. They can determine the likelihood of it being an original, examine the chain of ownership, examine the condition of the item in great detail, and arrive at a current appraised value.

They are experts in provenance. The online encyclopedia Wikipedia says about provenance that "The provenance of works of fine art, antiques, and antiquities often assumes great importance. Documented evidence of provenance for an object can help to establish that it has not been altered and is not a forgery, reproduction, stolen or looted art. Knowledge of provenance can help to assign the work to a known artist and a documented history can be of use in helping to prove ownership. The quality of provenance of an important work of art can make a considerable difference to its selling price in the market; this is affected by the degree of certainty of the provenance, the status of past owners as collectors, and in many cases by the strength of evidence that an object has not been illegally excavated or exported from another country. The provenance of a work of art may be recorded in various forms depending on context or the amount that is known, from a single name to an entry in a full scholarly catalog several thousand words long."

How Art Auctions Are Run

Art auctions are similar to other auctions in procedure. Catalogs are ready to view weeks before the auction. Onsite preview times are provided. Attendees are asked to be extremely careful not to damage valuable artwork on display during preview times, when children are sometimes brought to previews and cause accidents that damage art.

Artworks are held up high by ringmen so the audience can see the pieces, or the art may be displayed on large video screens. However the atmospheres can be different depending on whether the art is merely part of a general estate auction or if it is a high-end specialty art auction.

In some cases, the auctioneer's chant is slower at art auctions. There is less desire to entertain the audience with a fast rhythmic talking, and more desire to provide extra time for buyers to think about their next bid, and to give an experience different from an everyday auction.

Terms and conditions at art auctions are usually not different, but be sure to read them carefully. Items are sold "as-is," but not by every auctioneer.

For example, the auctioneer from Los Angeles said all his items are sold "unconditionally guaranteed." "If we don't notice that it was broken and repaired, we take it back," Chait said. "If it turns out to be a fake, which is possible even though it hardly ever happens, we take it back. No questions asked, even if someone buys thinking that it's a certain size and they're really upset when it's not what they expected."

Where can you go to find art? Buyers (and sellers) of fine art don't need to travel to big cities to buy and sell their treasures anymore, as was the case years ago. In the Midwest, for example, Jackson's International Auctioneers and Appraisers outside Cedar Falls, Iowa, sells only fine art and antiques (and millions of dollars worth annually) in a range of items from furniture, paintings, jewelry, coins, and silver, all sold from their simple block auction facility.

About 95 percent of clients come from outside Iowa, with 14 percent outside the United States. Jackson's is a *regional-national market*, one of about 36 auction businesses in the United States that size. Jackson and his staff of 22, which includes three auctioneers, give their customers an estimate of what they can expect their goods to bring at auction based on computerized records the company keeps.

Jackson's Auction, which does 10 to 14 auctions annually, has two types of sales. There's a Collector's Choice auction several times annually, with goods that generally bring from $250,000 to $500,000 in sales. Twice each year Jackson's holds their Class A sale, which offers better-quality fine arts. Bids are taken in a gallery form at the rate of 100 items per hour. About 80 percent of items go to end users and the other 20 percent to dealers, figures that Jackson says have flip-flopped in the past 20 years.

Bidders can bid by phone during the auction. The firm also uses its website and full-color catalogs for each major auction, sent via an extensive mailing list.

Buying Antiques

America is having a love affair with *antiques* at auction and in other settings. Antiques have become part of mainstream America thanks to many factors, including PBS television's *Antiques Roadshow*, and newspaper stories about yard sale discoveries bringing big money on Internet auction sites.

An online catalog of arts and antique items in a live auction.

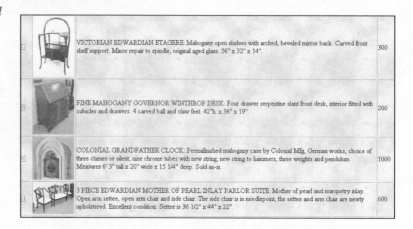

	VICTORIAN EDWARDIAN ETAGERE: Mahogany open shelves with arched, beveled mirror back. Carved front shelf support. Minor repair to spindle, original aged glass. 56" x 32" x 14".	300
	FINE MAHOGANY GOVERNOR WINTHROP DESK: Four drawer serpentine slant front desk, interior fitted with cubicles and drawers. 4 carved ball and claw feet. 42"h. x 36" x 19".	200
	COLONIAL GRANDFATHER CLOCK: Permafinished mahogany case by Colonial Mfg. German works, choice of three chimes or silent, nine chrome tubes with new string, new string to hammers, three weights and pendulum. Measures 6' 3" tall x 20" wide x 15 1/4" deep. Sold as-is.	1000
	3 PIECE EDWARDIAN MOTHER OF PEARL INLAY PARLOR SUITE: Mother of pearl and marquetry inlay. Open arm settee, open arm chair and side chair. The side chair is in needlepoint, the settee and arm chair are newly upholstered. Excellent condition. Settee is 36 1/2" x 44" x 22".	600

def•i•ni•tion

An **antique** is an item 100 years old or older, according to the U.S. Customs Department.

What qualifies as an antique? The U.S. Customs Department says it's an object 100 years old or more. But the term "antique" is used much more broadly. Generally speaking, antiques are artifacts from earlier cultures—that may or may not be 100 years old— but do possess some aesthetic, artistic, or culturally historic merit.

Antiques include much more than furniture, although that is one of the strongest categories of antiques. Other forms of antiques are dishware, electronics (phonographs, televisions, radios), photographs, pottery, rugs, coins, carvings, clothing, boats, automobiles, and so on.

Antiques are also sold at live auction with general household items such as at the weekly Tuesday night auctions of auctioneer Michael Anstead, of San Diego, California. He sells about 800 lots on a busy evening, with antiques accounting for about 100 of the items. About 60 percent of the 175 buyers at his auctions are dealers, who will resell the items. Although many come looking for antiques to stock their shelves, they're often as likely to pick up a bargain from Anstead's variety of furniture, collectibles, art work, appliances, and more.

Small antiques are hot sellers at general auctions in recent years because resellers look for items to sell on eBay.

Auctioneer Anstead runs his auctions with no reserves (no minimum price). Sometimes buyers walk away with a hot bargain, he said, but that keeps the dealers coming back for more. Also they are great for word of mouth advertising with the general public.

Because antiques can have cultural and aesthetic appeal, they can spark some lively bidding. At a recent auction, Anstead expected a Hunters cabinet to draw a top bid of $650. Fortunately, a bidding war broke out between the regular dealers, but the spoiler turned out to be a private party who chased off the dealers with a bid of $1,750. It was a new customer who spent additional thousands on other merchandise.

Just as with artworks, you must know the value of antiques to be a good bidder, says Ken Farmer, one of the appraisers seen on TV's *Antiques Roadshow*.

"Is it worth $500, $5,000, or $50,000?" he asks. "If you don't know what you're looking at, find somebody locally that you can trust. You need to know the difference between something good and something great."

Farmer is also an auctioneer who conducts antique auctions. He takes some merchandise that is not great, but is good, and it ends up at his twice-a-month Tuesday sale, where prices average about $50 to $100 per item. "They're fun, just like a country auction," Farmer says.

Bidding on Art and Antiques

As the baby boomer generation hits their senior years, more art and antiques have come to live auction, although some go straight to Internet auction sites such as eBay. And many bidding baby boomers have more wealth than past generations and are willing to spend it.

So what is a good bidding strategy on art and antiques? The basic one described earlier in this book is the best. Bidding up in small increments will often win your piece. Jump bidding to your maximum is an option, but may not work against wealthy dealers. Try to know your competition.

Auction attorney Stephen Proffitt gives this example of a bidding situation that occurs sometimes in antique auctions: say that a nice antique chest comes up for bid at an auction. The piece has a reserve, but the auctioneer predictably doesn't announce the amount. The bidding moves along quickly. When a bidder bids $2,500, the auctioneer exclaims, "We now have an absolute auction!" (Because the reserve of $2,500 has been reached, the item will definitely sell to the highest bidder.)

The bidding continues upward in $250 increments to $3,000 with only a man and a lady left bidding. The man holds the high bid. When the lady won't bid $3,250, the auctioneer asks her for $3,100 and she bids that amount. The two bidders then trade $100 bids for the piece until she is again the high bidder at $3,500. The man refuses to bid further.

Just before the auctioneer sells the chest to the lady, she hollers, "I don't want it!" The auctioneer immediately turns back to the man and asks if he can put the man back in at $3,400. He declines.

The auctioneer restarts the bidding and it opens with the man's bid for $500. At $1,500, he is the high bidder for the chest and no one will bid more. The man is happy, because he wins the piece for less than half of what he originally bid. Then the auctioneer announces a "no sale" inasmuch as the piece has failed to meet its reserve.

The man challenges the auctioneer that there is no reserve to be met, because the auctioneer previously declared it was an absolute auction. Others in the crowd openly agree with the man. The audiotape recording that the auctioneer is making of the auction continues to capture every word spoken.

This auctioneering technique is commonly used by numerous auctioneers who feel it will spur further bidder interest and drive bids ever higher. And it can, but it can also backfire.

Let's consider what happened here. First, the chest started with a reserve that was $2,500. After the man's bid satisfied the reserve, the auctioneer changed the terms of the auction from an auction with reserve to an auction without reserve (i.e., absolute auction). He did this in an effort to further excite bidders with the hope this would cause them to bid even more knowing that the highest bidder would claim the lot. Whether this change in terms played any role in driving the bidding to $3,500, we can't know for sure. What we do know is that the lady bid $3,500 and would have claimed the piece, except she retracted her bid before the auctioneer sold it to her. The commercial code provides that a bidder can retract a bid at anytime before the completion of a sale, so what the lady did was perfectly legal.

Second, the commercial code further allows that a bidder's retraction of a bid does not revive any previous bid for the lot. Although it was good auctioneering technique for the auctioneer to ask the underbidder to come back in at the amount of his last bid, there is nothing that provides for this to happen without that bidder's voluntary agreement to do so.

Indeed, it was a good bidding technique by the underbidder to decline to revive any previous bid, because his main competitor had just dropped out indicating the price might end up lower in a subsequent round of bidding.

Third, following another bidder's retraction of the high bid price, when an underbidder refuses to revive a previous bid, the result is that the bid price falls back to zero. The auctioneer is then left only with the choice of not selling the lot or restarting the bidding from the beginning.

So be aware of bidding situations such as this, as well as be prepared with your own bidding strategy.

Learn More About Art and Antiques

The wise bidder will continually learn more about his target type of property. Books and articles abound on details about every type of art and antiques. Check your bookstores, libraries, the Internet, and other locations.

In fact, fine art and antiques stir many collectors to near obsession and passion to learn about their category of interest. Art auctioneer Robert Baker, CAI, GPPA, CES, of Long Island, New York says that "Very few experiences in the world rock the very fibers of ones body with the same emotional intensity as does fine art. Whether looking at a uni-dimensional painting or a multi-dimensional sculpture both styles evoke reactions that can range from hate and outrage to love and jubilation. All the senses are ignited into action being stimulated by color, texture, form, line, and a host of other interactive stimulants."

As an example of what you'll find as you learn, let's discuss a few factors here. First is color and line. The colors in art and antiques have an effect on you. Reds make you feel alive, energized, excited, angry; blues make you feel peaceful, relaxed, cool; yellows make you feel happy, alive, electrified. Jagged lines make you feel uneasy, restless, agitated; smooth curved lines make you feel comfortable, safe, relaxed.

Auctioneer Baker also advises collectors to learn the difference between *fine art* and *decorative art*. In general the phrase fine art refers to paintings, sculptures, and graphic art and was not in use until the fifteenth century. Prior to that time artists were considered to be crafts persons. On the other hand decorative art is an application of segments of fine art to common or decorative objects which mirror the motifs of common society.

def•i•ni•tion

Decorative art is an application of segments of fine art to common or decorative objects which mirror the motifs of common society.

John Canaday of the Metropolitan Museum of Art defined a painting as follows: "A painting is a layer of pigments applied to a surface. It is an arrangement of shapes and colors. It is a projection of the personality of the man who painted it, a statement of the philosophy of the age that produced it, and it can have a meaning beyond anything concerned with one man or only one period of time."

There are eight major categories of paintings to identify and segregate: Fresco, Tempera, Oil Paint, Watercolor, Gouache (pronounced gwash), Acrylic, Mixed Media, and Pastels/Charcoal/Chalk.

Fresco is a method of painting calling for the application of paint to wet lime plaster on a wall. As the pigment penetrates the plaster it actually becomes part of the wall. The most famous of these paintings are those in the Sistine Chapel done by Michelangelo. The height of these creations was during the Renaissance; however, the twentieth century had its masters of this form of art, most notably was Diego Rivera.

The dry fresco or *fresco secco* in Italian is not a true fresco but rather painting with wet paint using a binding agent such as glue or egg. The dry fresco does not bind and become part of the wall but rather is surface art and is a less durable showing with chipping or flaking. Paintings such as these are seen in the missions and churches of the Southwest and Mexico. The wet fresco or true fresco, in Italian *buon fresco* is usually found painted on thick plaster walls and because the artist needs to work quickly before the plaster dries, great detail in the art is not evident.

Cracks in the walls display the depth of the art and its oneness with the wall. The colors are somewhat flat and in earth tones. Finally a third type of wall art is the cartoon. This is a drawing on paper that is transferred to a wall. A small spiked wheel, not unlike a pizza cutting wheel, is run over the outline of a drawing and then the paper is placed against a wet plaster wall and a dark pigment is rubbed over the surface causing a transfer of the outline to the wall.

These are considered works of art and are quite valuable but should never be confused with a true fresco.

Tempera is usually referred to as egg tempera and results by mixing pigments with egg yolk. Primarily these paintings were done on panels of wood in Europe during the fourteenth and fifteenth centuries. This type of painting was rarely seen after the 1500s but was rediscovered in the twentieth century by artists such as Andrew Wyeth. The paintings can be characterized as tedious at best due to the limited color range and the depth and richness of the painting is only achieved by layering on thin semi-transparent colors giving a luminosity not found in the fresco. In distinction to the fresco the tempera art is characterized by detail primarily because it was used in small quantities and applied with very fine pointed brushes line by line and layer by layer resulting in paintings that are very linear and detailed.

Oil paint is the binder for the color pigment and as such artists use it for the slow drying nature of the oil. Artists mix their colors on their palette or the work surface. Artists using oils can paint with the detail of the tempera artist or paint with a more fluid approach laying layer on layer presenting a surface with a thick texture or impasto. Old Masters build delicate layers called glazing creating a depth and richness never before achievable. Transitions between light and shadow are accomplished with a natural gentleness and such results in a piece of art that is referred to as being done in a "painterly" fashion. The nineteenth century introduction of tube oil paints revolutionized painting.

Watercolors, unlike other paint mediums, permitted the artist to accomplish very light tones by thinning the paint to the point where the ground or paper showed through and became an integral part of the work of art. Initially watercolors were used to hand color or tint other works on paper but in the nineteenth century it became its own art form. Spontaneity in the art is its form marker.

Gouache is a form of watercolor; however, unlike the watercolor a gouache is opaque and not transparent. This again is a form that appeared in the nineteenth century.

Acrylic is a synthetic or plastic paint which is water soluble and became commonly used in the 1940s. This synthetic can display properties of a watercolor or oil and is a quick drying medium.

Mixed Media combines two or more types of painting on one surface and is not a newcomer to the art scene. The fifteenth century often saw the mixing of oil and tempera on one surface. Today it is common jargon to describe prints and paintings with multiple elements including three dimensional objects attached to flat surfaces.

Pastels/Charcoal/Chalk are used in drawings and paintings and are marked by pure pigment mixed with a minimum of gum, resin, or other binder to hold the pigment together on a surface. Pure color presentation and soft delicate lines are the hallmark look for this art and it was originally used in Italy in the sixteenth century and then later chosen by nineteenth century impressionists. The surface of the art is perishable and many times the art shows with a smeared surface either intentionally or unintentionally.

This knowledge will begin to help the buyer determine the types of paintings offered at auction.

The Least You Need to Know

- Art at auction can look like original art, but may actually be reproductions.

- Whenever the price is significant, hire an appraiser to evaluate your target piece.

- Many antiques auctions are held without reserve, to draw in more bidders.

- A large part of the bidding crowd at art auctions are dealers, decorators, and collectors.

Chapter 12

Personal Property at Auctions

In This Chapter

- ◆ What exactly is an "estate auction"?
- ◆ An American tradition: consignment auctions
- ◆ Special items at specialty auctions
- ◆ Unlocking the doors of storage unit auctions

Personal property at auction generally means any items owned by an individual, except real estate. This includes everything from big furniture to small dishware, cars to artwork. In this chapter we discuss auctions where personal property is found, except the specialties of autos and artwork, which deserve chapters of their own.

There are four main types of auctions where personal property are sold: estate auctions, meaning usually after someone has died and their personal items are sold; consignment auctions, meaning sellers consign items to a general auction to be sold with many other sellers' items; specialty auctions, where an entire collection of one type of item, such as guns or coins, may be sold; and storage unit auctions, where a renter has defaulted or abandoned a rental storage space, so the landlord arranges an auction of the items in the space.

Each type of auction is conducted a bit differently, and bidders should know what to expect there.

Estate Auctions

At some time you've probably seen yard signs along the street saying "Estate auction here today." What does that mean? It means that someone's personal items are being sold at that location today. Often it is after someone has died that their children and legal representative hire an auctioneer to sell the items.

The *estate* is everything a person owns, including real estate and personal property. It can be anything from a small house with many items to a large farm with land, farm equipment, vehicles, and so on. Often the auctioneer must come in to the home to clean it, organize the items, appraise their value, set the auction, work with numerous heirs, and get the highest revenue possible for the seller.

def•i•ni•tion

An **estate** is everything a person owns, including real estate and personal property.

How do you find estate auctions? The common methods apply: see the advertisements in the auction section of the classified ads in your local newspaper and its website; visit the website of your local auctioneers (and get on their e-mail notification lists); notice yard and street signage.

The best way to find out what items are for sale at estate auctions before auction day is to go to the auctioneer's website. Click the link for the auction you are interested in, and often an online catalog of items is available to see, including photos and descriptions of the items. There will also be a description of whether pre-auction bids are accepted.

Here is an example of what may be offered in an estate auction: antique furniture, oriental rugs, lighting fixtures and mirrors, figurines, lamps, pottery porcelain, depression glass, stemware, antique jewelry, vintage costume jewelry, Bakelite, wristwatches, bronzes, oil paintings, and collectible books.

Two Rings Simultaneously

Because there can be a huge volume of items that take many hours or multiple days to sell, some auction firms have two auctioneers selling in two different rooms, also called *rings* (because people gather around in a ring formation).

Each ring will start at a specific time, and the lots in that ring will be sold in number order. The auctioneer's website listing and the cover of the printed auction catalog will denote which lots are selling where and the time the auction will start in each ring. If you plan to bid on items in more than one ring, you have several options. First, some bidders move from one ring to the other when a specific item of interest is coming up. This is made easier by TV screens in each ring showing what lot the other ring is currently selling. Second, if you have someone accompanying you, you can request a duplicate bid card and each sit in a different ring. Third, you can leave absentee bids for one ring and bid live from the crowd in the other.

Onsite at the Estate Auction

Estate sales can be conducted in the home of the seller, or at an auctioneer's building, where he or she has moved all the estate items for better display, if the home is a less desirable location (the home could be hard to reach or too small for an auction).

When you arrive at a home site, park in designated areas and register at the registration table. As you begin looking at items for sale, there may be items inside the home and some outside on the lawn for better display. Items for sale will have tags, and there may be items remaining in the home that are not for sale, and therefore, not tagged.

Perhaps the most prevalent type of items at estate auctions is furniture, including antique furniture.

Although furniture can be a specialty auction all its own, because it is so much a part of estate auctions let's look at it in that setting. The furniture for sale may be left in the home (a bedroom set in the bedroom, for example) or it may be displayed outside on the lawn so more visitors can gather around the items and inspect furniture better from all angles.

Be sure to examine the condition of furniture. Open all doors on cabinets, look for loose legs, stains, and other problems because you will be buying in as-is condition.

Most estate auctions have a full day of previewing the day before the auction. This establishes a relationship with the bidder and allows him to ask questions. Participants can also sign a request list so they know on what day an item is scheduled to sell. By doing this, bidders don't have to come every day during a multiple-day auction.

Auctioneers also conduct a mock auction so new bidders can familiarize themselves with the whole process ahead of time, and not while the actual auction is in full swing. Estate previewing usually closes two hours before the auction begins.

The auctioneer should already have made sure that there are no liens or other claims on the furniture, so it is sold with clear ownership title. Normally an item will not be sold with any encumbrance to clear title.

Lot Order in Estates

Auctioneers decide in what order items will be sold in an estate auction, so you can find out roughly when your desired items will be sold and you can come back at that time (for example, all furniture may start at 1 P.M.).

Some auctioneers prefer to alternate bigger items and smaller items to keep the crowd seeing a variety. "I'll usually sell a bedroom suite, and then an accessory item," said auctioneer Jack Earlywine, CAI. "This allows time to put the bedroom suite away."

Bidders at estate and consignment sales are often antique dealers, online resellers (hoping to sell online for a quick profit), collectors, and individual users. Normal bidding strategies apply.

After making your purchase at an estate sale, some auction firms may allow you to pay and take your item immediately, while others will make you wait until the auction is over so there is no confusion among attendees and staff about which items are leaving the location. "I don't allow individuals to pick up their items during the auction," said auctioneer Earlywine. "Not even a lamp or a picture frame can be taken during the auction."

Earlywine said this allows for a secured environment, and auction personnel don't have to worry about someone dropping furniture on a customer's head while trying to get it to the auction block. His buyers can pick their items up after the auction, and usually the next day as well. His buyers must also have a checkout form signed showing they bought the product as-is. The form also lists the buyer number.

Heirs, Feuds, and Emotions

Estate auctions are sometimes the site of feuds and strong emotion among grown children of the seller. You may see this as an attendee and bidder.

When grown children are inheritors, often they have to decide what to sell and what to keep among themselves, which can lead to anger and disagreement before the auction day arrives. And sometimes, if the children have not inherited anything, they may show up at the estate auction and want to buy special items as any bidder does, or they may try to make trouble.

One auctioneer described how he handled an estate auction with grown children who had not inherited any items. The auctioneer allowed the children to visit his auction facility prior to the auction to determine what items they might want from the estate. Some came equipped with appraisals in hand on certain items, which they then viewed. No items were sold before the auction. The children had decided to take their chances at the auction.

On antique auction day, all attendees arrived. None of the grown children were willing to pay the prices offered by regular clients. Some had traveled four hours to get there. The same happened on the next day of the auction. The auctioneer ended up educating the children about the auction process and auction goals to get the highest price possible for the seller.

Auctioneer Deb Weidenhamer, CAI, of Phoenix, Arizona, says that "The auctioneer has to deal with family members who are both emotionally unstable and often unfamiliar with the auction process. The survivors may have unresolved issues with the decedent and even more unresolved issues with remaining family members. People who cannot get along under normal circumstances can turn into real monsters with disputes about what will be sold, what the reserves will be, and who will get to withhold items from the sale. I've learned to watch for the warning signs of feuding relatives and will avoid booking an auction that has the signs of degenerating into a war."

She contractually requires a single family member be selected to make all decisions about how the auction will be conducted. Inability to settle on a single leader is a sure sign the family will be difficult to conduct business with. As a bidder, you may see such a single family member making decisions onsite, and sometimes running into opposition.

Other Auction Options Families Use

Someday you may be a family member considering an auction of a deceased relative's estate. A traditional auction may be a great option for you to maximize the revenue available. But an auctioneer may also be able to give you other options.

Auctioneer Weidenhamer said sometimes a traditional auction is not a fit for a family because "People usually have an over-inflated idea of what their items are worth and this is even more so the case when people have an emotional attachment to the items being auctioned. Often the estate will just not bring enough money to justify an onsite auction because of the high level of setup to properly prepare the estate for sale."

She offers families alternatives to traditional estate auctions. "If the estate has a burdensome setup, we will instruct the family on how to do the auction setup and then will perform the auction for a reduced fee. If the estate only contains a few high-value items, we will suggest some items be consigned to a regular consignment auction and the remainder of the estate sold in a yard sale or given to charity for a tax write-off. If the estate consists of highly specialized collectibles, tools, or hobby items, which will require extensive research, and a family member is already an expert in the subject, we may suggest the family prepare the descriptions for posting on the Internet. We then handle the posting, collection, and shipping for a reduced fee," she said.

The "Living Estate Auction"

Many elderly people have a *living estate auction* when they move into a smaller home or into managed care. It is very difficult for these people to give up the possessions of a lifetime and many of the same contentious issues arise among their family members.

def•i•ni•tion

A **living estate auction** is an auction of estate property while the seller is still living.

At a living estate auction you may see the elderly seller there. Many auctioneers strongly encourage the elderly family member to not attend the auction because of the emotional stress it will cause. But, in some cases, the seller may be well able to handle the situation and may even wander around talking with bidders, answering questions and seeing friends who came to the auction.

If the elderly seller is not capable of being in charge of the auction, another family member may be designated to make decisions. The elderly seller is encouraged to review the auction setup prior to the preview to say goodbye to their possessions and to identify any remaining items they may insist on pulling out of the auction.

Estate auctions can also present surprises for those involved. For example, if a family member wants to dispose of a dozen boxes of "worthless" old clothes, and the auctioneer finds several boxes filled with highly collectable beaded dresses from the 1920s, the auctioneer is required to represent the best interest of the seller and so must inform the seller of high value clothing. If an attendee finds such hidden treasurers and wishes to bid, they have no such requirement to inform anyone of the suspected higher value.

Sometimes estate auctions sell things that would seem to have great sentimental value, and you may think it is a mistake that love letters or similar items are being sold, but such is not the case. Auctioneer Weidenhamer said "The number of families that have absolutely no interest in old letters, journals, and photo albums astonishes me. I once sold hundreds of love letters written by an Army officer and his wife during the years before and during WWII because the family didn't want them. It is hard not to feel some emotional empathy at the casual tossing aside of once cherished mementos."

Weidenhamer adds that sometimes she personally purchased these items and found good homes for them. "Local museums and libraries are often happy to receive donations of old letters and photos if they portray events or people of historical interest. An organization called The Legacy Project is currently collecting war letters from all American wars and can be contacted at WarLetters.com. Some items may be of interest to people who share a common interest or background with the decedent."

Terms and Conditions of Estate Auctions

The terms that you, as bidder, agree to may be different at an estate auction and will vary depending on location and auction firm. Here is an example of terms from a New York estate auction:

1. Purchases are cash, Visa/MasterCard, guaranteed funds, or approved personal checks.

2. All lots are sold subject to New York State Sales Tax unless bidder has filled out a New York State Sales Tax Exemption Certificate and has such certificate on file with the auctioneer.

3. If the auctioneer determines that any bid is not commensurate with the value of the article offered, he may reject the same and withdraw the item from the auction, and having acknowledged an opening bid, he decides that an advance is not sufficient, he may reject the advance. Auctioneer reserves the right to bid on behalf of buyers/seller/secured parties.

4. Ownership title passes with the fall of the auctioneer's gavel, and thereafter, the property is at risk of the buyer with neither the seller nor the auctioneer being responsible for loss or damage.

5. Every item is sold as-is. Neither the auctioneer nor the seller makes any warranties or representations of any kind or nature with respect to said property. All sales are final. Catalog descriptions are for simple identification purposes only, no representations are made as to authenticity, age, origin, or value. Buyer relies solely on his/her own inspection and judgment when bidding.

6. All purchases by attendees shall be paid in full by close of auction, and preferably removed same day. Any items not removed within 48 hours of auction/sale shall be deemed abandoned by bidder and shall be disposed of at bidder's expense without recourse. (Exception: absentee and phone bids)

7. Purchasers are responsible for all costs involved with removal of their purchases and any and all damages incurred during removal of purchases.

8. A 13.5 percent buyer's premium shall be added to the top bid to become part of the purchase price; 3.5 percent discount applied for cash or check payments. The buyer's premium is defined as … that portion of the commission(s) which is being paid by the buyer. It is clearly understood and agreed by both the buyer and the seller that both the auctioneer and broker only represent the seller.

9. The highest approved bidder to be the buyer. In all cases of disputed bids, the property shall be resold, but, auctioneer will use his judgment as to good faith of all claims and his decision is final. Where a lot has a stated quantity that is more than 1 (one), the bid shall be multiplied times the quantity to determine the total cost of the lot.

10. All bidders are required to register and give full identification prior to the beginning of the auction and are required to use the number issued them when identifying themselves as the successful bidder.

11. Should a dispute arise after the auction, auctioneers' records shall be conclusive in all respects.

12. This is a privately owned and operated auction. We reserve the right to refuse admittance to any person(s). No transfer shall be recognized from one buyer to another.

13. Bidder agrees to pay any and all charges and expenses incurred by reason of any breach of terms and conditions of auction or in case of default, including, without limitation, reasonable attorney's fees, as well as any dollar deficiencies which may result in the resale of the property, and the cost of re-marketing said property. Additional commissions shall be due and payable.

14. As a courtesy to other bidders, please do not sit with small children in the first 6 (six) rows.

15. Auctioneer reserves the right to withdraw any property prior to auction.

16. Bidder agrees to the above terms and conditions of the auction prior to receiving a bid card for this auction, and all other auctions said bidder attends of this auction firm in the future.

17. The above stated terms and conditions of auction cannot be altered except in writing by all parties of the contract, or by verbal changes to terms given by auctioneer at time of auction.

17. Bidder does hereby indemnify and hold harmless auctioneer and seller from any and all damages, claims, or liabilities from injuries to persons or property of any type whatsoever, caused before, during, or after the auction.

Consignment Auctions

Consignment auctions are those where multiple sellers consign items (place items for sale) to an auction. Often it is a general property auction, a collection of household items, and is held in an auctioneer's facility. But, the term *consignment auction* can also apply to a vehicle auction with many sellers, or a firearms auction or other types.

The weekly or monthly general consignment auction at a local auction center often draws a crowd of regular bidders who enjoy the social interaction with friends as much as the bidding process and finding property to buy.

The types of property consignment auctions is obviously widely varied, and is similar to estate auction items mentioned previously. In fact, almost all advice about estate auctions also apply to attending consignment auctions, including bidding strategies.

An example of a large weekly consignment auction is at Christy's of Indiana Auction and Realty, in Indianapolis, Indiana. The weekly auctions every Wednesday occur from 9 A.M. to 5 P.M. and draw an average of 800 to 1,000 people.

> **From the Podium**
>
> If you're a seller, the best time to bring consignment items in is the day or two after the last auction. This allows plenty of time for the auctioneer to advertise your item.

Here's a typical day at this consignment auction, which auctioneer/owner Jack Christy, CAI, GPPA, CES, CAGA calls "Market Day." At 9 A.M. three auction rings open simultaneously in three different areas. Art, antiques, collectibles, and glassware are auctioned in the main building. TVs and other electronics, plus box lots and miscellaneous items are sold in a building attached to the back of the main building. Tools and business liquidation items are sold in a second building and include surplus desks, sofas, fixtures, and computers.

At 10 A.M. the furniture auction begins in a third building which also has antiques. At noon people gather between the furniture and main buildings for auctioning of automobiles, motor homes, campers, motorcycles, and riding lawn mowers.

Who attends this type of big consignment auction? "We have flea marketers and secondary eBay people (who buy so they can resell on eBay) who like to buy in large quantities," Christy said. "And that's what our auction is."

Auction attendees may often find that an estate's properties are offered as part of a large consignment auction with other sellers. That is the case at Christy's. "Most of our consigners are estates," he said, "so we are dealing with heirs. They need to be nurtured a bit because they are going through a traumatic time."

And some auction attendees may also go to an estate or consignment auction expecting to see for sale specific items they knew were in the estate, but not every item given to the auctioneer ends up in the live auction. With Christy's as an example again, this firm and others sell some items on eBay or other online venues because they believe that is where the most money will be obtained for the seller, especially for unique items. For example, Jack Christy said "We sold a woman's Chicago Bulls (basketball team) leather jacket and a lot of memorabilia we thought would do better on eBay."

What else will you see at some consignment auctions? Large screens at the front of the room to display clear images of small items such as jewelry. Videocameras may be posted as the auction is carried live on the Internet. Security guards may be posted to provide protection for staffers handling cash, and for crowd problems.

Storage Auctions

Storage auctions typically occur when a renter has fallen far behind on payments at a self-storage unit, or has abandoned a rental space. The recent growth of the self-storage business, with units that look like small garages, has led to a rise in *storage auctions*.

def•i•ni•tion

> **Storage auctions** are an auction of items stored in a rental unit that has been abandoned or fallen behind on rental payments.

These are also called lien auctions because there is a lien, a debt of months of unpaid rent, which the renter owes to the storage company. The auction is arranged by the storage company manager to satisfy the debt.

Rental unit auctions can be found in advertisements or on a local auctioneer's website. The auctioneer may set up 12 rental unit auctions in one day, driving from one to the next site with bidders following him or her in a caravan. Sometimes you may have an idea of something in a rental unit, and sometimes not.

Rental items may include valuable motorcycles, clothing, tools, and artwork, as just a few examples, or they may be boxes of worthless items. The auctioneer typically does not open the unit to examine it until the time of the auction.

For example, auctioneer Fred Reger, of Manasses, Virginia, frequently conducts auctions at storage facilities where the lock to the unit is cut and, following a quick inspection, the property is sold as either a single unit or in separate lots.

He also conducts auctions for businesses such as moving companies where the items are moved to his auction house. At least 46 states have laws governing the enforcement of liens on self-storage units. Federal Uniform Commercial Code law can also apply in many cases.

Sometimes you may find the renter of the storage unit is attending the auction, and he or she may be very unhappy their property is being sold.

"One of the key things to remember is that it is an involuntary auction," Reger said. "You're dealing with an involuntary seller who is not happy this is happening. It's not the willing seller-willing buyer concept in these cases."

Reger makes it a point to find out if the owner of the property is attending or someone representing the owner is in attendance at the auction. Because it is a public auction, those owners are welcome to bid on the items.

"We always ask if the person in default or a representative is in attendance and I talk to that person individually," he said. "I want them to know what's going on and explain there's nothing personal, that this is a legal process. You're selling storage today but you're in the community every day."

Price Ranges and No-Sale Decisions

Prices can be high or low, but typically are on the low end because the crowd is small and they are not aware of items inside until the unit is opened.

"There's many times I open up a unit of self-storage and say if anybody will bid today, life is good," Reger said. "Many times that unit is sold for $1 to the storage facility. But the auction needs to take place to satisfy the process and a $1 bill is legal tender."

Reger has also had situations where he's discovered valuable items inside. Experience has taught him that if the items look too good to sell or cause doubt in your mind, there may be a glitch.

"I close the storage unit back up and announce we aren't going to sell it," he said. "There's nothing that says the auction has to take place that day. There may be a problem, or you know you haven't brought the crowd you need to satisfy your responsibility to get the highest price."

Sometimes a lien auction is stopped just before starting because the debtor pays the outstanding bill. Reger has also opened up storage units and found vehicles or equipment he couldn't auction because of the potential of other liens on those properties.

Buyers Are Resellers: Identity Protected

Many of the buyers at storage auctions intend to resell for a profit. "If you give them (these reseller buyers) five working days to clean out the storage unit, they're going to follow you around (to the next storage auctions), and then clean out within the five days." Reger said he allows five days to clean out purchased items.

Buyers should also know that the auctioneer and storage owner can never release the name of the buyer. That is to protect you from harassment from the unwilling seller who may be angry his property was sold to satisfy his debt. He may want to get his motorcycle back, for example.

Specialty Auctions: Firearms Example

A specialty auction is where only one type of property is sold, such as cars, coins, or guns. The specialty auction brings out many dealers seeking to buy these items to resell, collectors seeking to add to their collections, individuals wanting one item, and curious spectators.

To buy effectively at the specialty auction, you must know the value of the items you want. Look closely at the catalogs of items available from the auctioneer, or posted on the auctioneer's website. Then research the value of the item and be prepared to bid against people similarly well prepared.

Firearms auctions are an example. They can be of everyday guns, from pistols to hunting rifles. Or there can be a specialty antique gun collection at auction. It helps to know the applicable laws as well as the monetary values of the guns.

Steps to Purchase at a Gun Auction

During auctions, guns are often held in racks in display cases. Each has a tag with an item number. Bidders can examine and handle the guns prior to the auction, under the watchful eye of auction staff. When a gun is sold, the buyer's number goes on the tag. But the gun is not handed to the buyer at that time. The buyer must first pay for the gun and fill out an ATF 4473 form.

That form asks the buyer if he is a felon, an alien, has any legal convictions, is under indictment, and so on. The auction clerk then looks at the buyer's ID to check age (complying with local and other laws) and address (may need to be an in-state resident), and makes sure that the face on the ID matches the buyer's face.

If the auctioneer is a licensed federal firearms dealer, he or she is required to check the buyer with the National Crime Information Center's computer system run by the FBI, which quickly sends back a message to the dealer telling whether the buyer is approved, denied, or delayed until more information is available.

"When we call you in (a buyer) and that comes back denied, there's nothing we can do," firearms auctioneer Larry Garner said. If the check is approved, Garner can transfer the weapon in accordance with all laws. "At that point, I feel that I've done everything I can do to ensure that firearm goes to a responsible party," Garner said. "However, I can't go home with that party and tell him what to do with it when he leaves my premises."

A Bit About the ATF

Enforcing the rules and regulations related to firearms in the United States belongs to the U.S. Bureau of Alcohol, Tobacco, and Firearms. The bureau's vision is to decrease criminal misuse of firearms and to curb violent crime.

There have been changes in the way this nation regulates firearms and their sales. In 1934, Congress passed the National Firearms Act, which regulated "gangster-type" weapons, such as machine guns, sawed-off shotguns, and silencers. The Gun Control Act was enacted in 1968.

More recently, in 1993 there was the Brady Handgun Violence Prevention Act, and later the Violent Crime Control and Law Enforcement Act of 1994. These made it harder for criminals to get their hands on firearms from federal firearms licensees. In part, that means criminals are looking to other avenues to get firearms including flea markets, gun shows, and auctions, where criminal background checks are not routinely required. But, that depends, in part, on whether the seller is required to be a federal firearms license holder.

If the auctioneer takes possession of guns and sells them on a repetitive basis, that business requires a federal license as a gun dealer, and they may be required to get more information from their buyers than nonlicensed auctioneers.

Auctioneers try to keep good records of the sale of each gun. They write down information such as serial number, purchaser information, and more. They don't want to be sued in case the gun is used in a crime.

Who Cannot Buy Guns at Auction

As a buyer at auction, you should also know the following about buying guns at auction: you often can't legally buy a gun at auction outside your home state. Firearms laws are complicated. For example, some state laws allow the sale of a rifle or shotgun to a resident of an adjoining state, but some states prohibit that. Superseding that is a federal law that says auctioneers cannot sell these items to an out-of-state resident unless the auctioneer has a federal firearms license.

Another twist is that in Chicago, Illinois, the sale of all handguns is forbidden within city limits under a city ordinance, Garner said.

So don't be surprised if you hear about complexity and even contradictions of gun laws when you attend a gun auction. Ask the auctioneer or the AFT any questions you have about whether you can purchase the gun you desire. Also read information on their websites.

Also bidders should know that auctioneers cannot sell guns to the following:

- Anyone who has been indicted for a felony.
- Anyone who is a fugitive from justice.
- Anyone who is a user of narcotics or controlled substances.
- Anyone who is an illegal alien.
- Anyone who suffers from mental deficiencies.
- Anyone who was dishonorably discharged from service.
- Anyone who renounced U.S. citizenship.
- Anyone who has a court restraining order against them.
- Anyone who is younger than age 18.

Also, it is illegal to make a "straw purchase," meaning to have someone else purchase a gun for you, if you are a person unable to legally purchase a gun. Auctioneer Garner discourages this practice by announcing before his auctions that straw purchasing is illegal and not tolerated.

"I announce before every sale that straw purchasing is a federal felony and that I and my auction crew will be watching closely for this activity," he said.

There are also certain guns that have additional specific regulations and procedures to sell. These include fully automatic weapons, an H-and-R Handyman (a shotgun that looks like a handgun), an "Ithica burglar gun" (a short-barreled 12-gauge), and so on. The Feds watch these guns closely, Garner said.

In addition to live gun auctions, there are online gun auctions that can give bidders exposure to the values of guns found at all kinds of auctions. Auctioneer Eric Smith, of Reidsville, North Carolina, said, "There are a few websites that offer gun auctions, however, you must contact a class 2 or 3 federal firearms licensee to help you with the transfer. www.ebang.com and www.gunsamerica.com are two of the sites I use. You should also be able to advertise (specialty guns) with a few gun-related publications and get quite a few offers. I would try *Gun List*, *Shotgun News*, *Guns and Ammo*, *Shotgun Sports* magazine, *Guns*, *Shoot*, *Shooting*, and even *Military Trader*."

Auctioneer Charles Brobst, CAI, CES, of Anchorage, Alaska, also recommends the website www.gunbroker.com for successful gun sales.

Exceptions for Antique Guns

One area not covered in the federal code is antique firearms. Auctioneers can sell to out-of-state buyers without a license, as long as the firearm meets the federal definition of an antique. An antique is described in the U.S. Firearms Code as any firearm with a matchlock, flintlock, or percussion cap manufactured in or before 1898, or a replica of such item.

The same applies to a gun using ring-fire or conventional center-fire fixed ammunition that is no longer manufactured in the United States or is not readily available in the ordinary channels of commercial trade.

Safety at Gun Auctions

When it comes to guns, you can't be too careful, especially when in a crowded public place. The first thing an auction staff does is check all the guns and make sure

Buyer Beware

Don't assume a gun at live auction is unloaded. It should be, but accidents have happened. Always check the safety latch when handling guns, and do not point them in the direction of people.

they're empty, but the occasional accident will happen. One time at live auction a gun went off and blew a hole through a wall, an event that could have ended in tragedy if the gun had been pointed toward the crowd.

Yet auctioneer Larry Garner supports letting buyers handle the guns. "A discriminating buyer isn't going to buy it unless he can handle it and be sure of its condition," he says. "You've got to let them handle the guns, you just have to be sure they're empty."

The Least You Need to Know

♦ To find estate auction items you like, review the online catalogs of estate auctions on your local auctioneers' websites.

♦ Weekly consignment auctions are held in most towns and are a social event for many attendees.

♦ Specialty auctions feature only one kind of item and draw experienced dealers.

♦ Never try to have someone else buy a gun for you at an auction. Such straw purchases are illegal.

Chapter 13

Buying at Real Estate Auctions

In This Chapter

♦ Residential real estate

♦ Agricultural and vacant land

♦ Commercial real estate

♦ Multi-parcel real estate sales

Real estate auctions, especially single family home auctions, are the fastest growing of all categories of auctions. By understanding how real estate auctions work, from the buyer's and seller's perspective, you can be a more efficient bidder and buyer. We will talk about home auctions first in this chapter, and many of its procedures will apply to other forms of real estate auctions, also.

Homeowners (the auction sellers) are choosing auctions because they see at least three big advantages (which you as the bidder need to understand). First, they see that an auction with a set date creates a sense of urgency and firmness about the sale: everyone expects that buyers will show up and the home will sell. Bidders feel that urgency, too, a feeling that often does not exist when a home is in a traditional real estate listing for months or years. At an auction, if you don't buy it on auction day, you'll lose that home you're interested in.

Secondly, sellers also like the idea that the home will sell as-is, with no promises to fix problems or provide any services after auction day. All the seller must do is disclose any problems with the property, and bidders make their bidding decisions with that information in mind. But clearly the responsibility is on both the seller and bidder to make sure the full condition of the property is revealed and understood. This could include faulty heating, plumbing, lead paint, or other problems.

Thirdly, the seller can set a reserve price, a minimum amount they will accept. This way, if the reserve price is not met, they do not have to sell at a lower price than desired. The seller will have spent a very modest amount on advertising and other auction expenses, but is not obligated to sell. You, as the bidder, should understand that sellers want a fair price for their home, or there may be a mortgage on the home that must be paid off, and this drives many to choose the reserve auction format.

In this chapter we examine the steps involved in a real estate auction, how to attend and bid successfully, the absolute auction format, and other topics to help you in a live real estate auction.

Residential Real Estate Auctions: Homes and Condos

First, let's go through the basic order of steps in a real estate auction in the usual six weeks leading up to the auction, including the many aspects that involve bidders. Notice the many points where you, as a bidder, should get involved, including getting your *property information package (PIP)* and attending an open house to examine the property.

Week 1: The auctioneer reviews the property and discusses with the seller the type of auction desired (reserve versus absolute). The auctioneer makes recommendations to the seller regarding how to market the property (upscale marketing, target moderate incomes, media selection, and so on).

def•i•ni•tion

A **Property Information Package (PIP)** is a file of information about real estate for sale, listing all details of the property, including physical location and descriptions, financial information, physical conditions, plus any problems and so on.

A home real estate auction in process.

Deed, title, liens, and other paperwork associated with the real estate are checked. Environmental concerns are investigated. Even if it is not required as a condition of sale, an environmental audit (an assessment of whether a property has any environmental problems) is usually a good idea in that it may help alleviate potential uncertainty among bidders. A clean environmental audit can be used as an advertising tool along with favorable zoning regulations, and so on.

The auctioneer helps the seller and bidders by recruiting financing for the property. One of the prime candidates to provide financing for real estate is the seller of the property. Regardless of who finances the property, it is important to identify potential bidders in advance of the auction and work to get them pre-qualified with a lender.

Week 2: Bidders are often not troubled about buying a property if it has a few problems, as long as they know about them. That is why a comprehensive "Property Information Package" is developed for bidders, and can be a very important asset in the marketing of a property—even if a few problems are listed. Some auctioneers order a home inspection to include in the PIP.

At this point, preparations for a real estate auction begin to resemble those made for any other type of auction. Advertising is ordered; auction site plans determined, and so on.

Week 3: A pre-auction seminar for prospective bidders is organized, and agreements are made with traditional real estate brokers who can refer buyers to the auction. Auctioneers offer a brokerage agreement that would allow brokers a commission if they bring a buyer to an auction.

In many cases, potential bidders at a real estate auction have never bid at auction before, let alone a real estate auction. These bidders must be shown how the auction process works and also give some advice as to financing. Potential bidders can be told the preparations they should make in advance with their own banker and/or directed to a financial institution that has agreed to provide financing for the property.

Week 4: The How to Buy pre-auction seminar can be held this week for novice bidders. Bidders are responding to ads and getting due diligence packages and information off the auctioneer's website.

Open houses begin this week. In addition to the primary purpose of showing potential bidders what they might be buying, an open house gives the auctioneer a barometer of how successful the auction will be. One auctioneer says "My previews take place only for an hour immediately before the auction. It's a frenzied hour that builds excitement. People generally look at a property to eliminate it. At an hour preview, people will stay."

Week 5: During this period, an initial evaluation of the marketing campaign is made based on the response at the open house and calls requesting bidders' packets.

Interested and qualified bidders are being identified and their deposits to bid are placed in escrow accounts.

Week 6: Final details such as site preparation and posting additional signs to the auction site are being done. Bidders are contacted to make sure they have directions to the live auction site and any questions they have are answered.

Basic Course of Events at a Home Auction

Finally, it is auction day. You've planned adequate time to arrive early, you've read your due diligence packet, inspected the property at an open house, placed your deposit with the auctioneer, and decided on your bidding strategy and maximum bid price. You park at the site and are ready for the auction to begin.

Go inside the home and go to the registration table to get your bidder number. If you only want to watch this auction, explain that to the clerks. They will be glad to welcome observers.

The home auction may be held inside the home, with bidders standing in the living room, or it may be on the front lawn, with the auctioneer standing on the steps by the front door.

The auctioneer will welcome the bidders and read the terms of the auction. He will describe if there are any changes since the advertising was placed and due diligence packages given out. He will tell if the auction includes live phone bidders, advance bidders or other types of bidding, and if the auction is being broadcast live over the Internet.

Most auctioneers will not answer questions from the podium. If you have questions get them answered before the auction starts.

The auctioneer will then open the auction and call for bids.

Home auctions typically have smaller crowds than other types of public auctions. There may be 5 to 15 people at a home auction, most being serious bidders, already pre-qualified to buy and having placed a deposit. The bidding goes very quickly and is often over in a few minutes.

As at other auctions, the auctioneer opens the bidding at a moderate amount and asks for a next higher increment. Bidders raise their bidder numbers. When there are no higher bids, the auctioneer will declare the auction over and he will announce if the bid offer is accepted by the seller (in the case of a reserve auction, the reserve must be met).

SOLD! _____

If you are the backup bidder (the second highest bidder), be sure the auction clerk has your phone number because, if the sale falls through, you might get a call to purchase at your bid price.

The buyer then signs a real estate contract, the contract is then presented to the seller, and the auction is done. Closing and title transfer is usually done within 30 days.

Types of Bidders and Behaviors

Who are the bidders and observers at a home auction and other real estate auctions? There are several types.

One is the "bottom fisher," the person looking for a basement bargain, an extra low price for a good property. They think "auction" means a forced sale for distressed or foreclosed property, which is sometimes true, but less so today than in the past. A minimum opening bid may or may not discourage this type of bidder.

Another is the serious buyer. In fact, most buyers at real estate auctions have to be serious because of the deposit and pre-qualifying requirements. This is not an impulse purchase as compared to something such as an antique auction. Don't look at bidders in real estate auctions in the same way as you do at a local consignment auction of small items.

Neighbors, vacation-home buyers, and investors are other categories of buyers. Neighbors sometimes want to buy a home next door to control a property that has been a problem in some way, or to prevent a problem from moving in. A vacation-home buyer is likely someone with financial capital to spend and a serious bid in hand.

Real estate investors are also common at home auctions today. They may want to "flip" a house, meaning sell it quickly to make a fast profit, or they may hang on to it. Investors can be savvy auction buyers with the ability to bid high and work the angles for a good purchase.

But the market is flooded with schools offering seminars, books, tapes, and all kinds of information designed to turn everyday people into overnight millionaires via real estate investing, including at auction. Auctioneer George Richards says that "Many are using investments or using other forms of credit to finance their dreams. Some folks are coming to auctions and purchasing speculative properties using funds drawn from home equity lines of credit in combination with cash advances from credit cards."

Another real estate auctioneer says "The buyers are often a tough crowd. I had a building with an office on the bottom floor and two apartments above, and we had a lot of bottom fishers, but also some educated buyers that checked in the basement for water damage. Even though we make all of our disclosures they know what to look for. You have to be able to be on top of that."

Who else is at the auction? Real estate agents who bring their clients or have come alone. You'll see the agents talking with their clients and perhaps the auctioneer. The seller will also likely be there, standing near the auctioneer.

Bidder behavior at real estate auctions can be unusual. Some unethical bidders even tell lies to other bidders to scare them away from the property, a tactic called "poisoning the well."

"They're brutal because they're trying to talk down the property so they can keep the bidding low. They come in saying how terrible the property is, but they're right there with their deposit when the property is ready to auction," said a veteran auctioneer.

Don't be swayed by other bidders' comments. Stick to your plan and trust that the auctioneer has provided full disclosure of all property conditions. That is his or her job. Ask questions if you have concerns.

The Opening Minimum Bid: Bidding Strategies

Not all real estate auctions have a minimum opening bid, but many do. Some advertise "No minimum opening bid," but the final bid is subject to acceptance by the seller.

But when there is an opening bid, how do the auctioneer and seller arrive at an opening minimum bid amount? Here's a look.

"If there is a home valued at $100,000 at auction, a typical offer in my market would be $95,000," said auctioneer Gardner. "After the seller pays the costs (advertising and others for the auction), they are going to have $83,000 to $84,000."

> **SOLD!** _____
>
> You can make an offer to buy a home before or after an auction (if it does not sell that day). The auction date drives the sale toward that one point with urgency, but it's not the only day on which you can make a deal.

She uses this as a marketing tool to establish a price point. "I tell them that if they're going to net around 84 cents on the dollar, why don't you let us start it at a $79,900 minimum bid," she said.

Then, she uses that $79,900 figure to market the property. Sellers are informed that commissions and closing costs will be added (as a buyer's premium on the buyer, usually around 10 percent). The bottom line is that the $79,900 figure draws attention.

"When sellers are searching in that neighborhood of homes marketed at $100,000 and they see the one for $79,900 do you think they are going to go there?" she said. "Absolutely! The deal is going to bring them in, the intrigue of why it's going to auction and how come it's so much less."

After bidding has started at a home auction, the same bidding strategies can be used in any auction: incremental bidding, half-balling, and maximum bidding. Start out with incremental bidding, guided by the auctioneer's requests for the next high bids (maybe at $5,000 or $10,000 increments). Begin jumping to higher amounts only if you see strong competitors. Set your maximum bid and stick to it. Getting carried away at a home auction will cost you much more than on a low-priced item.

And don't be surprised when fair market value, or higher, is reached. Sometimes local real estate brokers come to auctions expecting low prices and leave astonished at final prices auctioneers have produced.

But, in those times when a home is drawing low bids and not getting up to its reserve price, the auctioneer may call a break in the bidding and privately step aside to ask the seller to lower the minimum. But that intention will not be announced to the crowd.

Auctioneer Pamela Rose, CAI, AARE, says these breaks are short and the bidders are kept occupied. "When we take a break, one of my assistants is talking to the crowd about the property," she said. "If you don't, the crowd will talk among themselves or begin wandering off. I keep them occupied and keep them thinking about the auction on my terms."

Auctioneers call this the danger of "buyers cooling off." They remember that the high bidder can withdraw his or her bid up to the point that the auctioneer's hammer falls to sell the property.

How to Set Your Bid Amount

For a real estate auction, you must know your financial ability to set your bid.

Many buyers think they know their price range, but actually don't. Here is what some have said before auctions:

"We are paying $500 a month rent. We should be able to afford $1,000 a month on a house payment."

"We are living with my parents and are saving $800 a month. We should be able to afford that much for a monthly payment."

"Our parents have given us $20,000 for a down payment. We should be able to afford a $230,000 home."

This type of reasoning sounds like a sure sale, but only at first blush. When the auctioneer informs the clients that a $230,000 loan at 9 percent for 30 years is $1,850 per month, they don't believe it. If they can only afford $1,000 per month, they can't buy a $230,000 home. This couple needs a home in the $120,000 range.

After you have your range, go to a bank or credit union and apply for a loan. Auctioneers may require pre-qualifying because they need to know you have the ability to close the deal, which a bank translates as your ability to make the promised payments. The auctioneer does not want to risk having a buyer sign a contract and then have to forfeit their deposited earnest money when a loan cannot be approved.

After the Auction

The steps that occur after a home auction are, typically that an attorney prepares the deeds and may do all the legal work, or a broker may complete all aspects of the closing. Title insurance on the property should have been available at the auction. That will head off surprises at closing. In addition, have all courthouse work handled properly before closing. Taxes need to be prorated and deeds need to be properly executed and signed by both buyers and sellers. Only then can deeds be recorded.

SOLD!

The National Association of Realtors has an auction division and encourages realtors to use auctions, evidence of the credibility of the auction method.

The successful bidders are now new owners of the real estate, and they have a tremendous story to tell about obtaining a home at auction.

Licensing Requirements

Many states regulate the auctioning of real estate. In some states, a real estate auctioneer must also have a real estate brokerage license so the auctioneer has training in real estate issues.

"If an auctioneer only has an auctioneer's license, he or she is limited to selling the property at the auction or shortly thereafter," said Stephen Karbelk, CAI, AARE. "If the auctioneer also has a real estate license, he can sell the property at any time."

Some auctioneers hold licenses in multiple states. State regulatory licensing agencies are increasingly recognizing other state licenses. Some states may require additional requirements. Check with your state's licensing group to be sure your auctioneer is licensed.

Absolute vs. Reserve Auction

Many auctioneers agree an absolute auction will produce a higher offer than a reserve auction. But many (if not most) prospective sellers of real estate at auction are unwilling or unable to offer their property unreserved because they can't cope with the risk.

This is particularly true of sellers with liens against their property that must be paid at closing. However, under the proper circumstances, the vast majority of reserve auctions offer a good chance to sell property.

Some auctioneers have an auction listing agreement with a clause that allows them to encourage buyers to the auction by identifying the client as a motivated seller who accepts the possibility of selling at or below market value. When prospective buyers call to inquire about a reserve auction, they ask about the "minimum," Or no minimum starting bid. The auctioneer explains to prospective sellers that they will tell prospective bidders that the client has instructed the auctioneer to dispose of the property for what the market will bear. Telling a prospective buyer that he must meet a seller's pre-determined expectation is "de-motivating," auctioneers said, and reduces attendance at the auction.

Sellers pass the motivation test if they understand about possibly selling at a discount and if they clearly understand that buyers must be lured to the auction.

Knowing why the prospective seller is attempting to sell the property also helps the bidder know how much lower the price can go. Is the prospective seller an individual, financial institution, or a corporation? What is the mortgage balance? How over-priced is the property? Is the market improving or declining? What did the owner pay for the property?

Bidders are excited by a must sell seller. Bidders smell the low price potential. But, a seller who says he "doesn't have to sell" or "isn't about to let anybody steal" his property may be excluded from auction services indefinitely.

Consider if the seller is an individual, financial institution, corporation, and so on. These entities can range from excellent to inferior as auction sellers. Financial institutions and corporations will occasionally participate in an auction (even though they have no intent to sell) so they can reduce property taxes or to convince regulators and shareholders of an earnest attempt to sell property.

On the other hand, companies and financial institutions often are directed to sell properties quickly, with lessened emphasis on obtaining initial purchase prices or aggressive appraisal amounts. A seller's indebtedness also is critical.

> **From the Podium**
>
> In the early 1900s, auctions of homes and other real estate in New York City were extremely popular and widely accepted by the public.

Questions Bidders Should Ask

Bidders should ask at least basic questions of the auctioneer (representing the seller) to make sure the bidder has all the information needed.

Ask the following questions:

♦ What minimum price, and price range, are you looking for?

♦ How much is the deposit, how do I submit the deposit, and what else is needed to pre-qualify to bid?

♦ Will you take offers before the auction? (Some states require the auctioneer to submit all offers to the seller, including pre-auction offers).

♦ When can I get the Property Information Package and inspect the property?

Take detailed notes.

When you make a pre-auction offer, point out the lost time and opportunities and extra carrying costs possible if they don't take your offer.

Agricultural Real Estate

Bidders can get good values on vacant agricultural land that can then become the site of your dream home, recreational land for fishing or hunting, or a place you can develop as a subdivision for rural homes on large lots.

Where do you find these and how can you buy at auction? Contact your local auctioneers who deal in real estate.

Farm credit banks, which deal strictly with agricultural lending, often turn properties over to auctioneers to sell vacant land. So do absentee landowners. Estate sales are also a place to find vacant land that was owned by someone now deceased.

"Estate sales seem to draw large crowds and more money, for some reason," says auctioneer Tommy Rowell, CAI.

The steps for home auctions also apply to agricultural land auctions, but buyers and auctioneers must also be sure they are dealing with the person who has the authority to sell the property. "If it's a corporation, that might be the president or one of the officers. If an estate, make sure you're speaking with the executor or the administrator. In partnerships, make sure you are speaking with every person you need to," auctioneer Rowell said.

Here are some essentials to check:

- ◆ Clear title, no liens, as on any real estate.

- ◆ Placement of access roads, with a legal description of the property and information on the total acreage and makeup, if it's wasteland or cultivatable acres or timber acres, pasture land or orchards.

- ◆ Allotments on a farm. To determine allotments they have value go to the Agricultural Stabilization and Conservation Service office for the information.

- ◆ Improvements on the property.

- ◆ Know if it's leased. Learn about the property's financing and what's owed on it.

- ◆ Look for surveys or any photographs, including aerial.

- ◆ Structures on property. It helps them describe improvements room by room and they learn information about utilities and more.

Some information could come from the tax office. Often times the soil conservation office will have a great deal of information and sometimes by checking records "you can tell a great deal about a farm without setting foot on it," Rowell said. "You can tell a great deal about the quality of a farm and its worth."

A very important thing to do is to check on local governmental regulations on subdivisions. Before you take a farm and subdivide it, make sure to visit the planning and zoning office and get the regulations on how to subdivide legally in your area. Otherwise, you could be asking for trouble and officials could stop you. Ask for a copy of the subdivision ordinances and make sure what you would like to do is something you can do.

When you visit the property to inspect it before auction, get the outline of terms and conditions, order of sale, possession of property information, closing information, and any other information you feel is important.

If acreage varies from surveys, the price will be varied upward or downward. Be clear on what chemicals have been used on the property and discuss owner financing. Get a sketch of the property if there's one available.

Commercial Real Estate Auctions: Stores and Offices

Want to buy a small business, such as a gas station? They're available at auction. How about an office or apartment building, a warehouse or shopping mall? All these and more are sold at commercial real estate auctions.

The basic steps are the same as at home auctions, but the higher prices make it even more important to do your homework on all aspects. And once again, do not expect bargain prices when these serious, professional bidders and auctioneers are at work.

A recent *Wall Street Journal* article described commercial real estate auctions this way: "In the past, auctions were almost exclusively the last resort for desperate owners or banks eager to get a failed property off their hands. Now an auction is one of the first options many owners think of to sell commercial properties. Sellers now include blue-chip companies and building owners under no imminent financial pressure to sell. The range of buyers has expanded to include more institutional investors and small entrepreneurs with long-term goals, not just opportunists looking to make a quick buck by turning around a distressed property. And the properties in many cases are well-leased office and apartment buildings, shopping centers, and hotels, in good condition."

For example, commercial real estate auctioneer Kim Hagen, CAI, AARE, CES had an auction of four car washes in Dallas. The appraised value of the businesses was $3.8 million; Hagen sold them for $5.5 million.

These auctions can include the land, buildings, and contents. Get all details from the auctioneer and be sure exactly what you are bidding on. Find out all financial details, including taxes due yearly on the properties. Also the previous checklist for agricultural land also applies to commercial auctions.

Commercial real estate is that used or to be used for a business or investment purpose, said auctioneer William Fox. This includes multi-family residential properties or apartment properties.

Sellers of these properties are often a bank's real estate department. "Sometimes loans go into default and collateral needs to be disposed of," including commercial and industrial real estate, he said. "And many times people leave businesses and business assets in trust as part of their estate."

In buying industrial buildings, make sure you are familiar with things such as the ceiling height, crane bay span widths, floor load factors and things of that nature. "If you're going to deal in this kind of real estate at auction, you need to become educated before you go into it," Fox said.

Commercial Real Estate Foreclosure Auctions

If you're buying commercial property, you should know how sellers decide to use an auction instead of a general real estate listing. It will help you set your bidding amount.

Auctioneer Stephen M. Karbelk, CAI, AARE, said that the decision is a simple cost-benefit analysis of the most likely net to the lender at the foreclosure auction versus the most likely net selling the property in their Real Estate Owned (REO) inventory via general brokerage. With commercial real estate, the cost savings of selling the property at a foreclosure auction are significant.

For instance, here are the lender's benefits by selling at auction: immediate recovery of the value of the property; ability to immediately commence recovery against the borrower for any deficiency in those jurisdictions that permit deficiency actions; no closing costs paid by the lender because the buyer pays them at closing; interest accrues and is paid by the buyer from the date of auction until closing; no extended marketing time as an REO property; avoids buying back undesirable or troubled properties; none of the other burdens of ownership.

Therefore, if the value of the property will not increase by the lender taking it back and owning it, the decision should be to simply sell the asset for the highest price at the foreclosure auction.

Also at the foreclosure auction is this situation. In many cities the rights tenants have over property owners prevents many good brokerage deals from ever happening.

For instance, in Washington, D.C., tenants can stop a general brokerage sale from occurring by simply matching an offer accepted by the seller and "trying" to get financing, sometimes delaying a sale up to a year. In most of these cases, the tenants have no intentions of buying the building. They just want free rent or money, and then suddenly "lose interest" in the purchase. Unfortunately this maneuver is common practice in some urban areas.

However the one caveat to being held hostage to tenants is to sell the property at the foreclosure auction where they have no rights. The buyer knows they will not have to pay off the tenants and the lender knows that it can close in 30 days, not 12 months.

The bidder/buyer of leased real estate should also do these preparations: this includes receiving copies of leases, accurate rent rolls, and operating expenses. The seller and auctioneer get this information because they know the more information bidders know about the property, the higher the price at the foreclosure auction.

You may also seek an appraisal, environmental report, survey, and/or an engineering report on the property to disclose all conditions. This may already be available from the auctioneer, but that is a legal and marketing decision made between the auction company, foreclosure attorney, and lender.

Finally, invest in an auction marketing campaign that will generate significant interest in the property.

Prepared by the auction firm, this campaign will focus on attracting the target market to the property by attention-grabbing newspaper advertisements, first class direct mail, high-quality brochures, informative property information packages, telemarketing, Internet marketing, and signage.

It is important to note that the marketing budget will be in addition to the cost of any required legal notices.

Foreclosure is a drastic remedy, the requirements of which vary from state to state. Because the result of a foreclosure is to divest the owner of the property from title to the property, care must be undertaken to ensure that the foreclosure complies with all provisions of the loan documents and all applicable state and federal statutes.

Some states provide for nonjudicial foreclosure whereby a third party conducts an auction pursuant to a power of sale contained in a deed of trust with only minimal involvement by the court; others have quasi-judicial foreclosures where the sale is still conducted by a third party via a power of sale, however, the courts monitor and regulate the foreclosure process.

Still other states have judicial foreclosures that require an adjudication of the indebtedness and a decree from the court ordering the foreclosure sale.

Senior vs. Junior Mortgages at Auction

Here are a few legal matters to consider when buying at foreclosure auctions:

When a senior mortgage or lien (one filed first) is foreclosed, all the junior liens and mortgages (filed after the earlier ones) are extinguished (with some statutory exceptions). In some states, a deed in lieu of foreclosure may have the same effect on extinguishment of junior liens as a sale by foreclosure, nonetheless, the most prudent assumption should be that a conveyance pursuant to a deed in lieu of foreclosure conveys title subject to all encumbrances and that only the foreclosure sale itself effectively purges the title of the subordinate liens.

Because the deed in lieu of foreclosure may not extinguish subordinate liens on the property, the lender whose borrower is willing to transfer title via a deed in lieu of foreclosure should consider what is typically termed a friendly foreclosure.

A friendly foreclosure is nothing more than a regular foreclosure whereby the borrower agrees not to contest the foreclosure or declare bankruptcy in exchange for some type of accommodation by the lender, typically either full or partial forgiveness of any remaining debt. By conducting a friendly foreclosure, the lender is able to advertise the foreclosure sale as required by the deed of trust and local statutes, and also market the property via the use of a professional licensed auctioneer.

Use of the friendly foreclosure will permit the lender to conduct the foreclosure against the property and purge the real estate of any subordinate liens, while also allowing the lender the opportunity to aggressively market the property in an effort to maximize the price at the foreclosure sale and perhaps dispose of the property altogether by a sale to a third party.

Multi-Parcel Real Estate Auctions

A growing number of real estate buyers today are buying condominiums, vacant land, and other properties in a format called *multi-parcel auctions*. These are not just investors, but also average homebuyers and vacation-home purchasers.

def•i•ni•tion

A **multi-parcel auction** is an auction in which more than one piece of real estate is sold during one auction. This can include vacant land split into many tracts, multiple condominiums, homes, or other real estate.

In these auctions, a seller offers, for example, 100 condominiums in one building for sale at one auction. Buyers come from across the country to get a condo in Florida or a Colorado ski resort. The buyers can bid on the condos of their choice, with the size and layout they like. The buyer may even buy two or three condos, so he can keep one and sell the other two.

Hundreds of bidders attend these auctions and the bids are kept track on a bulletin board at the front of the auction gallery.

Although there's some variety in multi-parcel auctions, they all work basically the same. A room is filled with the auctioneers, crew, sometimes an advisory team, tables and bidders. The crew often uses projection screens to show maps and photos of the properties, dry erasable boards to post bids for the audience to see, and computers to sort and track the bids. A mock auction can be held before the real auction to show attendees exactly how the bidding and posting will work. The auction then proceeds with several rounds of bidding offering first individual parcels followed by combinations of parcels, continuing with more rounds to group and re-group (or combine) again and again throughout the day as needed.

A winning bid on one parcel affects prices of all combination parcels by a percentage factor or dollar amount, as can be predetermined by the seller and/or auctioneer. Computer programs figure subsequent bids needed for bidders to remain as the highest bidder on their single parcel or combinations. Throughout the auction, crew members work with bidders to keep the sale running smoothly and efficiently. Trained bid assistants are vital to the success of multi-parcel auctions. Although most multi-parcel auctions involve property owned by just one seller, this is not a requirement and parcels from several different, possibly adjoining, sellers can be included.

Auctioneer Richard Lust, CAI, of Madison, Wisconsin conducts this method, especially with farmland, and says the method produces more money for the seller by selling individual parcels of land.

"The sum of the parts will always total more than the whole," he said. "Six different buyers instead of one. What makes the multi-tract work is that you've just created more buyers." The key to selling multi-tracts is to let buyers purchase only the portions they want, even if the property as a whole isn't the most desirable.

Auctioneer Scott McCarter, CAI, from Sevierville, Tennessee, sold 25 acres in 13 lots in 45 minutes for $2 million to four buyers. The development property, sold as commercial and residential lots, was located on a four-lane highway. Bringing out the property's winning points, he said, is key.

"We're big on promotion. When you list a property as an agent you get the property for six months. You're limited to what you can spend (on marketing)," he said. "It's just one of many. At auction, we know that property is going to sell that day," he said.

"The most unique feature of this auction is the use of the individual and in combinations, par bidding, and high-bidders choice auction methods," said auctioneer Stephen Karbelk.

To illustrate the first method, let's assume a property is composed of 26 building lots. The auctioneer can offer at auction each building lot, then offer them in any variety of combinations, and only accept the bids that realize the lender the highest net proceeds.

> **Buyer Beware**
>
> Multi-parcel auctions are designed to encourage bidders to bid against each other. Runaway emotions can lead to over-paying in these auctions.

Some jurisdictions may require an offer in separate parcels and in total in an effort to maximize the sale proceeds. This is an excellent way to encourage individual lot buyers and builders to bid against each other, thus driving up the net realized by the lender.

This encourages the first round of bidding to bring in the highest price so the market is set high by the bidders for the rest of the auction (if the first buyer does not take them all).

The benefit of this auction method is the ability to have bidders interested in several different lots bidding against each other for the right to choose the lot they want to buy.

Where to Find Real Estate Auctions

Real estate auctions are easy to find in most areas. Look in the "auction block" section of your local newspaper. There are many real estate auctions listed in large towns, with the ads referring the reader to websites for more information.

Small yard signs are increasingly prominent today saying "Real estate auction here" and listing the date of the coming auction. Stop and write down the information when you see it.

The website of the National Auctioneers Association at www.auctioneers.org has a "Find an auction" search section. Enter "real estate auctions" and your city or state, hit the Enter button, and a list of all real estate auctions offered by NAA members will appear on your screen.

Also check the website of your local auctioneers and real estate agents, or call them to ask when their upcoming auctions are scheduled.

Marketing is a critically important element in auctioning real estate, according to Mary Jean Agostini, a licensed Connecticut-based real estate broker.

"When you auction a property you have to advertise in a very short period of time. When we take a regular listing we spread the advertising over a six-month period. With the auction business you pack it all into a 30-day period." That means the auctioneer, seller, and real estate broker are all trying to make it easy for you to find these auctions.

Timing the distribution of advertising is also crucial. Agostini and others have mailing lists of investors as well as brokers, and send their auction notices about three weeks ahead of time. In this way her prospects won't forget about the auction, yet they'll still have time to look at the property, attend a preview, and get their financing in place. So as an interested bidder, get on these lists.

With all these types of real estate auctions, keep in mind that real estate live auctions are expected to continue to grow and gain wider acceptance among the public, real estate agents, and all parties involved. You should be able to continue getting good values as a buyer and good prices as a seller of your real estate if you keep learning how the process works.

Baby boomers are inheriting property at an unprecedented rate in history, and auctions offer a faster and viable method of liquidating these assets.

The Least You Need to Know

- Most real estate is sold at auction in as-is condition, with no promises to fix problems or provide any services after auction day.

- Be sure you're buying property with clear title, meaning no liens (owed money claims) against the property.

- Most bidders of real estate must put down a deposit and be pre-qualified for a loan to assure the seller they are serious bidders with the ability to pay.

- Real estate auctions can be absolute (no minimum price) or reserve. Find out early which type your auction will be.

Charity Auctions: A Different and Festive Animal

In This Chapter

- ◆ A party for a worthy cause
- ◆ Bidding with a different outlook
- ◆ Most items are sold "absolute"
- ◆ A peak behind the curtain

Charity auctions are a growing auction niche. More buyers are attending more charity auctions than ever before. You may have already attended local charity auctions for your school, church, or civic organizations.

These auctions are growing more sophisticated each year by using professional auctioneers, marketing and technology to draw more donated items and bidders to raise more money. In this chapter, you'll learn how these auctions operate and how they differ from all other auctions.

Charity Auctions 101

Charity auctions are those that raise money for charities, or nonprofit groups. These are also called benefit auctions and fundraisers. They are opportunities for buyers to get a variety of items and help a good cause at the same time.

def•i•ni•tion

A **charity auction** is an auction that raises funds for a charitable organization. Also called a benefit auction or fundraiser.

In charity auctions, typically an auctioneer sells donated items to raise money for a nonprofit group such as a church, Heart Association chapter, or Special Olympics. Volunteers of these groups have worked for months to obtain these donated items. The auctioneer may donate his or her time, or he may get paid to manage the event with the help of volunteers. Most of these auctions are conducted in one night, but some last an entire day. And sometimes, they are formal affairs where the attendees dress elegantly while enjoying a party atmosphere and may pay a fee to attend the dinner and auction.

Many nonprofit groups hold a charity auction each year and it is the biggest fundraising event they have. The crowd may be made up, for example, of mostly the church's congregation and friends, but visitors are often sought because they bring in extra money, and that's the point: to raise money.

What's Sold at a Charity Auction?

Typically the items for sale at charity auctions are a mixture of travel trips (a weekend at a timeshare condominium in Colorado or Hawaii); wine; sculptures; jewelry; golf clubs; sports memorabilia; electronics (computers, music players, televisions donated by local stores); gift cards from local stores; lessons for skills such as golf, swimming, or horseback riding; services donated from hairdressers or tax preparers; imported rugs; dishware; and possibly donated cars or motorcycles.

Often there are hidden treasures that auction regulars know how to find and acquire at their local charity auctions. The charitable organizations routinely advertise their whole item list to draw bidders from their in-house audience and from the general public. The organization may run local ads and then refer you to their website for the complete item list. But look closely to see if there are items you want.

Charity auctions are the best place to buy unique experience packages not available anywhere else. "At a charity auction I once bought a dinner for 12 at a Moroccan ambassador's home with he and his wife. It cost nearly $4,000 but it was worth every penny," said Stephen Karbelk, CAI, AARE.

Attendees also enjoy the silent auction section that is typical at charity auctions. In the silent auction, normally held one hour before the charity dinner/auction, attendees walk around tables to see items placed there for sale. In front of each item a bid sheet and pen are placed where attendees can compete with others on paper by placing bids for their items of interest. The attendees have a set time to continue to stroll around and raise each other's bids. When the time has elapsed the silent auction is closed and the last person who placed the highest bid purchases the item.

You write your bid for that item on a sheet of paper, and then the highest bidder wins. You may go back two or three times to check the last high bid and raise your bid.

Items in the silent auction are usually lesser-priced items that the organizers expect will not generate the competition or high prices of items in the live auction. But there are still many good items at good prices available.

What Are the Next Steps?

Now that you've decided to attend a charity auction, call to make a reservation (often required for a dinner), pay any upfront fee to attend, and find out the dress style required. It may be a tuxedo is required for men, but that is not typical of most charity events.

Next, go over the item list to spot any special items you want, and then decide on your bidding strategy and high bid amounts.

SOLD!

Be ready for the auction to start during the dinner salad. Position yourself so you can see the items, bid, and continue eating dinner.

At a charity dinner auction, bidding usually starts during the dinner salad to get the auction moving quickly. Auctioneers say that after dinner, people begin thinking of going home soon, so the auction needs to begin during the meal.

The timing for dessert is just as important, adds auctioneer Jay Fiske. "It should be orchestrated like a play with precision," he explains. "Use the dessert to make sure everybody is in their seats before you sell the biggest item. The whole evening must be choreographed. That means lighting, sound, and even musical bumps between items."

Fundraiser audiences are different from the typical buyers that come to commercial auctions to bid for bargains. They expect dinner and entertainment for the price of their ticket, and some are auction rookies that need to be coaxed into bidding.

Bidding and Expectations Are Different

You can get excellent values at charity auctions on some items, but there is also a higher chance that some items will sell for inflated prices than at regular auctions. Why? Because many people in the charity auction crowd know and expect to pay a higher price to support their favorite charity. And the charity auctioneer is trained to make that happen.

In fact, when friends with money start to bid against each other, the prices rise fast and the crowd enjoys the show.

Auctioneer John Stone in Trenton, New Jersey said "I ask the (charity) organization to point out people or groups that might compete with each other. That way I can say 'Are you going to let Sam have that for such a low price, Harry?' That lets you give the auction a personal touch."

Auctioneer Cheryl Parker said that charity auction prices are planned to rise and fall like a wave. She keeps the audience ready for the bargains by letting them know they will return. "I remind people when I'm selling the high-end items that lower-priced items are coming back," says Parker. "I'll say, 'Okay, we just sold that Italian vacation for $5,000, but wait until you see what's coming in just a few lots. You'll all have a chance to bid on something low again.'"

But the basic bidding styles of incremental and jump bidding still apply as a starting point. Auctioneers start the asking price in a moderate range, and bidders begin bidding with small increments, soon someone jump bids substantially more than what is considered normal at other auctions.

This is where you have to expect the action to change dramatically. When a bid is made that doubles the last bid, you have to decide if you will stick to the high bid you've planned. The bold bidder who just doubled is making a statement to the crowd. He's saying: "I'm donating to our cause, and I want this item."

It's time for you to escalate or back away, but don't be confused about what is going on. This is a show and an auction. Personalities and pocketbooks are in the mix to a greater degree than usual.

At this point you may see two competing friends going for the high price, both wanting the trip to the Hawaiian condo. The trip donor may be present, and the auctioneer may ask the donor to donate one more similar trip because the strong competition presents a large amount of money for the charity. The same can occur for other items, such as rugs, computers, or professional services.

It will also help you be a more successful bidder by knowing how the auction items are ordered for sale.

Auctioneer Stone advises his clients on how to arrange the order of the items for auction. "Their normal tendency is to hold the big items until the end, but the big items sell better in the middle. Holding items does not hold the crowd," he said.

While bidding, charity attendees should also remember that auction laws generally remain the same at charity auctions as at most others, even though there is a more-festive, less-serious atmosphere. For example, you cannot retract a bid later if you change your mind on a purchase. A bid made at an auction creates a contract between the seller and bidder, according to the Uniform Commercial Code (UCC). This provides the legal framework for contracts for sale formed at auction (with the exception of real estate to which the UCC does not apply). Take a moment to read the following few short paragraphs about the three sections of the UCC important to the formation of contracts for sale.

First, when an auctioneer offers an item for sale, it is called a *lot*. Section 2-105 of the UCC defines a lot in pertinent part as "a single article which is the subject matter of a separate sale or delivery …." Thus, each offering by the auctioneer is a lot that will be the subject of a separate contract for sale. A dining room table and six chairs could be one lot, or two (table in one and chairs in another), or even seven (each piece separate). An auctioneer has reasonable discretion in defining the lots offered for sale.

Second, UCC section 2-206 (1) (a) provides: "Unless otherwise unambiguously indicated by the language or circumstances an offer to make a contract shall be construed as inviting acceptance in any manner and by any medium reasonable in the circumstances." So, a highboy offered for sale in an antique shop would invite acceptance in a different manner than the same piece offered in an auction.

Third, UCC section 2-204 (1) provides that "[a] contract for (the) sale of goods may be made in any manner sufficient to show agreement, including conduct by both parties which recognizes the existence of such a contract." Therefore, when an auctioneer cries for a $450 bid on a dresser, and a bidder signals "yes" by a nod of the head, this conduct shows agreement sufficient to create a contract for sale.

When an auctioneer introduces a lot, the seller and bidders go through the process of offer and acceptance. If the lot is sold, a contract for sale is formed between the seller and the highest bidder, as defined by the terms of the auction. Auctions are all about contracts.

From the Podium

Charity auctioneers will sometimes chant slower so auction rookies can clearly understand the bids, but the momentum of the auction forward to the next item moves quickly.

Stone says charity auctioneers keep the pace moving quickly. "You've got to keep it moving because most likely 30 percent of your audience has left within the first hour. So the pressure is on."

As a result, bidders seeking a lower price for an item may be more successful in the second half of the auction.

Bad weather can also play to the advantage of bidders because fewer bidders sometimes show up. Auctioneer Kurt Johnson said "One cold and snowy night resulted in more than half of the paid attendees not showing up. Those who did show were almost an hour late. We had to make changes on the sly to salvage the night."

And occasionally, bidding may be more difficult at charity auctions if a professional auctioneer is not used or an adequate number of trained ringmen are not used to spot the bids in the crowd. This occurs less frequently than in the past because many charities now choose to professionally run their auctions, but it is good to be aware of the possibilities.

For example, auctioneer Wilbur C. Mull, CAI, said one black tie gala he worked at presented problems: There were 2,000 people in the audience, plus the press, and the lights were right in my eyes," Mull recalls. "You've got all of those people out there wearing black or tuxedos, so when one person puts their finger up in the air, you can't possibly detect it. I had no bid assistants, but luckily I had a friend that was an auctioneer at the event and he was able to help me."

Help yourself as a bidder by sitting in a well-lighted spot, near a ringman if possible, and yell out your bid if necessary.

Become a Regular Attendee

You may come to enjoy charity auctions so much, and the items you find, that you will want to become a regular attendee. You may look for their advertisements in your local media.

There are several reasons to become a regular beyond finding good items to purchase. Obviously, you can also help good causes. You get to know people in those groups, which you may want to join yourself and become active (even helping to organize their auction!).

When you attend a charity auction, sign up with the organization to receive their newsletters and notices about their future auctions.

Some regular charity auction attendees get hooked on the silent auction portion. Charity auctioneer Kurt Johnson says that "Depending on the event, the participation rate in the silent auction can be close to 100 percent. My opinion is that the average participation rate falls around 75 percent. I define silent auctions as 'the ultimate in competitive shopping.' There are many types of individuals who just love bidding at silent auctions. Some will bid on items they do not even want just because it was a good deal. Others are what I call Silent Auction Vultures. They are constantly circling the silent auction area watching the bid sheet for their special item. There are the early bidders and the last minute bidders. And sometimes there are late bidders who bid after the silent auction is closed."

He says some attendees will only spend money in the silent auction. They might never bid in the live auction. That is why silent auctions are an important revenue stream to many fundraising events and the people who plan them.

Charity Auction Formats and Technology

We discussed three basic types of auctions in Chapter 2: the absolute auction, the reserve auction, and the subject to seller confirmation auction. Which applies to charities?

Usually, most items in charity auctions are sold absolute, meaning no minimum price. Most items are donated items, so they have been given to the charity, which will get whatever amount possible for the item.

But, sometimes charities may buy an item to resell for more, so they estimate they can sell an item in another venue for a certain price and do not want to take an extremely small price for an expensive item. And why should they? The point of the auction is to get fair market value or higher, not allow people to get unfairly low value.

If there is a minimum price required, a reserve, it will be announced by the auctioneer, just as in any other auction. The same is true if an item is offered at charity auction "subject to seller confirmation." An official with the charity may decide to accept or reject the high bid for some reason. But, these circumstances are usually rare.

A technological auction format that is becoming more frequent at charitable auctions is live Internet bidding, which allows customers to bid from home or elsewhere, if they cannot attend.

As with other auctions, some charitable auctions these days also take phone bids and absentee bids to help their success. The auctioneer usually explains this to the audience when these bids are in play because auction rookies will not understand what is happening without explanation. However, local charity auctions run by small groups such as churches remain one of the simplest auction formats, often having only the live auction crowd on the floor bidding. This retains the fun and simplicity that small groups often enjoy.

But, at larger benefit auctions you will see technology used such as large video screen, electronic payment options, and software management.

When a charity has a worldwide audience of supporters and the products being sold are of global appeal, the online auction is increasingly becoming another fundraising tool. For supporters who cannot attend the actual benefit auction, some events are now incorporating real-time Internet bidding, as well as online absentee bidding from auction catalogs published on websites. Technology definitely will be a driving force in how the benefit auction continues to change.

Behind the Scenes

Now that you know the visible part of the charity auction, it will also help you to know what goes on behind the scenes with the auctioneer and organizers. You'll be a wiser attendee and bidder and you may also be involved in organizing a charity auction someday (or maybe you already are).

Some auctioneers only do charity auctions. In years past it was common for organizations to hire a local TV personality to act as auctioneer/emcee. Such a local celebrity is well-known and can draw interested attendees. But recently, more charity groups find that a professional auctioneer can raise much more money using advanced techniques, and can put on a more enjoyable event than having an untrained emcee. A professional also knows auction laws and can avoid problems arising from bidding disputes and other legal issues.

Some charity auctioneers advise the organization on all aspects of auction, including item donations, sending attendee invitations, dinner planning, and timing, lighting, sound systems, payment software systems, and so on.

So, as you look around at the auction, or help organize one yourself, realize that the auctioneer may be the expert suggesting all aspects.

For example, charity auctioneer Jay Fiske, of Bellevue, Washington, advises his clients to consider using an evaluation copy of MaestroSoft auction software. The program covers such steps as setting up committees, milestones, budget tracking, sponsorships, and bid tracking. Similar software may also be available from other companies.

"I don't see myself as an auctioneer; I'm a consultant," says Fiske. "The real work is in the planning, and that's where the money is. I work with clients three to six months prior to the event, and we can affect their bottom-line by 50 to 75 percent in the planning."

Many organizations acquire terrific items, but don't build the audience with buyers who can afford higher-priced items. Or they let much buying power slip away on undervalued items.

"Both sides have to be matched," Fiske said. "Many organizations make the mistake of doing their planning in a vacuum, with one part of their team looking for items, and the other looking to fill the room. It's another opportunity for the auctioneer to offer their expertise and build a relationship."

Planning and donations start at least six months ahead of the auction, often a year ahead. Volunteers go to businesses and their membership for donations.

Lot order is a crucial behind-the-scenes issue. Auctioneer Cheryl Parker, of Solano Beach, California, said "Don't put 10 dinners in a row and don't put the most expensive things first. It's like riding a wave, you start out low, then go up a bit, and back down again, then take it up a little higher." Ultimately, Parker sees the lot order as a balancing act.

> **From the Podium**
>
> See where your item is in the order of lots to be sold. If you have to leave early, ask that it be moved up to sell earlier in the evening.

If there are too many expensive items at the start, the audience assumes the entire offering is out of their price range and they leave. Too many low-priced items and the high rollers will lose interest. "I announce that everybody should have a chance to make a donation and bring in items that allow me to start the bidding low," says Parker.

Many items at fundraising auctions can't be viewed at the event. Nonetheless, vacation trips, dinners, sporting events, and such still need visuals to add to their appeal and their value, so you'll often see these displayed on large video projection screens.

Meet your auctioneer. It can help when he or she needs to recognize you and your bid. Auctioneer Chuck Robinson of Overland Park, Kansas, said "I go around before the auction starts and introduce myself to all the tables and make a special visit to the tables closest to the stage where the money is. You want to make sure they know you're all there to have fun, so I sit down and get to know them a little."

Some charity auction staffs issue *request cards* to discover which items will be in demand. That can set the tone of the auction with an item that will generate some lively bidding. The cards also help make sure an item sells before the interested parties have to leave the event.

def•i•ni•tion

A **request card** is a card identifying which item you have an interest in, or special request about.

"I've had people tell me they really liked a certain vacation package, but it's number 20 on the list and they have to go to another fundraiser tonight, so I'll change the lot order for them," said auctioneer Cheryl Parker.

Another behind-the-scene occurrence is to pre-sell items. If the charity knows someone interested in buying an item, they sometimes choose to call the person before the auction, and sell it before auction day to be sure to secure the sale. Keep this in mind as a buyer. It's worth a try.

Also, notice that there is an intentional festive atmosphere at a charity auction, more so than any other auction format, and that may show in different auction activities.

For example, auctioneer Ron Stricker of Gardner, Kansas says he and his partner sometimes stand on tables. "We make it fun for the people," says Stricker. "On a high bid of $2,200, I might stand on top of the bidder's table and ask for $2,500 while my partner is doing the same thing at a different table. We'll have a bidding war against each other."

The Least You Need to Know

◆ Find the charity auction item list from the organization, and decide on your bid strategy.

◆ There are still bargains at charity auctions, but some items sell very high as people donate to their cause.

◆ Be ready for the auction to begin while the dinner salad is served, early in the evening.

◆ Meet the auctioneer so he or she will recognize you and your bid easier.

Chapter 15

Auto Auctions

In This Chapter

- ◆ Public versus dealer-only auto auctions
- ◆ Police auctions of seized and government vehicles
- ◆ For experts only: Salvage auctions
- ◆ The luxury and collectible car auction

Auto auction is a general phrase today that really means vehicle auction. Trucks, sport utility vehicles, buses, fire tucks, and many other vehicles are also sold at auto auctions.

Used cars are the commodity of the auto auction: slightly used, heavily used, rebuilt, and every other condition imaginable is seen at weekly auto auctions in cities across America.

Advertisements in media proclaim "Buy used cars at auction that are practically new, with some still under factory warranty!" Indeed, car auctions can be a great place to get a good value, but you also must be careful to do your research on a car's condition and the price you are willing to pay.

Car auctions are very fast paced, with cars coming into a driving "lane" in front of the auctioneer's podium. The auctioneer describes the car, and bidders often sit or stand close to the car. The auction chant is fast and the sale is completed faster than many other types of auctions because a large volume of cars must be sold.

Bidders often include many auto dealers, who resell the cars for a profit. Most of the largest auto auctions are "dealer only." Dealers know the prices they need to make a profit, and they've done their research on the car's condition. You should do the same.

Let's take a look at the varied types of car auctions, starting with those open to the general public.

Public Car Auctions

Public car auctions is the phrase for a general used car auction with average to good vehicles, not classic or collectible cars, where the general public is invited to bid. These cars come from banks, dealership fleet returns, governments (cities, counties) reducing their fleets, and other sources.

> **SOLD!**
>
> Auto auctions are the largest category of all auctions, generating more revenue than even real estate auctions.

Many public car auctions are held on Saturday mornings or Wednesday evenings to make it easy for working people to attend. An online catalog of the sale cars is often available to view a few days before the auction. And you can preview the cars on the auction lot the day before the auction. Check with the auction firm to see exact times and procedures allowed.

A typical local auto auction may sell 100 to 300 cars during an auction. Each car may take one minute to sell.

A public auto auction crowd with a car up for sale.

Check the value of the car you want to buy in a *Kelley Blue Book* (often available onsite at the auction) or similar book, and base your bidding on that.

Also find out if the car is still under warranty. If not, get an extended warranty, but do some research online about warranty scams, also. If you buy a used car and an extended warranty, and if the car is found to have a salvaged title, it will void your extended warranty. Learn about warranty issues.

Run a Vehicle History Report

It's very important to run a vehicle history report, using the Vehicle Identification Number (VIN) on the car. You can find the VIN on the plate on the dashboard by looking through the windshield. Some cars also have the 17-digit VIN printed on stickers on the driver's side door or trunk.

A vehicle history report will provide title information and history of whether the car was rebuilt after an accident. A popular site for car title checks is autocheck.com. A history report provides background on the title, damage (frame or water damage), odometer rollback, theft, fleet car history, and other situations.

The 17-digit VIN did not become standard until 1981, so you cannot get a similar report for a car made before 1981. Every car manufacturer had their own format, and each state tracked them differently with unique formats.

Buyer Beware

Always run a vehicle history report on every vehicle you consider buying so as to determine previous repairs and help determine current condition. A popular site for getting such a report is at www.carfax.com.

The Scene at Public Auto Auctions

At auto auctions there is usually a "traffic light," similar to the one at intersections, hanging behind the auctioneer. This has red, yellow, and green lights. These lights are used to indicate the status of the car's title.

When the auction company writes up your purchase, they will indicate the color of the light on your contract. Here is what the lights mean, as described by CarBuyingTips.com:

Red Light—Usually means there are issues with the title, rebuilt, not actual mileage, or some other problem. This is important, because you would not expect to pay as much for that car as one which had not been in a wreck. At wholesale auctions as the cars come up to the block, the ones with bad titles trigger the red title warning light to come on over the auction box. At this point, usually 50 percent of the bidders take off. The remaining 50 percent don't know what the heck to do, and the price ends up dropping usually 30 percent. The reason is a rebuilt car is just bad news. It's one thing to have a quarter panel replaced or door dent removed, but a rebuilt title means something very bad happened to this car. It means the car was totaled in an accident and then rebuilt, and the title was "branded" back to used car status again.

Yellow Light—Usually means the title is in transit, or there is some frame damage, but not enough to brand the title. Usually the seller is right there next to the podium and they have the owner's manual and title ready to hand over to you, and you settle in the closing room. Ideally, when you buy at a car auction, you'd like to have the title right there because you are required to pay in full on the spot. Unfortunately, many titles at auctions are in transit. They expect you to pay in full for that car now, yet they won't give you the title now. Sounds very lopsided. Each car is usually on the auction block for about a minute or two, and the bidding moves fast. There are a couple of hundred cars there, and they have to get them all through. If the car does not sell, they just roll it right on out the door and the next one comes in. Sometimes they will pass cars through the auction lines a few times hoping they will sell.

Green Light—Means everything is okay with the title.

Cars Sold As-Is, in Current Condition

Vehicles at auction are sold as-is, in current condition with no guarantees of repairs. Don't trust sellers to reveal the full extent of any body damage or operational problems. That's why you do your research. Many auto auctions use a very simplified car title check, and some do no car title check at all, so do your own.

The sale is final unless the title turns out to be fraudulent. At some auctions you can pay a fee to guarantee the engine, frame, and body for 30 days.

How Good Are Previous Rentals?

A used rental car brings the image, to some people's minds, of a car driven roughly by a renter, so they assume the rental may likely be damaged and a poor car. Not so. Rental cars are probably maintained better than many privately owned cars. They were kept in constant care and maintenance during use. The companies tend to take them out of service by one to two years of age, so you may be getting a decent car which the rental company has already absorbed the largest portion of the depreciation.

Police and Government Auctions

These are also open to any consumers, just as with public auto auctions. Police auctions often have cars seized in criminal cases, or cars that a government agency no longer keeps in its fleet.

All the advice for public auctions applies to police auctions. The cars are sold as-is. There is also a widely held myth that you can get cars at police auctions even cheaper than at public auctions. Not so. If everyone thinks that and goes to the auctions and bids against each other, you've got real price competition!

From the Podium
It is a myth that police auctions offer better car values than other public auctions.

There are often decommissioned police cruisers at these auctions, and normal other cars. Set you own price point to pay well under market value, which leaves you room for profit if you desire to resell. Don't forget that a buyer's premium and other fees (see other chapters on payments) are included, so figure those in to your bidding.

Salvage/Insurance Auctions

These auctions are usually open only to dealers. Salvage auctions (also known as insurance auto auctions) are not open to the public because of the serious damage to these cars, and only experienced professionals who know what they are doing should be buying from these auto salvage auctions. Often the cars are not operational, but some bidders just want the cars for spare parts.

Generally, if a car's damage is estimated at more than 75 percent of the car's value, then usually the law requires the insurance company to declare the title of the car as "totaled in a wreck." The car cannot then be sold as a regular used car. A vehicle history report will show that car was salvaged and rebuilt, and it may show it as passing through a salvage auction.

When a wrecked car has been determined by the insurance company to be totaled, the title is branded and the car is sent off to the auto salvage yards and the insurance company pays you whatever they determine to be the going rate for your car being totaled. Once in a while the auto salvage yards have a salvage auction, where dealers can go in to inspect rows of totaled cars and bid on them.

Typically the cars sell for 20 to 50 percent of their market value, reported CarBuyingTips.com. Honest dealers will find a buyer for a totaled car before buying the car then tell the buyer how much it will cost to rebuild the car. Then the dealer buys it from the salvage auction, fixes up the car, rebuilds the title, and sells it to the buyer for a price that is hopefully 25 to 30 percent below market value.

Wholesale (Dealer to Dealer)

These car auctions are for car dealers only. The general public is not allowed to attend. At the wholesale auction at Manheim Auto Auction in Manheim, Pennsylvania, the cars come from the following sources:

◆ Cars that are returned after their lease expires.

◆ Rental cars from car rental agencies.

◆ Brands of used cars that a dealer received as a trade-in, but does not normally sell.

◆ A new hot seller that a dealer may be able to sell for more than the MSRP in the car auctions.

◆ Exotic cars, either new or used, that some collector dealers are trying to sell.

◆ Used cars more than 4 years old that most major dealers don't want on their lots.

To attend these auctions, you have to be a licensed dealer, even if you only sell a few cars a month from your home. To become a registered car dealer, for example, in Florida you must complete a two-day school, take a car dealer test, be bonded, get a Tax ID, get approved by your city, buy insurance, and have a clean record—and then you also need an occupational license (about $150).

Some people try to get a car from these auctions by knowing a licensed private dealer who will attend. The dealer shares the catalog with you, and you tell him the price you want to pay. He will also likely charge you something for his service to buy the car.

Dealers at wholesale auctions use a car pricing book that is updated at least monthly with regional selling prices from wholesale auto auctions. It's like a *Kelley Blue Book* for auto auctions. It lists most vehicle makes and models, and what they should sell for if the vehicle is in bad, fair, or good condition. Dealers would like to bid on a car and pay less than the book price for the car to be sure they are getting a good price. Some other dealers use the NADA guide for their pricing.

Dealers often use a small device that measures the thickness of paint on a car body. If paint is extremely thick, it indicates body work has been done, and the car may have been damaged.

This *elcometer* digital coating thickness gauge has an LCD readout that shows how thick the paint is. Factory paint jobs are usually 4.5 mils thick. When a body shop paints a panel, it often paints over existing paint and can double the thickness. So if the gauge reads 8 to 12 mils, you can be pretty sure body work has been done.

If the car had previously been damaged, sometimes the windshield will have the word "Unibody" written on it, indicating prior accident damage that had been repaired. Mercedes and BMW leasing companies usually do this, some others do not.

def•i•ni•tion

An **elcometer** is a digital coating thickness gauge that tells how thick a car's paint is.

And sometimes auctions have the mileage written on the windshields so you can walk up to a row of cars in the lot and determine if it meets your mileage requirements without having to open each car and check the odometer.

Small and Large Auto Auctions

You can attend a big public auction or a small auction. Small does not mean less quality.

For example, auctioneer Ron Faison, president of Delaware Auto Exchange, runs a public auto auction every Thursday night when cars roll through four lanes while bids are taken. "We're a mom-and-pop small operation. We know all our customers. We sell about 200 vehicles a week. I don't want to get so big that I can't joke with our customers." Faison feels he can provide better service than the big auto auctions.

He says most of his vehicles sell for around $2,000, but the range is from $400 to $15,000 per vehicle. His revenue comes from charging a buyer's fee (starting at $65 and up) and a seller's fee ($45 and up) on each vehicle, for which he provides the buyer and seller all necessary sale documents. He says about 25 percent of his business is from the public. People drive two or three hours to get to him.

But auto auctions come in all sizes, ranging from a city block of about 3 acres—to a small city—248 acres. They feature from 2 to 26 lanes, with as few as 5 employees to as many as 1,550 employees.

In contrast to the small operations is the largest auto auction site in America, the Manheim Auto Auction in Manheim, Pennsylvania, which has more than 90 acres of cars. Manheim's 27 auction lanes move cars very quickly.. Nevin Rentzel, along with 26 other auctioneers, work themselves nearly hoarse every Friday at the Manheim Auto Auction. He says Manheim's 27 lanes move that many cars in a minute.

The Manheim auction is a continuous constant flow of steel, glass, rubber, and chrome. "This is a fast-paced business. There is nothing leisurely about this at all," says Rentzel. An almost circus-like atmosphere pervades the auction held in picture postcard-like Lancaster County, as thousands of automobile dealers swarm through the gates in search of late-model cars to fill their lots. Vendors sell soft pretzels and popcorn. Some car manufacturers offer incentives, such as free stadium blankets or leather valises with purchases. Colorful flags and banners hang from the rafters.

Check-in and registration at Manheim is streamlined. With the swipe of a card, regular bidders receive their auction number and other information from ATM-like machines set up in the lobby. The spacious lobby, which features a large sit-down restaurant as well as a snack bar, resembles an airport concourse. The popularity of automobile leasing—40 percent of new cars are leased—has increased the amount of cars available for auction dramatically. Fewer people buy cars and keep them, but instead lease them for three or four years and then turn them back to the car dealer.

Classic and Luxury Cars

Classic cars are older, rare, or collectible cars. These include popular "muscle cars" of the 1960s and 1970s, such as the Plymouth Barracuda. Baby boomers with money have elevated the muscle car/classic car auction in recent years to a booming business.

Classic car auctions such as the Barrett/Jackson auction in Phoenix draws hours of televised coverage on the Speed channel of cable television. The Kruse International Auto Auction in Auburn, Indiana is another that offers acres of classic autos.

A classic car auction at the Kruse International Auto Auction.

For an example of prices, these are the Kruse company's top 10 sales at the fall 2007 Auburn Fall Auction:

1. 1932 Duesenberg J340 Murphy Coupe for $1,000,000

2. 1954 Chevrolet "Star Spangled Collection" Corvette for $327,000

3. 1937 Cord Sportman Cabriolet for $265,000

4. 1995 Mercedes Benz 1000 Race Car for $227,500

5. 1957 Dual Ghia for $227,500

6. 1930 Cadillac Imperial for $200,000

7. 1931 Cord L-29 for $175,000

8. 1966 Batmobile for $175,000

9. 1929 Rolls Royce 33WJ Phantom II for $170,000

10. 1929 Cadillac Dual Cowl Series 341 for $165,000

Luxury car auctions can include classics, but can also be current used hot sellers, including recent model Jaguars, Mercedes, Porsches, Rolls-Royces, Humvees, and BMWs. At the big Manheim company, they call their luxury auction the "Exotic Highline Sale."

There, auctioneer Nevin Rentzel said "I just sold a Ferrari. The seller wanted $115,000, I got him $141,000. In my whole life, I never thought I would see a car worth that much, let alone offer one." These sought-after vehicles, including the Corvettes, evoke memories of actor Martin Milner and the TV show *Route 66* while the Aston Martins call to mind the early glory days of James Bond, when Sean Connery was king.

At that sale, auto dealer Bob Lutz, of Vindevers Automobiles, Toledo, Ohio said "There are not a whole lot of sales with this variety." Everyone turned almost in unison as a powder blue 1969 Volkswagen Beetle convertible rolled through the lane to the auction block. People swarmed around it.

There are some tricks to the trade. Red corvettes, for example, always sell high. There also is a color in the auction business called "no-sale blue"—a dark Navy-type of blue that fails to generate any emotional interest. Timing is also important. Everyone wants to have their cars auctioned between 11:30 A.M. and 1:30 P.M., when the crowd and interest are at their peaks. Running in the first 11 cars usually means a low price for a car. Auctioneer Rentzel said he gets a special rush when he is auctioning the exotics. "There are people from 15 to 20 different countries and 40 states here today. The pace and variety of people here is amazing."

The Least You Need to Know

- Public and police car auctions are open to the general public. Salvage and wholesale car auctions are open only to licensed car dealers.

- Examine the car auction catalog online closely a few days before the auction for details of cars available.

- Run a vehicle history report, using the VIN number, to get a history of its condition.

- Small local auto auctions do not mean less quality than larger regional auto auctions.

Chapter 16

Farm and Livestock Auctions

In This Chapter

- ◆ A day at a farm auction
- ◆ New methods at cattle auctions
- ◆ Horses for sale at all prices
- ◆ The boom in goat and buffalo auctions

Farm and livestock auctions have gone hand-in-hand in rural America since the country was founded. Farmers sell their land and equipment, and also, in separate auctions sell their livestock, including cattle, horses, pigs, goats, and other stock. But both these categories of auctions are undergoing massive changes.

Farm Auctions

A *farm auction* refers to either the auction of an entire farm—including the land, buildings, and equipment—or it can be the small property used in farming, such as planting or harvesting vehicles, tractors, and related equipment. A farm equipment auction is also a term often used just for equipment auctions.

def•i•ni•tion

A **farm auction** is an auction of an entire farm, including land and buildings, or individual property used in farming, such as tractors and related equipment.

Auctions of entire farms, and auctions of farm equipment, are declining in number because the small family farms of past eras are being sold to large corporations, or large families, that run massive farm acreage as big business enterprises. Small families are less able to afford the rising cost of farming, such as from equipment (a $150,000 combine), gasoline, taxes, and so on. And often declining prices of crops, combined with drought creating poor crop yields, make their small businesses unable to sustain throughout the years.

Also the children of established farm families today often want to move to cities to pursue new careers for more money, so the farming parents decide to sell their business rather than pass it down to their children.

A Typical Farm Auction

A typical farm auction, where a farmer is selling his whole business, draws buyers ranging from other farmers looking for good used equipment, to resellers seeking to turn a quick profit, the occasional antique dealer looking for a hidden treasure, and average auction enthusiasts looking for small items such as a wheelbarrow or pitchfork at a good price.

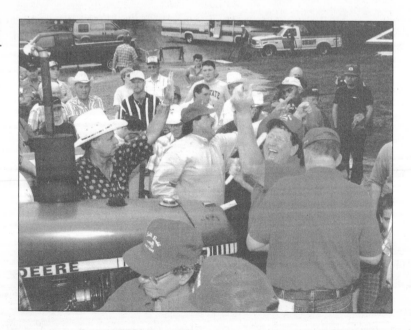

An auctioneer sells a piece of equipment at a farm auction.

For example, farmer Allen Peris had a farm auction recently. His big combine was a Massey Ferguson 850, a boxy, red thing. When Peris bought the machine, in the early 1980s, it was top of the line. At his auction he sold the dated Massey machine, along with his old tractors, augers, grain bins, and all manner of odds and ends accumulated during a lifetime of farming, as reported by Citypages.com. After almost 40 years, Peris got out of the business.

His wife Mary said about farming that "The thing that drove me crazy about it is that a person can go out and do the very best job. You can work yourself into the ground. And if it doesn't rain, it didn't do any good. If the prices are bad, it didn't do any good. I wanted to go crazy, thinking, how can you do all this work and you don't know if you'll get anything out of it?"

The day of his auction, a Thursday, dawned mercilessly hot. By 10 A.M., when the sale began, there were two dozen trucks parked in the Peris's long driveway. Many of the neighbors had dropped by for support or out of curiosity. But some of the license plates were also from as far away as North Dakota and Missouri. Most of the farmers in attendance were older.

Auctioneer LaDon Henslin worked the microphone, and his son Allen served as ringman. As usual, they began with the smaller items: welding torches, wrenches, battered old oil cans, and anything else that might catch a farmer's eye or an antiquer's fancy. Normally, Henslin explained, they saved the machinery for last, because farmers who are interested in bidding on the larger items usually show up late. Henslin sat in an enclosed booth on the bed of a pickup and chanted "Ten dollar, ten dollar. Now five dollar. Who'll give five dollar? Two-and-a-half. Two-and-a-half. Who'll give a dollar? Dollar, dollar, dollar. Now two-and-half. Now five, now five, now five. SOLD! for five dollar. What's your number, buddy?"

Peris walked silently at the back of the crowd as the tools of his life's work were sold, including his hand-carved ice-fishing lures, a rickety old motorbike that hasn't run in years, and even a battered suitcase that still has Northwest Orient tags attached.

SOLD!

Because farm auctions are typically outside and last for hours, take plenty of sunscreen, water to drink, and a vehicle large enough to take home your purchases.

By two o'clock, everything of consequence was gone. People drifted off, some empty-handed, others carting away bits of the Peris farm.

Peris's obsolete combine sold for $2,800—not, perhaps as much as he'd have hoped, but perhaps, as much as could be expected. Even the rusty old Ford truck belonging to his father sold. He still isn't feeling sentimental about it, though. "It's just stuff," Peris said.

This is an example of a typical farm sale with large and small items for sale.

Farm Equipment Auctions

A farm equipment auction can be from a working farm or can be the liquidation of a farm equipment store.

Here's another real example: Dave Kautzman, co-owner of D&K Farm Equipment Inc., had to sell his 46-year-old family business in North Dakota.

"We had a really good working relationship here with a lot of people," Kautzman said in a story in *Hobby Farm* magazine. "But business was getting to be less and less every year. I think in the last few years the drought has had a lot of impact on things."

Because equipment from a store liquidation is often new, prices may be considerably higher than 20-year-old equipment on a working farm. But, good values are always possible at auction. Research the price values and be an informed, ready bidder.

Where to Find Farm Auctions and Values

Farm auctions are found in newspaper ads in the "auction block" section of the newspaper or on the website of your local auctioneers. Also check for them on the following websites, some of which can also be used to find recent sale prices for farm equipment. Visit and explore these websites to learn more about the whole field of farm auctions:

- www.farmauctionguide.com
- www.machinerypete.com
- www.farmauctions.com
- www.farmandranchguide.com
- www.midwestauction.com
- www.auctioneers.org

Full Range of Bidding, Technology

Farm auctions are an old category, but they include the latest and full range of bidding options and technology used. Sometimes farm auctions are held indoors at an auctioneer's building or a local rented facility, especially in bad weather, with photos of the equipment up on bid screens.

Also when you are at a farm auction, you will often see absentee bids, Internet bids, phone bids and others, just as at real estate and other auctions. If you cannot be present at the live farm auction, don't forget that you can place absentee bids to compete as if you were present. Below is an example of the absentee bid agreement from a farm equipment specialty auction firm, Musser Brothers.

"Absentee bids are submitted with the following understanding:

◆ Bids are executed in competition with the audience on an alternate basis as if the bidder were present at the auction and the bidders purchase will be obtained at the lowest bid possible. Due to uncertainties of bidding, a lot may sell to the audience for the same amount authorized by the absentee bid. To avoid this possibility, the bidder may authorize Musser Bros. Auctioneers to increase their bid by an increment by placing a (+) sign beside the bid price for that item.

◆ Absentee bids are confidential and bidding will not commence with the highest absentee bid.

◆ The bidder agrees to be bound by Musser Bros. Auctioneers standard bidder registration agreement. A copy will be forwarded at request. All items are sold "AS IS, WHERE IS!"

◆ Musser Bros. Auctioneers does not guarantee the year, condition, description, or suitability of any item.

◆ Bidder acknowledges that the absentee bid is accepted on the express condition that the bidder will not have any claim against the auctioneer or its employees if the auctioneer fails, for any reason, to bid on behalf of the bidder.

◆ Successful bidders will be called by the morning after the auction with bid information unless specific arrangements are made with the auction company.

◆ Musser Bros. Auctioneers appreciate the time you take to participate in our auctions and we will do everything possible to submit your absentee bid. However, there are no guarantees—just our "best effort" promise!

◆ Absentee bids must be received 24 hours in advance of auction."

Dig In to Box Lots

Often at farm auctions (which can be a form of estate auctions), a family will sell tools and other hobby items from their home. These are put in boxes, and are termed box lots.

It is important to look carefully at box lots. A story about this comes from a doll collector who found valuable doll items at a local auction, and wrote about it on About. com.

"Some of my finds at local auctions have included dollmaking molds ($40 for an entire box of them)," she said, "sewing items galore (usually in mixed, unsorted boxes—I have found things like wonderful silk thread and even a gold thimble once—boxes usually go for about $5 to $25, depending what people have spotted in them!), fabric, trims, laces of all sorts, and dollmaking patterns and magazines. One recent estate auction I attended was from a dollmaker's estate, and I think the most valuable item I purchased was a hand-cart full of boxes of old patterns and doll magazines for $25!"

She added that "It is imperative that you go to a preview before attending the actual auction and that you carefully look the items over, especially the box lots. Here is a cautionary tale for you about why it is important to check every item carefully. Well, at the auction, I am sitting with a dollmaking/collecting acquaintance. One of the dolls I hadn't even looked at comes up for bid—and the bid goes to $125! I turn to my friend and ask if she had looked at the doll (no, she hadn't either—it had been up on a shelf, in a *very* purple polyester dress). After the auction I asked the lady who purchased the doll about it—turns out that the doll was a very nice Kestner on a composition body, not a reproduction at all! And, as for the boxes of doll parts—underneath the parts were several pairs of lovely glass eyes (I learned this later from the lady who won those). So, look at everything, assume nothing, and dig in those boxes!"

Livestock Auctions

Bidders at livestock auctions include the hobby horseman, the cattleman building a herd, a slaughterhouse owner, and others. Across America and the world, all kinds of livestock are run through rings in livestock auction barns as the auctioneer sits on a podium above the stock and watches the bidders in front of him or her.

But, in general, the number of livestock auctions is declining as the bulk of cattle are being sold directly to slaughterhouses for pre-negotiated prices. Instead of competing at auction, slaughterhouses make contracts with cattle raisers. But this is for nonpurebred cattle, also called feeder cattle. Purebred, high-quality animals rise above being treated as a commodity, and remain at auction.

However, industry's highest dollar markets remain in cattle, hogs, and horses. Sheep and goat auctions offer a good deal of business, but nowhere close to the volume of the big three. Poultry was a viable market at one time but it's fallen into the business of direct contract sales.

A livestock auction in Indiana.

As a savvy bidder, prepare for livestock auctions well. Preview the animals on the auctioneer's website catalog, if available, learning of their condition and background. Research values of similar animals recently sold at auction by looking at auction websites for prices posted.

Some livestock auctions allow sellers to set a reserve price, and some do not. As a bidder, ask if there is a reserve.

Cattle Auctions

Cattle auctions move quickly with feeder cattle moving through the ring continually as professional buyers bid quickly. Unless you are buying breeding stock, the higher-quality bulls and cows to build a herd, the cattle auction is a routine business.

The professional buyers for slaughterhouses (those not working by contract with cattle raisers) examine the weight and condition of the cattle and know the current prices.

Auctioneer John Korrey sells cattle at the Livestock Exchange, in Brush, Colorado. He's one of two auctioneers employed by the Exchange, and works two auctions, alternating every hour with the other auctioneer. About 200,000 head of cattle, destined for the slaughterhouse, move through the Exchange in a year. Feeder cattle (classified by a weight of 500 to 800 pounds) make up the bulk of the sales. "The industry is changing and there are only three or four major buyers of that cattle now," says Korrey. "Years ago they'd come to your farm and buy them if you had 25 head. Now the packers won't even come to a feeder that has even 100 heads."

"There can't be any lull in these auctions," he says, "because these buyers are professional and you have the momentum built up, so you've got to keep the crowd alert and the action moving." Sometimes the sprint can turn into a marathon. Korrey has had the experience of selling without any real break for eight hours straight.

Streaming Video of Cattle Auctions

It's more common today for live cattle auctions to be broadcast live on the Internet and even on a major TV cable network, called RFD-TV, where buyers across the country watch and bid.

Superior Livestock Auction, of Ft. Worth, Texas uses live moving video (also called streaming video) of its auctions broadcast on RFD-TV, a 24-hour cable television network targeted to rural America, through which SLA markets more than 1.5 million heads of commercial cattle and other livestock to buyers across the country each year. The real-time video transported via Streambox shows cattle or horses, the bidder, or the consigner selling his or her lot. Although each shot may last only 30 seconds, the short minute or two that it takes to sell the lot may represent the entire yearly income for the consigner. Thus, image quality is important not only for showcasing lots for sale, but also because each sale is a significant event being watched on RFD-TV by friends, neighbors, and colleagues.

California auctioneer John Rodgers, of Stockman's Market, started offering video auctioning services in 1990 after years of watching California's feeder cattle industry (and his auctions) dwindle away.

His company takes its cameras to Nebraska, Wyoming, Colorado, California, Oregon, Washington, Idaho, Nevada, and Utah. Stockman's Market services include videotaping the cattle, along with the information a buyer needs, and of course, broadcasting the auction, which is also attended by live bidders. Twenty phone lines accommodate the bids from the video viewers.

"Video auctions take a little longer," Rodgers explains, "because you've got to make sure the buyers on the phones are keeping up. When I sold only live auctions we'd move 60 draft an hour, but with the video it's about half that. All of our auctioneers are world champions of the Livestock Marketing Association." Another testimonial to the power of contests.

Horse Auctions

Types of horse auctions range from small local general auctions, where you can buy a horse for $50, to million dollar thoroughbred and quarter horse auctions, where champions and breeding stock are sold.

To find horse auctions, read the various horse magazines that are readily available at most bookstores; check online for local horse auctioneers; ask at a local horse stable; or ask at the local cattle and general livestock auction.

After reviewing the catalog days earlier, show up at the location of the auction early to preview the horses and talk to their owners. You can also bring a veterinarian or horse trainer with you who can examine the horses you desire for soundness (no lameness in feet or legs).

Horses are sold in as-is condition, but you can ask the owners if the animal has any problems in physicality or behavior. Some buyers say you can't rely on truthfulness from an owner who wants to receive top dollar for his horse.

Lead the horse around and pick up its feet. Ask the owner if you can ride the horse. This will give you an even better idea of how the horse will be after it comes home with you.

> **From the Podium**
>
> Before the horse auction, lead your target horse around and ask the owner if you can ride it. This is important to evaluate condition and behavior.

Horses are usually led individually in to the auction ring, with the lead person showing all sides of the animal to the crowd. Horses often act nervous because of the lights and noise of the auction ring, so do not think this is always the normal behavior of the horse.

The same bidding strategies apply for horse auctions. Try incremental bidding unless you feel jump bidding will defeat your competition. Pick your maximum bid and stick to it.

Bidders can include the amateur horse owner, the professional trainer or stable owner, ranchers, or others. Horse slaughter plants are nearly gone in the United States, so few of those buyers are at auctions.

As of this writing, the last horse slaughter plant in the United States was in Illinois and was fighting off closure in its state courts. And the United States Congress, concerned with slaughter methods, was considering a federal horse-slaughter ban that passed the House of Representatives.

<table>
<tr><td>

From the Podium

Bring a trailer to transport the animal you buy at a livestock auction. If you buy an animal, it is normally ready to take home with you immediately.

</td><td>

Until recent plant closures, roughly 100,000 American horses were slaughtered every year after being purchased primarily at local auctions.

Almost all American horse meat was shipped overseas for human consumption, where horse meat is common cuisine in many parts of Europe and Asia. But the horse slaughter industry has been under attack by the Humane Society of the United States, which

</td></tr>
</table>

claims the industry purchases people's healthy pets for inhumane slaughter, often without their knowledge. Facilities and transportation used in the slaughter of horses are meant for cattle, they say, so horses are abused by long trips and inhumane killing measures.

Some horses have a tattoo on the inside of their lip for identification, especially if they have been in professional races. You can track information from this tattoo number and find out the history of that horse.

A registered horse (registered with a horse association such as the American Quarter Horse Association) may also have a public record of information if it has been in horse shows. You may be able to find that through the associations.

Goat Auctions Rising

Americans are eating more goat and buffalo as these low-fat specialty meats are carried by more grocery stores and restaurants. So it follows that more of these animals are being raised and sold, many of them at auctions. If you have acreage, or are an investor, you may wish to get into this livestock business yourself.

Buyers are slaughterhouse owners and hobby ranchers starting their own herds of these animals. These buyers study conditions of the animals for their purposes, and target the values they believe applies in the current market. They visit the websites of ranches that raise these animals to see the animals' photos and descriptions. They subscribe to the goat and bison trade magazines, and they follow prices obtained at auction by visiting specialty auctioneers' websites.

Randy Bush, CAI, is a goat auctioneer. Bush, of Elizabethtown, Kentucky, raised and sold his own herd goats before he started conducting goat auctions when a group of breeders hired him to do an auction in North Carolina. In Sonora, Texas he sells about 700

Buyer Beware

Don't believe all that a seller tells you about his animal. Although he should be honest, he may distort or conceal important information about a horse, cow, or other animal you want to buy.

goats in one of the largest goat auctions in the United States. He conducts about 5 to 10 goat auctions per year.

"People can't raise goats fast enough to meet the demand today. The U.S. imports about two million pounds of goat meat per month," he said. "Americans are finding out that goat meat is lower in cholesterol and fat than most other meats. In Nashville, Tennessee, for example, there are three restaurants with goat on the menu. In New York there are Wal-Marts and grocery stores that sell goat meat. Muslims also buy goat for their holiday meals, and Latin people buy it."

Bush estimates there are about five goat auctioneer specialists in the country, including himself. Goat auctions are similar to purebred cattle auctions, he said.

"You have to know your product," he said. "You have to know about bucks and does, about average daily weight gain, genetics, and other details." South African Boer goats (male breeding stock) are among the highest-quality animals and are greatly sought by breeders, Bush said. He has seen a male Boer sell for $56,000.

Learn the lingo and animal behaviors, too. For example, suckling kids stay near their dam. But weaned kids or yearlings do not.

At the auction, the order that animals enter the ring is at the manager's discretion. And sellers sometimes get to know the buyers and talk with them about what kinds of animals the buyers will want in the near future. Sellers ask buyers what local auctions they will be attending, and sellers urge buyers to watch for the seller's animals.

At auctions, sellers may be handing out their business cards to buyers who are looking over animals before the auction, or after bidding is done. Sometimes an auction firm will share buyer contact information with a seller.

Goat and other livestock producers often seek out large regional auctions that are supported by numerous buyers and have good prices. Several large auctions have their average prices publicized on the web or in various marketing publications making it easy to track price trends.

Two of the largest goat auctions are the Monday morning sale at New Holland Sale Stables, Inc., of New Holland, Pennsylvania; and the Tuesday morning sale at the Livestock Co-op Auction Mkt. Assoc. of NJ in Hackettstown, New Jersey. Information about these and other northeast U.S. auctions is available on the web.

Other bidders at goat auctions are Muslims who use the goat for food during religious periods. Their desired goat is usually characterized as still having milk teeth. However, older goats are also in demand for the Muslim trade during the Festival of Sacrifice. These animals must be "unblemished." Different Muslims have different interpretations for unblemished. For all, the animals must be sound with no open wounds, broken horns, deformities, and for some it must be uncastrated.

Extremely fat goats are penalized by most cultures because this fat is viewed as a waste that will drop out of their body cavity at slaughter. A standard Boer buck in show condition would be considered extremely fat. The same applies to dairy does at the end of lactation.

Buffalo Auctions Charging Forward

Much of the same information applies to buffalo auctions. The big shaggy bison that once roamed the plains of America by the millions were driven to near extinction, but rebounded by careful breeders and demand today for their lean meat.

"The buffalo auction season is November 1 to April 15," said Jud Seaman, CAI, of Rapid City, South Dakota, a buffalo auctioneer who does about 10 buffalo auctions each season. South Dakota is the largest-producing state for bison. Pennsylvania has many producers also, Seaman said.

Buffalo meat tastes sweeter and richer than beef, and has fewer calories and less fat, according to the National Bison Association.

Being a producer raising the animals is pretty profitable now, Seaman said, but the market has had ups and downs in recent years. Buffalo are sold by the head, not by the pound as beef and cattle are.

Seaman has seen a 2-year-old bull sell for $101,000. Buyers such as that are buying top-quality breeding stock to increase herd quality. Many other buyers are taking bison to slaughterhouses.

A major promoter today of buffalo meat is former CNN owner and buffalo rancher Ted Turner, who has opened Ted's Montana Grill restaurants across the country and specializes in serving buffalo meat. Turner has run 30,000 head of bison across his ranches in South Dakota, Nebraska, Kansas, Oklahoma, and New Mexico, said Seaman.

The Least You Need to Know

◆ Farm auctions can be a good place to get a used small tractor and other small items for the average bidder, even the city-dweller.

◆ Examine the auction catalog closely for details of the cattle or horses you want to buy, and look on the auctioneer's website.

◆ Arrive at a horse auction early, bring a veterinarian if possible, and ask to ride the horse.

◆ Learn about goat and buffalo industries from the many associations that cater to these specialties.

Part 4

Sellers' Success at Live Auctions

You may be a seller at live auction someday (or are even considering one now). Or you may wisely just want to know what sellers are motivated by and how they operate, so you can be a better buyer. Smart idea! Sellers at live auction want to get a good price for their property, and they have many decisions and pressures to get to a final sale. This part tells you all about it. It tells you how to find and evaluate an auctioneer to hire, what an auction contract includes, how to research your property's value before auction (very important!), and what to do when problems arise.

Chapter 17

Finding and Evaluating an Auctioneer

In This Chapter

- ◆ Finding a professional auctioneer
- ◆ Contacting the auctioneer
- ◆ Meeting and evaluating the auctioneer
- ◆ Pausing before you decide yes or no

One of the most important decisions in holding an auction is at the very start of the process, when the seller finds and hires an auctioneer. You've got to hire the right person for your specific auction. In this chapter we will review how to locate auctioneers, evaluate their experience and suitability to work with you, and how to make the decision to hire the right person.

The more thorough you are in choosing an auctioneer, the greater the chance for a successful auction. You should ask about the auctioneer's experience in selling your type of property, as well as about their licenses, references, and fees to be charged. Let's explore more to help in your choice.

Using the Internet to Find an Auctioneer

To find an auctioneer, in today's Internet-connected world, many people turn first to the Internet to find auctioneers and other business professionals because it is the fastest and most comprehensive way to get lots of information. Certainly not everyone uses it, but the numbers are increasing every year. Before the Internet became commonplace in the 1990s, people searched the local telephone book, newspaper advertisements, called their local Chamber of Commerce, and asked friends for referrals to auctioneers. You still can use those good methods, but if you have access to a computer, the process takes much less time and is more focused by using the Internet.

Let's look at one brief but real example of how someone used the Internet to find an auctioneer and what occurred afterward. A person in California found a painting in their attic that their grandmother brought over from Italy many years before. It was a classic-looking painting of a bushy-bearded man (who looked a lot like Charlton Heston in his role as Moses) with some astronomical instruments in front of him. The owner knew the picture looked old, but there was no signature or any way of telling just how old it was, or what it might be worth. What would the average person do? Give it away maybe, because it doesn't fit with the decorating style in their home?

As it turns out, the smart thing to do was send it to an auctioneer for evaluation, and that's just what they did. They went to the Google website (www.google.com) and searched for names of auctioneers in their area.

> **SOLD!** _____
>
> Whenever possible, transport your items personally for appraisal. When this is not possible, use a reputable carrier and insure the item appropriately.

This mystery painting was then placed with an Oakland, California auction firm. The auction company did research as best as possible on this unsigned painting and put a modest price estimate on it of $3,000 to $5,000, and described it as "Portrait of a Man with Armillary Sphere," a framed seventeenth century oil-on-canvas. The auction company then marketed the painting effectively, getting the word out among potential art buyers across the world with the description and photos of the painting before the auction. And, bingo, some art investor experts out there knew more about it.

The painting came to the auction block and the bidding began at $5,000. With about 16 people bidding by phone from both sides of the Atlantic and throughout the United States, the bidding soon rose to $300,000 (the bidders knew it was a special piece, and reacted). Suddenly, a New York bidder joined the competition, turning the auction into a real battle royale, until only the New Yorker and a French bidder were left. Finally the French bidder dropped out, and the final sale price (including a buyer's premium) was $620,900! (Some people say that the auction company should have known much more about the true value of the painting.)

Why the worldwide interest? The painting is thought by experts to be done by Pier Francesco Mola, who was born in Coldrerio, Italy, in 1612 and died in Rome in 1666. His works are in some of the greatest museums in the world, including The Louvre, The Hermitage Museum, London's National Gallery, and the J. Paul Getty Museum in Los Angeles.

Most experts expect this painting to come back on the market in a year or two, with a much higher estimate.

Be Specific in Searching the Internet

On the Internet there are thousands of websites with a Search For box at the top that you can use to enter the word "auctioneer" to find a list of auctioneers. Google and Yahoo! are only two of the larger websites that have powerful search capability. When you enter words into the search box, be as specific as you can. If you live in New York and have a painting to sell, you may want to enter "auctioneers, New York, art," and that will bring up websites of auction companies in New York that specialize in artwork. Another Internet option is to find an auctioneer through the website of the state auctioneer association where you live. Most states have their own association of auctioneers who reside in that state and whom gather regularly for educational seminars and networking.

> **From the Podium**
>
> Every auction house has a specialty. Be sure to select a place with a proven track record in the specific category of sale you need.

Perhaps the only nationwide and specific search database for auctioneers is found at the National Auctioneers Association's website at www.auctioneers.org. At that homepage, you can click the Find an Auctioneer button. A new page appears with boxes you can fill in to search for either a specific auctioneer's name you already know, or you can search by city, state, and auction specialty to find auctioneers in those areas.

After you fill in those boxes and hit the Search button, a list of auctioneers' names meeting those criteria will pop up on your screen. These auctioneers will all be members of the National Auctioneers Association.

The Telephone Book and Newspaper

Using the printed Yellow Pages telephone book of business listings is also a simple option. Just turn to auctioneer, auction firms, or appraisers (because some appraisers are also auctioneers they will list under multiple headings). Following conventional wisdom, the larger an advertisement in this book, or other venues, sometimes the larger the firm that placed it.

Many newspapers today also have multiple sections where you can find auctioneers. One is the Business Services section where auction firms advertise along with plumbers and other service providers. They often have a business card-size ad. Another section is the Auction Block, a common heading in the classified advertising section where auctions of all types are advertised. Many times estate or home auctions are advertised, but any type can be there. See which auction companies advertise there and get their contact information.

The Personal Touch

Call your local Chamber of Commerce, that local business organization that has monthly luncheons and other events where business people gather. Ask if the Chamber has local auction firms as members. If an auction firm is a member, it's a good indication the firm is well-grounded in the community. If there are several auction firms as Chamber members, the Chamber may hesitate to recommend one over another, as a way of being fair to each member. This is a common policy.

Buyer Beware

Utilize the Better Business Bureau in your city or state to check on the background of any auction firm you are considering working with. If they have a bad reputation, they will likely have negative information with the Better Business Bureau.

Should you ask friends to recommend an auctioneer? Yes, absolutely! You might be surprised how many people you know have employed an auctioneer in the past to sell a relative's estate, a car, or other property. Because you are friends you probably put value in your friend's judgment of people and events. Ask about details of the auctioneer, how he or she treated the seller, and how the auction process was conducted from start to finish.

A good auctioneer wants to leave sellers and buyers happy so they will come back to do business again. But, take all advice with a grain of salt. Be a bit skeptical. Whether they had a good or bad experience may depend entirely on that specific situation. Sometimes a seller expects an unrealistically high price at auction for a property, and the auctioneer knows that price cannot be obtained. You may have a different experience with the same auctioneer. Use your own best judgment.

Contacting the Auctioneer: Research First

So now you've got the auctioneer's contact information such as phone number, address, and website. You want to call the auctioneer to describe your property and ask questions, and maybe set a meeting. Stop right there! You're not ready yet. You want to do a little research. After all, you're thinking of hiring this person to work for you. He will be your representative.

The auctioneer's first and main responsibility is to you, the seller: not to the buyer or the attendees or anyone else (although all parties must be treated ethically). He or she contracts with you to get the highest money for you within the terms agreed and specified. So before you even contact him or her, look on their company website for a biography of the auctioneer and a profile of the company.

You want a company with substantial experience in selling the type of property you have. Their website should explain that experience and will likely show preview information about upcoming auctions in that category. If you want to sell grandma's house and its contents, look for similar home sales discussed in their company profile and auction lists.

Also look at their Past Auctions section, where auctioneers tell of auction successes. This section often tells details of exact prices obtained for similar property to yours.

Now with research in hand on the auctioneer and his company, you're ready to either call, or send an e-mail or letter to the auctioneer. Introduce yourself and briefly describe the property you have for sale. Tell him or her if you are the owner or if you are an agent for the owner, such as if you are handling the sale of a painting for your grandmother, who is still living but has authorized you to direct this sale.

Tell the auctioneer that you have questions about the live auction method for this property and you have researched the auctioneer. This letter need not be lengthy. You can get into your detailed questions at your next meeting or phone call. However, don't leave out any vitally important information, such as whether you've had an appraised value on the property previously, or maybe there is a signature on the back of that dusty old painting and you are pretty sure it says Van Gogh. Be sure to leave your name and phone number clearly so the auctioneer can get back to you.

If the auction firm you contact initially refers you to an auction staffer other than the auctioneer for an initial evaluation of your situation, don't feel you have been insulted. The senior auctioneer may be unavailable at that moment, but the staff wants to answer your questions promptly, so you may be referred to an auction apprentice or another experienced staffer who can set a meeting or answer many initial questions.

Making an Informed Decision

It's vital you ask the right questions to make an informed decision to find the right auctioneer to sell your specific property.

Here are things, as a potential seller, you want to ask:

- **Auction specialty.** Many auctioneers specialize in only a few types of auctions. You want one that specializes in the property you have for sale. They will best know the market, the value of your property, and how to attract the buyers most interested in your property.

- **Career experience.** Auctioneers can conduct anywhere from a few dozen to more than 100 auctions in a year. But volume alone does not indicate professionalism or a success for your auction. Seasoned auctioneers know the market and know how to get the best price for your property.

- **License and references.** Many states require that auctioneers meet professional licensing requirements. Municipalities may also require auctioneers have permits or licenses. Also auctioneers have plenty of success stories to share. But don't just take their word for it. Ask former clients for their thoughts on their sales, especially on the same type of property you plan to sell. Also see success stories on the auctioneer's website.

- **Professional affiliations.** If the auctioneer is a member of his national or state auctioneer associations, it indicates they are likely to be interested in keeping abreast of their respective specialties, regulatory requirements, and changes in the market. They also subscribe to a code of ethics that requires them to treat all parties ethically, protecting you and the buyer.

  Ask if the auctioneer has any professional designations such as CES, which indicates a graduate of the Certified Estate Specialist program offered by the National Auctioneers Association. These graduates learn extensive procedures about conducting estate auctions. And, if you are selling real estate, ask if the auctioneer has both a real estate license in addition to an auctioneer's license.

Even if their state laws don't require the auctioneer to have a real estate license to auction real estate, auctioneers committed to that specialty typically hold both licenses.

♦ **Fees and billing.** Each auctioneer or auction firm has its own fee structure, and it may vary substantially from the way other auctioneers in your area are paid. Here are a few basics. Auctioneers typically are paid a percentage of the price received for the item (or for all items added together in an auction, if there is one seller for the whole auction).

This percentage, which comprises the auctioneer's commission, can be paid for by the seller or it can be shifted to the buyers through a *buyer's premium*, which is a small fee added to the winning bid price offered by the buyer. Auctioneers may or may not want to use the buyer's premium, and they may or may not want to negotiate on the amount of their commission.

As with any service provider, the lowest-priced auctioneer is not always the best choice to help you get the highest price for your property. Also, typically the seller pays for advertising, and may pay for rentals, catering, setup, and auctioneer staff. Those charges may also be deducted from the gross proceeds from the sale.

Which Type of Auction Is Best?

There's more than one type of auction, but which one is best for your property? Absolute auctions set no minimum amount for a piece of property, despite its appraised value. For example, if a car is appraised at $600 but only garners a high bid of $550, the high bidder purchases the automobile. Likewise if the car sells for $650 or more, you benefit from the greatest advantage of an auction the market determines the value.

Reserve auctions allow you to set a minimum amount you're willing to accept for your property. That amount may or may not be disclosed prior to or during the auction. You have the right to accept or reject any bids at a reserve auction, and you can remove the property from consideration before the auction is completed. The auctioneer will give you an opinion on which type of auction he thinks is best. You will also need to consider your desires, and put your decision in the contract with the auctioneer.

How Will You Market This Auction to Find Buyers?

Your auctioneer will need to generate interest in your auction, and the best way to get the word out is advertising. Depending on what you're trying to sell, the auctioneer could use a blend of newspaper ads, radio spots, ads in newsletters and specialty magazines, custom brochures, direct mail pieces, sales bills, maybe even cable television commercials.

The Internet now plays a significant role in marketing upcoming auctions. Many auctioneers post details about upcoming auctions on their websites, or they could use auction lists on other auction sites. Some sophisticated auctioneers develop e-mail lists of registered buyers who are interested in specific items that are offered for auction.

Ask About Their Contract or Written Proposal of Services

The auctioneer will likely tell you some details of the standard contract he or she uses, and that more details will depend on exactly what you and he agree to for your specific auction. He may also give you a written proposal with details that he has developed prior to your first meeting. But, as you both ask questions and learn more about each other, the proposal and the contract will also develop.

Those are the main questions. Yes, there is a lot of information and lots of decisions to make, so you want to take notes and take time to consider all that has been discussed. After you and the auctioneer have asked all questions of each other, set a time to meet again in person or by telephone to share your decision whether you want to move forward together to an auction.

Before You Make Your Choice

After you've researched and met the auctioneer, you'll also be wondering if live auctions are the right method for you, and if this auctioneer is the right person to hire. Before you decide yes or no, consider the following points.

Live auctions are geared toward getting you the highest possible price. This method is not aimed at simply putting your item in a store or antique booth or newspaper ad with a price tag on it. Every sales method has its place in the market. But because of

> **From the Podium**
>
> Have confidence in the auctioneer. You are hiring an auctioneer for his or her knowledge and ability to succeed.

the effort to get the highest price, there is going to be more work involved than in some other methods. That's why you are considering a professional auctioneer who knows the details of live auctions.

It's also logical (and smart) today for sellers to think about selling their item on the Internet. After all, so-called *auction websites* have the goal of getting the highest price for the posted item also, right? Not always. Sellers must also be aware of the Internet. Sophisticated auctioneers know when and how to use the Internet in conjunction with their live auctions, to attract more bidders and higher prices. Ask your auctioneer if it is right for your property. Sometimes the Internet works for a auction, and sometimes not. Many factors must be evaluated, and today's auctioneers are doing that almost every day.

As you're going through your evaluation, don't fall back on the myths and misconceptions discussed in Chapter 2. It's easy to let old opinions sneak in to your current business evaluations, even if the old opinions are no longer valid. The auction industry has changed from years ago. It is not primarily for distressed property that can't sell in another method. In fact, just imagine that when there are several interested buyers making offers on a property, it makes sense to have them bidding against each other until the highest price is reached (that's an auction!).

If you do decide to take your property to auction, the next major step is to work out all details, which will be set in a contract signed by both parties. The contract should describe all the aspects mentioned here, including fees and the type of auction, and many more details as well.

The Least You Need to Know

- Be very specific in searching the Internet for an auctioneer. Search for your state and type of property sold.

- Find an auctioneer with experience in selling the exact type of property you have for sale.

- Make sure to ask about the contract details that you would be expected to agree to.

- An auctioneer with substantial experience can tell quickly if your situation is good for an auction.

Chapter 18

Signing a Contract with an Auctioneer

In This Chapter

- ◆ Why you need a contract
- ◆ Know the three types of contracts
- ◆ Basic elements of most contracts
- ◆ Add special elements specific to your auction

A written contract between you, the seller of property, and the auctioneer, who represents your best interests while conducting an auction on your behalf, is not legally required to conduct a live auction.

Many times in eras past (and probably sometimes today) auctions were conducted with only a handshake and verbal agreement between the seller and auctioneer. But, the wise business person today puts down all in writing.

A contract can be verbal, and some people try to enforce verbal contracts by going to court with witnesses, but a written contract, signed by both parties, is the common procedure used in auctions today.

Purpose of an Auction Contract

The purpose of the written *contract* is to record the exact procedures, expectations, and responsibilities of the seller and the auctioneer.

def•i•ni•tion

A **contract** is a promissory agreement (making promises) between two or more persons that creates, modifies, or destroys a legal relationship (*Black's Law Dictionary*).

From the time they first meet, the seller and auctioneer begin discussing how the auction should be conducted: the location, the type of auction (with price reserves, or not), the payment to the auctioneer, and so on. These and many more factors need to be exactly agreed upon, written, and signed to avoid anything unclear, lapses in memory on details, and to provide methods of solving problems that may arise between the parties later.

Three Types of Contracts at Auctions

Although the main contract at work in a live auction is between the seller and auctioneer, there are actually three separate contracts at work. Let's take a look at them, so you as a seller are aware of all major legal relationships occurring.

The main one is called the *consignment contract*, the general contract where the seller wants to consign an item, say a dresser, to be sold at auction, or consign many items of a whole estate. This is between the seller and auctioneer, and states the terms of the consignment.

The second contract involves bidders. When bidders register to bid, they sign the Terms and Conditions statement, thereby agreeing to be bound by those terms of the auction. This agreement to allow bidding under these terms is a contract between the auctioneer and the bidders, but the seller should be highly aware of each element of that agreement, also.

The third contract originates from the auction itself, and is between the seller and buyer. For example, the auctioneer offers a dresser and a bidder buys it for $450. Legally, the seller is offering the item for sale, and the bidder is offering to buy it for that amount. There is a legal contract between the seller and buyer, says auction attorney Stephen Proffitt. The auctioneer is not a party to this particular contract. He is only acting as an agent for the seller.

So note the three different guiding legal relationships: seller and auctioneer; buyer to auctioneer; seller to buyer.

The consignment contract between the seller and auctioneer creates an agency relationship (auctioneer acts as agent) that empowers the auctioneer to sell the item under the terms of that contract. The dresser is sold when the auctioneer makes a contract for sale between the seller and buyer.

You might argue that "Well, the seller was not even present, and the buyer did not sign any paper, so where is the contract?" The answer is that this is an oral contract, and has as much legal force as a written contract.

Contracts for sale must contain three elements: an offer, an acceptance, and a consideration. The seller makes an offer to sell an item for a stated price. The buyer accepts the seller's offer to buy the item at that price. The seller's promise to sell the item for the price, and the buyer's promise to pay that amount for the item, represent the "consideration" that forms a binding contract for sale between them.

> **From the Podium**
>
> A seller/buyer contract is oral, but this type of verbal contract is fully enforceable.

A contract for sale vests both the seller and buyer with legal rights and responsibilities. If either party breaches the contract, the other may void the contract, or bring a lawsuit to force specific performance (carrying out the promise). They might also want to recover money damages against the breaching party.

The Uniform Commercial Code (UCC) is the legal framework for contracts for sale formed at auction (except for real estate, which is not governed by the UCC). The UCC is a model body of law that the various states have enacted to regulate commerce. By 1979, the UCC was enacted into law in every state, except Louisiana.

Why Written Contracts Are Needed: An Example

An auctioneer in New Hampshire tells this true story about why a written contract is needed: "Many years ago, a man's wife died and he engaged me to do an auction and sell his house out. It was well-advertised, and my crew and I arrived at 7 A.M. to set it up. The man greeted me with the news that he decided not to have an auction that day and, in those days, agreements were made with a handshake. I had no contract with him, as none was required and we did not need them. I explained to him that I had a lot of money invested in advertising; expenses in securing the help for the sale and that people might travel for miles to the sale and would be quite unhappy with our auction firm and him, as well. He still insisted he didn't want to do the sale that day. Nevertheless, we did the auction, gave him his accounting from the sale that day and his check. I never heard any more from him on it."

A written contract covering such situations may have avoided this disagreement. Attorney Kurt Bachman advises all auctioneers to have written contracts with each seller prior to doing any work. The contract should establish the terms of the sale and be fully executed. A written contract should clearly establish the terms and conditions for an auction and will help reduce the possibility of disputes and liability.

"Conducting an auction without a written contract is not a crime. It is, however, very risky," he said. "Years ago a verbal contract to sell property at auction was generally enforceable. A verbal contract may, however, not be worth much. One of the parties could forget or misunderstand the terms of the contract. In other cases, a party to a verbal contract may simply lie and deny any agreement."

Elements of a Contract

A typical auction contract has these main elements: it says the seller gives the auctioneer the right to sell the property; it describes the property, sets a reserve price, if desired; and states when and where the auction will be held.

The contract states that the seller is, in fact, the owner of the property without any liens against it (claims of full or part ownership by someone else).

The contract details whether a buyer's premium is used; all other fees, including their amounts; and how things such as earnest money or other deposits will be handled and where deposited. It also details, as closely as possible, all services to be performed by the auctioneer, including marketing and advertising, and typically explains that the auctioneer will not predict or promise a certain price will be obtained for an item, and that the seller must accept the price for a property to be sold.

A real estate auction contract will also contain language that describes that the seller authorizes the auctioneer to work with cooperating brokers, that the auctioneer is not charged with any maintenance of the property, that the auctioneer has not made an investigation of condition beyond the external and interior areas, and it may state that the seller will hold harmless the auctioneer against any claims that arise from the seller's associations with other brokers or parties.

The contract states that the property is sold as-is, with no guarantees. It can also mention a "no sale fee," meaning that if the seller declines to accept the final bid achieved at auction, the owner shall pay to the auctioneer a certain amount called a no sale fee.

Contracts also discuss that "If any of the property's structure was build before 1978, the owner will provide a disclosure of lead-based paint as required by the U.S. Dept. of Housing and Urban Development." Contracts can also clarify that the owner has the right to accept subsequent purchase offers until the close of escrow under certain conditions.

The following is a short typical real estate auction contract:

> This agreement, entered into this _____ day of _____, (month and year), by and between (*auction firm's name here*) called AUCTIONEER and the undersigned owner(s) called SELLER(s).
>
> 1. SELLER(s) grants to the AUCTIONEER an exclusive right of sale of SELLER's following described property by public auction: _____
> _____.
> SELLER(s) grants "Exclusive Right of Sale" from the day this agreement is signed to the day of the auction which is _____ (month) _____ _____ (day), _____ (year), and will continue for 90 days.
>
> 2. SELLER(s) represents that his title to the property is marketable and insurable, and that the said SELLER(s) has the full authority to enter into this agreement and to convey title.
>
> Minimum bid: $_____
>
> 3. A 10 percent buyer's premium will be added to the buyer's bid and will be the auctioneer's total commission.
>
> 4. All closing costs paid by the buyer. Taxes will be prorated to date of closing.
>
> 5. SELLER(s) will contribute $_____ in advance to help with all advertising and promotional expenses.
>
> 6. AUCTIONEER will post property on website and place auction signs on property.
>
> 7. SELLER(s) acknowledges that AUCTIONEER or agents cannot accurately predict the price the property will bring at public auction.
>
> 8. Property to be sold subject to owner's acceptance.

There are many websites that offer sample legal contracts, including auction contracts. Most auctioneers have a customized contract with elements and language they want to include, and wish to use in their contract.

It is highly recommended that sellers have their own attorney review any contract used for an auction. You can and should educate yourself by looking at sample auction contracts, but get advice from an expert to avoid liabilities.

Special Elements to Include

Fair housing and lead-based paint disclosure language should be in an auction contract of real estate. The auctioneer is required to inform the seller of the seller obligations under these acts and to ensure compliance.

The Fair Housing Act is a federal law that prohibits discriminatory housing practices. Under the law, an individual selling real estate generally cannot refuse to sell or rent to an individual who makes a legitimate offer based on race, color, national origin, sex, religion, family status, or disability. An individual selling real estate cannot treat a potential buyer differently because of his membership in any of the previous categories.

SOLD!

Exercise your right to put any special elements in the contract that you desire, if agreed by both parties.

The Fair Housing Act also prohibits auctioneers, real estate brokers, and others from persuading individuals to rent or sell housing by telling them that a particular race, color, or something else on is moving into the neighborhood. The Act also prohibits discriminatory advertisements and steering races or certain groups to a particular neighborhood.

The Residential Lead-Based Paint Hazard Reduction Act of 1992 is another federal law that applies to the sale of homes built before 1978. The Act was passed to protect families from exposure to lead from paint, dust, and soil. The seller must (1) provide the buyer with an EPA-approved information pamphlet on identifying and controlling lead-based paint hazards ("Protect Your Family from Lead in Your Home"); (2) disclose any known information concerning lead-based paint and/or lead-based paint hazards; and (3) disclose any records and reports on lead-based paint and/or lead-based paint hazards. In addition to these requirements, sellers must typically give a buyer 10 days to conduct a paint inspection or risk assessment at their own expense, unless it is waived.

Disclosed Seller Bidding

Sellers bidding on their own items is a legal practice when disclosed. The auctioneer and his staff can bid on items also, when disclosed. However, seller bidding is illegal fraud, plus a violation of the UCC, when practiced in the shadows of secrecy.

Sellers don't come to auction to give valuable assets away for fire-sale prices. Most want at least what they perceive to be reasonable market value for what they sell. The drafters of the UCC knew this and acted to protect auction sellers from an involuntary sacrifice of their goods in two ways—by providing for auctions with reserves, and by allowing sellers to make disclosed bids in their own auctions.

Commercial sellers often bid in their auctions. Mortgage companies do it all the time in foreclosures of real estate. Auctioneers who own the goods they sell frequently bid to boost prices and protect their interests.

Similarly, it is not uncommon for auctioneers' staffs to bid in the auctions they work. Some auctioneers themselves bid in the sales they conduct. Sellers' agents, employees, representatives, and close relatives frequently bid in these sellers' auctions. None of this bidding hurts good and legitimate auctions. Only when bidders are kept in the dark does seller bidding come out to hurt an auction.

Some bidders do not like it when sellers or auctioneers bid on their own items, but they should understand why it occurs. Auctioneers' bidding creates a problem because the auctioneer is primarily an agent for a seller. As an agent, the auctioneer owes a fiduciary duty to act for the seller's benefit, while subordinating one's personal interest to the other person. But, when the auctioneer is trying to buy at a less-than-top price, it is not representing the seller as best as possible.

Puffery, Puffing, and Fraud

It can also be put in a contract that the auctioneer and seller will avoid *puffery* (meaning exaggeration), *puffing* (meaning a shill bidder who is driving up bids), and fraud (meaning clear misrepresentation of facts).

Puffery is exaggerated flattery and commendation that a salesperson gives a potential buyer when describing what is being offered for sale. A seller or auctioneer can say flattering things about how beautiful a vehicle is and that it runs well, but any statements of operating ability must be true.

Buyer Beware

Beware of exaggeration and outright misrepresentation by any parties at the auction, and try to prevent that by putting a prohibition against it in your contract.

Many auctioneers love to give flowery descriptions of what they sell. Puffery is a legal sales tool, unless it crosses into fraud. That's a crossing that neither seller nor auctioneer ever wants to make.

A puffer in the crowd is a shill bidder, a decoy in an auction crowd who works in secret tandem with the auctioneer or others to drive bids up on the lots on which the puffer bids. The goal is to make buyers pay more for the goods than legitimate, competitive bidding would require them to pay.

The puffer does this by acting as a legitimate bidder in an effort to trick legitimate bidders into believing that they need to bid higher to buy the subject lots. The truth is that the puffer has no intention of buying anything and his bids are the hollow bids of a straw man. Think of a puffer as one who blows up (puffs) the price "balloon" and you understand how these tricksters work and why they were given this name.

Puffing is illegal fraud everywhere and that means the potential for both criminal and civil penalties for the auctioneer and puffer. Fraud has been a serious violation of law for eons before the UCC was ever imagined, let alone enacted.

Bid Increments

You can also specify which amount of bid increments you want the auctioneer to accept for your item or items.

An applicable case arose once for an Ohio auctioneer on an item where the bidding reached $1,500 for an item, and the auctioneer was asking $1,550. A bidder bid $1,525 and the auctioneer refused to take that bid, and so sold the item for $1,500. The $1,525 bidder filed suit, claiming the auction was advertised "selling to the highest bidder," yet the "highest bidder" didn't get this item. But the terms and conditions of the auction stated something such as "Auctioneer reserves the right to refuse bids which are but a trifling advance more than the prior bid ...."

Attorney Kurt Bachman says that even when a sale is advertised as "absolute, to the highest bidder!" the auctioneer has the authority to control the manner of the sale. But this right may be limited, however, when you have an absolute auction because there should be no limiting conditions, such as incremental bid amounts. Requiring bids to be at least $50 more than the previous bid may be considered a limiting condition. It could be perceived as a limiting condition by the courts. So consider that when you put bid amounts in terms for an absolute auction.

Who Is Authorized to Make Decisions

If anyone besides the seller is authorized to make any decisions, it should be spelled out in the contract.

For example, an auctioneer contracted to conduct an auction for an estate. The executrix was a daughter of the deceased. The estate's attorney has told the executrix that if the items in the auction are sold below 'fair market value,' she will be personally responsible for the difference. The executrix wanted to have an appraisal done. The attorney also advised her that she cannot have an auction unless she advertises the sale as being one for 'market value,' or otherwise establishes minimum prices on everything. The executrix was very concerned about all this and considered postponing the sale. The auctioneer advised her that it was too late to postpone the auction, because the advertising had been placed.

> ### From the Podium
>
> Auctioneers can run into problems with dealing with decedents' estate representatives and their attorneys. Different people can claim to have authority in an auction.

The sale was conducted for the benefit of the deceased's four children, but the executrix and her attorney created problems during the process. If you want your attorney to be authorized to act in some phase of the auction process, in case you are absent, indicate that in the contract.

Auctioneers sometimes worry about a client not doing what has been agreed to or about the client not paying. They often feel more secure if the client offers to place an indemnity clause in the contract. But how good is an indemnity clause? It's only as good as the other side. "An indemnity clause from a worthless bozo is worthless," said attorney Lynn Coyne.

"Sometimes you see people giving up major portions of a contract because they have an indemnity clause," he said. "Well, remember, an indemnity clause can be discharged in bankruptcy. If you're not sure of the financial strength of the other side, be careful." The paper isn't the person, he said, "Does the paper have any money? Then what good is the paper?"

As with indemnity clauses, disclaimers may not be worth as much as you think, Coyne said. Disclaimers often show up as trouble spots in the contract and negligence areas of law.

"You can always say 'not responsible for accidents,'" he noted, but you could be wrong. "It's much the same thing as driving around with a sticker on your car that says 'not responsible for accidents.' It doesn't work. You are responsible for your driving and any accidents you cause, no matter what the sticker on your car says."

You can buy insurance for many negligence-related problems, Coyne noted, "but most states won't enforce a disclaimer of negligence."

Document Everything

To protect yourself, keep copies of all contracts, related documents, and write down everything concerning your dealings with the auctioneer, bidders, and anyone connected to the auction.

Contracts also offer an opportunity to address potential problems before they become problems, and to make for a smooth business transaction. Make full disclosure to all parties of all items and procedures. Understand the contract, the auction process, and your obligations.

Also keep a good working relationship with your attorney so you can run these things by him or her on short notice when an auction is coming or shortly past.

The Least You Need to Know

- A written contract is not required to hold a live auction, but it is best for all parties in case disagreements arise.

- The auctioneer will likely want to use his own contract. Have your lawyer review it.

- Auction contracts should spell out all auction procedures and responsibilities for each party.

- You have the right to consider adding any special elements you want to the contract.

Chapter 19

Price Valuation of Your Property

In This Chapter

- ◆ How much should it bring?
- ◆ Who can really determine price?
- ◆ Why to do your own research
- ◆ What professional appraisers offer

Central to the live auction is the idea of the current price value of the item for sale. Everything is built around that. The key question is "How much are the same or similar items selling for on the market today?" That's the *current market value*.

Millions of people understand this idea from watching TV such as the PBS show *Antiques Roadshow*, where appraisers tell people how much they think the current market value of an item at auction is.

The bidders, the seller, and the auctioneer all should know the current market value of their target items, and often they have all done their homework to find out. Then, they base their bids, reserve selling price, and hoped-for price on that.

Savvy buyers at auctions are often seeking to buy rare items at bargain prices, then turn around and sell the items for big prices on eBay, or at live auctions. They search live auctions and the Internet looking for items that are vastly under-priced because the seller or auctioneer didn't discover the real current value. An example occurred a few years ago when an antiques dealer sold a thirteenth century Persian artifact for $48,000, but the item was soon resold at Sotheby's for $1.9 million.

When sellers don't know the value of an item, enabling a blunder such as that one by the antiques dealer, it teaches a hard lesson: appraise closely, and if you're not sure of a price, get professional help.

But how do you find out what the live auction valuation price is? Let's take a look.

Ways to Determine Price

Most people, sellers and bidders, do their own research for ordinary items of small value because they see no need to pay a professional appraiser when the prices are small. But when prices are large, it makes it worth it to get a professional appraiser.

To do your own appraising, the fastest way is to use the Internet. Search eBay.com and other websites, calling up similar items to the one you wish to sell or buy, and check the completed auctions for selling prices.

"Look at completed sales and individual results. Were there bids? Was the reserve met? Notice the condition, size, and weight in evaluating each item," said appraiser Lorrie Semler, CES, of Carrollton, Texas.

She also recommends Prices for Antiques (www.P4A.com) for regional auction house results. "It's reasonably priced for what they offer," she said. Another source that might help is www.ArtFact.com, which features big auction house results.

Another way is to consult price guides, either printed or online (do an Internet search for "price guides"). Also ask collectors, antique dealers, and your auctioneer, who all have experience in price determination. The auctioneer can be especially helpful in telling you if your particular antique is in our out of fashion with buyers this year. Ask for this guidance.

Auction House Websites Useful for Valuation

The websites of big auction houses are good for checking prices, especially for antiques, says auctioneer Shirley Baumann, CAGA, of Madison, Wisconsin.

"If you're doing some very high-end, great antiques, you'll want to turn to some of the big auction house websites. Christie's, Butterfield's, and Sotheby's all list their auction results on the Internet. Watch for similar items and the most recent sales," said Baumann, who specializes in antiques. "If I'm looking at art, I like either ArtNet or AskArt. There's free information from all such services, but you pay for details. The fees are worth it if you're researching something substantial. You wouldn't do it for every little household thing."

About eBay, Baumann says "You can't look at an item one time only. You have to watch it over time. Otherwise, you might be viewing a situation where a buyer has more money than sense, or a collector was finishing out a collection. Or if the price is low, it may be because a real collector missed it that day and the item went for a bargain."

She also recommends talking to your local dealers and asking what people are spending for certain types of items. Go to other auctioneers' sales as well. Notice if they've developed a different clientele which would explain prices different than what you're getting.

SOLD!

Most auction houses list their results (final prices) on their websites, which makes a good resource for your appraising searches.

She also recommends secondary market dealers as a great source for finding collectors of things. "That holds especially true in the collectibles market," she said. She also uses the book *Collectibles Market Guide and Price Index*, published by Collectors Information Bureau. "Hallmark Keepsake Ornaments publishes their own guidebook which lists secondary dealers. Use the indexes in these books," she says. "You'll find source people listed that way."

While you are finding the current sale prices for similar items, you must also pay close attention to the condition of the item, and make adjustments.

Condition Is Important

When it comes to evaluating an item, condition is most important. Is the item in *mint* condition, with no cracks, blemishes, or missing parts? The better the condition, the higher the value.

"The general public is under the misconception that just because something is old, it's valuable," Semler says. Other factors such as supply and demand go into determining appraised values, Semler said. "The Internet has been the great leveler. Supply and demand changes very quickly now."

Then there are external forces affecting values. Economic factors such as inflation and recession. Political forces affect values. If there's unrest in Africa, it could change the price of diamonds, for example. She noted that forces such as civil rights in this country have affected values of items such as African American memorabilia.

After you have determined the market price for similar items, and adjusted up or down for condition, you should also be familiar with different types of values that can apply to an item.

The following are different types of values:

- **Auction value.** The value expected at auction in a competitive bidding situation.

- **Retail value.** The price in a retail store setting for the general public.

- **In-place value.** This is a midway point between auction value and dealer retail. Maybe a son is buying out the father, with neither committed to either auction value or retail.

- **Insurance value.** What will it cost to replace this piece of equipment at dealer retail? If a particular part is worn out, what will the dealer charge to replace it?

- **Replacement value.** Equipment isn't usually replaced with used equipment. An old piece usually is moved out to make way for a new machine.

- **Liquidation value.** This is the value of equipment for a farmer who is going to retire, for example, or for a "fire sale." Such a sale probably would carry the bank's name.

- **Seasonal value.** The value likely in a particular season of the year. For example, farm equipment such as combines and plows appraised and sold in March are not going to bring what they would in August.

To evaluate how these values apply to your auction item, ask your auctioneer, a professional appraiser, or do research on websites such as that of The Appraisal Foundation (www.appraisalfoundation.org).

How to Use an Appraiser

Since the popularity of the TV show *Antiques Roadshow*, some people are under the impression that appraisers are wealthy, kind-hearted souls who are willing to tour the country, offering free appraisals.

Although some appraisers appear at free appraisal fairs, most charge for their services. They are trained and certified to use specific techniques to investigate and determine the value of an item.

Many appraisers will offer three ways you can get their professional opinion. These are the following:

♦ E-mail the appraisers a good photo, measurements, detailed description, all marks, serial numbers, brand and model names, and condition of the item, and the appraiser will provide an estimate for a nominal fee. This is commonly known as a "desktop appraisal."

♦ For a minimum one-hour charge, the appraiser will stop by your location to provide a verbal opinion.

♦ For the appraiser's hourly rate, based on actual time spent, plus expenses, he or she can come at the client's convenience, draw up a contract, and get a retainer (usually about half the estimated time) for services in doing the inspection and preparing the written appraisal. A contract is very important because it defines what both parties expect. Payment of the balance of the fee is due upon presentation of the appraisal report.

An appraiser's opinion must always be neutral and unbiased, so sometimes a client may get an appraisal that is higher or lower than he had hoped for, and he doesn't want to pay for it. An enforceable contract can be taken to court to ensure payment.

With banks, attorneys, accountants, and government agencies, appraisers get a *letter of specifics* also called a letter of engagement, setting out the specifics of what the client wants, because they often have detailed needs.

How do professional appraisers find value? A top appraiser of manufacturing equipment, Bernie Dworkin, uses at least these three sources to determine value: the Internet; the Thomas Register of American Manufacturers; and dealer and industry trade magazines.

He also spends hours on the telephone, talking to the owners of equipment, original manufacturers, used equipment dealers, and anyone else who might have even a sliver of a lead on how much an item is worth.

The Thomas Register, which used to stand in heavy volumes along Dworkin's office walls, has advanced along with the technological age and is now available online, at an easy-to-use and ultra-informative website. With just a few keystrokes, anyone can access detailed information on 168,000 American and Canadian manufacturing companies, almost 64,000 product and service categories, almost 7,800 online supplier catalogs, and even view thousands of CAD drawings of individual items.

Determining the value of a piece of equipment isn't as easy as finding its original value and calculating depreciation. It's not even as easy as finding similar items sold today and estimating a ballpark figure. There are numerous other considerations, such as the region of the country where the item will be sold, whether any new applications for the item have emerged and, if the item is unique (fabricated, instead of mass-produced), is there any particular value to anyone for its existence today?

High Value Today, Low Tomorrow

Appraiser Mike Odell, GPPA, CES, says one of the saddest things about being an appraiser is meeting clients who have been collecting for decades, and now that it's time to downsize and pass along their legacy, they often discover that their prize collections hold no interest for the next generation.

In many cases, they must also face the disappointment of learning that the treasures of a lifetime have shrunk in value to a pittance of their original cost. Many collectibles have gone out of style over the years, but the children of the collectors may not realize that popularity usually recycles, and what is out now may come back into vogue in the future.

Postcards and photos, for example, are being collected by more and more of the younger collectors. "I recently went to a postcard show and noticed that more 20- and 30-somethings were in attendance. So keeping up with new trends is of vital importance to auctioneers and appraisers alike. Reading *Antique Trader* magazine and other fine collecting and antiquing publications is important for us to maintain a working knowledge of the so-called new collectibles. We also need to follow the patterns of sales by our fellow auctioneers around and country, and also internationally."

Using an Auctioneer As Your Appraiser

Many auctioneers today are also trained and certified appraisers. They have always had greater knowledge of auction prices and expected values for the items they frequently sell, and auctioneers have therefore offered informal appraisals to many clients.

But in recent years this practice has changed. Auctioneers know that today they risk a lawsuit if they offer an opinion on value, and seemingly make a promise to try to get that amount. So for a valuable item, they may refrain from giving a judgment without getting details in writing.

If you are a seller, it's good to know that under most state laws, a licensed auctioneer must keep informed on current market conditions of real and personal property at all times to be in a position to advise and perform services for his clients.

> **SOLD!**
>
> You can ask your auctioneer for an informal appraisal of current market value, or you may be able to hire him for a detailed formal appraisal.

To reduce exposure in lawsuits, prudent auctioneers may also hire a professional appraiser. Auctioneer and former practicing attorney David F. Gerlach of Hartland, Wisconsin, who is also a senior appraiser in the American Society of Appraisers, recommends that auctioneers use price reserves or contract language to protect themselves. If you are a seller, or a bidder, it's good to know when the auctioneer may seek these conditions.

An auctioneer may also require, when working with a seller, that they make it clear that the auction house is not responsible for valuing the item and is relying entirely on the seller's representations and instructions as to an acceptable price at the auction.

The contract could also point out that if the item is incorrectly valued by the seller, it is possible that it may be purchased at an auction for an amount that is substantially less than its actual market value. In that case the seller, not the auction house, assumes all liability for the undervaluation.

Local or Regional Appraisal Shows

You can also visit local appraisal shows for a free or low-cost appraisal prior to taking your item to live auction. Professional appraisers are on tap there.

An example is a fair in Fishkill, New York at a Holiday Inn. The organizer, auctioneer Rob Doyle, CAI, of New York set up the Hudson River Antique and Collectible Roadshow and advertised it on local radio.

About 2,000 people came from a 50-mile radius with 20 specialty appraisers who worked from individual booths. "All the top gallery appraisers wanted to be a part of this show. They liked the exposure for their companies," he said. Their categories included: paintings, jewelry, furniture, lighting, military items, political buttons, posters, rugs, musical instruments, glass, clocks, coins, toys, dolls, porcelain, autographs, baseball cards, silver, and more.

SOLD!

Local appraisal shows are a good way to get a professional appraisal at low cost.

Large pieces of furniture were appraised in the parking lot. Some of the top items appraised at the show included a Colt handgun valued around $25,000 and a pink Lionel train set for girls valued at $8,000.

"People especially brought in a lot of china and porcelain carved figurines," said Doyle, whose staff also did appraisals. Visitors paid $5 for each verbal appraisal (they paid the money at the front door and got a ticket to present at the appropriate booth). Admission was $1 for people who did not bring an item for appraisal.

About $2,000 of proceeds was donated to the Salvation Army. The idea began when the Special Projects Director of the local radio station asked Doyle to organize the show by getting the appraisers. Doyle was chosen because he is well-known for auctions and appraisals in the area.

Fine Art Appraising

When you think of appraising, often people think of paintings or other fine art. Fine art auction specialist Bob Baker, CAI, ARRE, GPPA, gives a few guidelines that show when to get help in appraising.

"Do you know the difference between fine art and decorative art?" he asks. "It helps to know these definitions, and a few details about the several types of fine art."

In general the phrase "fine art" refers to paintings, sculptures, and graphic art and was not in use until the fifteenth century. Prior to that time artists were considered to be crafts persons. On the other hand, decorative art is an application of segments of fine art to common or decorative objects which mirror the motifs of common society.

Buyer Beware

Appraising fine art can be the most risky of all. Consider hiring a professional if you are unsure of your appraising methods and result.

There are eight major categories of paintings to identify and segregate: fresco, tempera, oil paint, watercolor, gouache (pronounced gwash), acrylic, mixed media, and pastels/charcoal/chalk.

Fresco is a method of painting calling for the application of paint to wet lime plaster on a wall. As the pigment penetrates the plaster it actually becomes part of the wall. The most famous of these paintings are those in the Sistine Chapel done by Michelangelo. The height of these creations was during the Renaissance; however, the twentieth century had its masters of this form of art, most notable was Diego Rivera.

Tempera is usually referred to as "egg tempera" and results by mixing pigments with egg yolk. Primarily these paintings were done on panels of wood in Europe during the fourteenth and fifteenth centuries. This type of painting was rarely seen after the 1500s but was "rediscovered" in the twentieth century by artists such as Andrew Wyeth. The paintings can be characterized as tedious at best due to the limited color range, and the depth and richness of the painting is only achieved by layering on thin semi-transparent colors giving a luminosity not found in the fresco.

Oil paint entered the art scene in the sixteenth century and the van Eycks of the Netherlands are credited with mastering its use. Oil is the binder for the color pigment and gave artists a panorama of colors to use. Due to the slow drying nature of the oil paint, the artist could actually mix their colors on their palette or the work surface. Artists using oils could paint with the detail of the tempera artist or paint with a more fluid approach, laying layer on layer presenting a surface with a thick texture or impasto.

Expert painters would build delicate layers called glazing, creating a depth and richness never before achievable. Transitions between light and shadow were accomplished with a natural gentleness, and the results are referred to as being done in a "painterly" fashion. The nineteenth century introduction of tube oil paints revolutionized painting.

Watercolors, unlike other paint mediums, permitted the artist to accomplish very light tones by thinning the paint to the point where the "ground" or paper showed through and became an integral part of the work of art. Initially watercolors were used to hand color or tint other works on paper but in the nineteenth century it became its own art form. Spontaneity in the art is what is enjoyable about this art form to many people.

Mixed media combines two or more types of painting on one surface and is not a newcomer to the art scene. The fifteenth century often saw the mixing of oil and tempera on one surface. Today it is common jargon to describe prints and paintings with multiple elements including three-dimensional objects attached to flat surfaces.

Pastels, charcoal, and chalk are used in drawings and paintings and are marked by pure pigment mixed with a minimum of gum, resin, or other binder to hold the pigment together on a surface. Pure color presentation and soft delicate lines are the hallmark. This art was originally used in Italy in the sixteenth century and then later chosen by nineteenth century impressionists. The surface of the art is perishable and many times the art shows with a smeared surface either intentionally or unintentionally.

Parts of an Appraisal Document

The main documentation pieces within a written appraisal are ...

- ◆ A title page.

def•i•ni•tion

A **certificate of appraisal** is the section of an appraisal that states the purpose of the appraisal.

- ◆ A *certificate of appraisal*. This states the purpose of the appraisal, and that, as of this date, it's our opinion that the property is valued at such an amount.

- ◆ Authorization. Names the person or persons who have authorized the appraisal and whether the owner of the property was present at the time of the appraisal.

- ◆ Overall description. Includes maintenance and condition of the equipment.

- ◆ Approach to value. States how the appraiser came to the value. States something such as, "This appraisal uses market analysis of comparative sales," then says if he consulted equipment price guides and dealers. Then there is a list of those resources, such as Hot Line Equipment Guide or Fast Line Guide.

- ◆ Description of values. Lists every possible thing related to that piece of equipment's value. Is the auto body rough? Is the motor weak?

- ◆ Appraiser's qualifications. Some appraisers want their qualification documentation to be thick with listings of licenses and memberships in state and national associations.

Some appraisals also include a disclaimer such as "We are not mechanics, and we rely on our client's description of the equipment's mechanical condition." Also mentioned is that the appraiser has no personal financial interest in the equipment and is only involved in appraising value as an independent third party.

As we've learned in this chapter, price appraisal of your auction item is vital to having a successful auction. Begin by doing your own research, know the types of appraised values that apply to your item, and don't hesitate to use a professional when needed. But also remember that an appraisal is usually one person's value estimate, while an auction is the market value on auction day.

The Least You Need to Know

- Find current values by looking for completed auctions on eBay.com or ArtFact. com.

- Condition of an item is very important in determining value.

- There are at least seven types of values, from auction to retail and seasonal values.

- Hire a professional appraiser for an item of high value. Don't rely on your own appraising skills.

Chapter 20

Choosing the Right Live Auction Venue

In This Chapter

- Top factors in choosing location
- Inside or outside?
- Marketing your choice to your advantage
- Using the Web to reach the world

If you are the only seller of property in an auction, such as a single estate, you are the boss and make the final decision where you want your live auction to be held. But choosing the right location is crucial to the success of the auction, and you should listen to the advice of your auctioneer, who likely has years of experience and has seen the advantages and problems caused by each type of location.

A basic decision is whether you want to have the auction where your property is currently located, or if you want to move it somewhere else, such as a rented building or the auctioneer's facility. There are good reasons to consider every option. This is where you must talk out the details with your auctioneer and examine the pros and cons.

Sale Items and Goals

Your sale items and your goals for the auction are among the top factors that determine where to hold the auction. Ask yourself: "Where can my type of property be displayed and sold to bring in the highest number of bidders and most money?" Normally that is the purpose of the auction.

> **From the Podium**
>
> A top consideration in choosing auction location is deciding where bidders will most easily get to your auction and see the items in a comfortable setting.

However, also ask yourself (and the auctioneer will ask you), "What is the goal of this auction?" It may be that your goal is a more speedy liquidation of your property at an acceptable price, rather than taking time to move many auction items to a different location that may be easier for bidders to reach, and therefore, bring higher prices.

The auctioneer will recommend the best location to you and tell you why that venue is the best for your type of auction. Here are some of the top factors to consider:

- Easy-to-find location for attendees.

- Comfortable seating and good lighting for attendees and auction staff.

- Adequate display space for auction items, storage, and conducting the auction.

- Adequate parking and vehicle movement around the property.

- Safety factors, attractiveness of the auction site, and rain protection.

A few comments about these five factors: put yourself in the position of the attendee who may want to come to your estate auction, for example. If the home with all the estate items is located 20 miles from the nearest city, on a winding dirt road that may be muddy after a rain, and is hard to find even with good directions, would that deter you from attending? It well might. In that case, you may want to heed the auctioneer's advice to move all the auction items to his or her auction building in town.

And as an attendee, would you not also want comfortable seating, good display areas, parking, a safe site to walk around, and so on? Of course, so your job as a seller is to provide that for the bidders as a means to reach your goal: a successful auction for you.

Onsite Options: House, Barn, and Outside

Your auction can be inside or outside. Each has its own advantages.

Auctions today are increasingly held indoors because of the many advantages. Bad weather is less damaging to attendance and having bidders stay at an auction if the event is indoors. Lighting and temperature is constant where displaying small and medium-sized items is better. Technology also works better inside, from sound systems to big video screens and running a simultaneous audio and video on the Internet. Working such technology outside creates problems with cables on the ground, wind noise, sunlight reflection, or dark shade under a tent, and so on.

A typical auction house is a commercial business that is set-up to provide the best setting for auctions in regard to all the factors previously mentioned. Consider this as opposed to a residential home for an estate auction, where parking can be cramped, rooms small, and so on. Also, regular auction attendees in your community are already familiar with the location and amenities at the auction house, and will not consider location a deterrent in their decision to attend your auction.

> **From the Podium**
>
> Most auctions are held indoors today to better accommodate technology and comfort. In past eras, outdoor auctions were more numerous.

The same applies to an auction barn for livestock sales. Parking, location, and display of auction livestock are all generally an advantage over going to a farm in a different location.

However, outdoor auctions have their charm and times when they are necessary. Gathering under a tent on a pleasant spring or fall day for an estate or personal property auction creates a fun atmosphere. Estate items displayed on a yard and around the property provide good space to walk around and an interesting presentation.

And in some cases, where there are many large furniture items at an estate, or many large farm equipment items, it is just not feasible or economical to take them to another location to sell. Leave them at your home location, hold an outdoor auction there, and do a great job of marketing the auction to bring in as many bidders as possible.

However, the outdoor auction and onsite home auction takes careful planning to provide comfort and efficiency for bidders and auction staff. The auctioneer is the expert in this, but as seller, you should be kept informed of the plans, and you should offer your own ideas and help.

Ask the auctioneer about the planned seating, tents, technology to be used, security plans, and so on. Find out all that will occur on your property. However, don't be overly concerned that an outside auction cannot be held safely and successfully. It happens every day somewhere in the world.

In fact, many auctioneers have all their equipment ready to roll to the outdoor site. As discussed in Chapter 4, some auctioneers operate from an auction topper truck while calling bids at an outdoor auction. The topper is a shell that fits on the back of a pickup truck. The auctioneer can sit in this camper-style shell with an open window, from which he looks out over the crowd. This keeps the auctioneer out of the sun and wind, reducing wind noise into his microphone, and he can sit comfortably during a long auction.

And, some auctioneers use a mobile office, also called a cashier trailer or registration trailer. This is similar to a recreational vehicle, with space inside for attendees to register, restrooms, and space for auction clerks to work with computers, printers, and other office equipment. These mobile trailers have awnings that fold out to provide weather protection, and other features. They typically range in size from 12 to 20 feet.

SOLD!

Take the initiative in preparing your home or other property for a live auction to be held there. Clean the grounds thoroughly. Don't wait for the auctioneer's staff to do it.

Also for a live auction at your home or farm, prepare your property for the event. You want it to be a clean and safe area. Install portable toilets, mow grass, remove any hazards, set a clear parking area, prepare road signs and onsite signage ("park here," "register here"), notify neighbors of the event, if needed. Work with your auctioneer on these and get additional ideas from the auctioneer.

Advertise the Venue Effectively

After you've chosen the venue for your live auction, advertise it clearly and effectively to your target bidders to draw as many of them as possible to the auction.

Take this approach: "This is a great location! The sale items are beautifully displayed. Here are the easy and exact directions to find our auction. Here is where you can go to see a full catalog of items before the auction."

Push that positive approach. Whichever venue you pick, communicate that it's a great location (unless it clearly is a problem area. Don't exaggerate when circumstances absolutely do not merit it).

Your auctioneer will coordinate and place the advertising and marketing pieces that you both jointly decide on. The auctioneer should have the experience in how to target bidders for your exact type of auction, from local bidders to those worldwide.

However, once again, it's to your advantage to check what the auctioneer is doing and to communicate any specific advertising desires you have. Here are advertising and marketing categories to cover in your auction, regardless of the venue you pick.

Newspaper Ads

In many cities and rural areas, the local newspaper is still the major way to advertise your auction. But, although some auctioneers say newspapers ads are still an absolute necessity in their local market, some sellers and auctioneers are pulling out of newspapers. "We have downsized our newspaper advertising to a bare minimum. The costs are outrageous for the results we are getting," said auctioneer Barbara Blake, of Blake Auction Company of Princeton, West Virginia.

The key is to know your own market. But before cutting back on newspaper advertising, take a look at how well-designed your ads really are, advises Larry Mersereau, advertising consultant. There are two common problems in most ads, he said. First, the information is not presented in the proper sequence that leads a customer to the auction. Second, the ad lacks a specific and persuasive call to action. Review your ads to be sure all the necessary information is there, including directions to the auction site, description of at least some sales items, language referring the reader to your website for more information, and language encouraging the customer to attend.

Websites

Promote your auction on your auctioneer's website and others. A website isn't a magic bullet that replaces all other forms of advertising, but it's an instant source of information about your auctions.

"Newspapers are the number one thing we always do, but the website follows next," says Joe Tarpley, CAI, president of JL Todd Auction Company of Rome, Georgia. "The Internet has been the biggest change for our advertising in the last five years. We put all of our sales on the website and we get all kinds of phone calls from it."

Auctioneers today are pulling customers into their auction websites through advertising in newspaper, magazine, radio, and cable advertising. All paid forms of advertising should drive the public to a website where the real bulk of information about an auction, including a catalog, is housed. Most other paid advertising is just a teaser, a referring tool, to push people to the website.

You and your auctioneer should also investigate what other websites to advertise on. Especially consider websites focused on your specific type of property. If you're selling a rare art collection, check out the price of an ad on a rare art website that is viewed by collectors worldwide.

E-Mail, TV, Direct Mail, and Other Formats

After advertising your auction in the two biggest formats—newspapers and websites—closely consider the other major marketing methods.

As a seller, you should know that a highly effective method to draw people to local auctions of estates and other categories is the local auctioneer's list of e-mail addresses of his or her regular attendees. The auctioneer should prepare an e-mail invitation to your specific auction and send it to all targeted possible attendees, especially those who have bought your type of property in the past from that auctioneer. Be sure to tell your auctioneer you want this service.

Direct mail of brochures, flyers, or printed catalogs to the auctioneer's regular customer list can also be effective, if you are willing to spend money in this area. It's a judgment call. Many times even a color flyer printed by the auctioneer's staff can be effective.

Cable TV and radio ads are a good way to target audiences in geographic regions. Some auctioneers have seen big results, some say they have seen few results, but many are trying cable in their areas.

The runaway growth of cable has resulted in low prices and targeted marketing. "It's one of the best deals out there, and auctioneers that are not using cable are missing out on a great form of marketing," said one auctioneer.

Trade magazines and guidebooks can target specific industries and buyers, and they're not just for the big budget sales. "Some of the collector magazines might be as low as $20 to $50 per year," said Judy Landino, co-owner of D & J Auction Service in Sterling Heights, Michigan. "We have found that putting a small ad in these magazines gets people to your website."

Billboards along roads can also be a highly visible advertising tool, but may be too expensive for a small auction. But, road signs at the auction location saying "Auction here on July 1" are effective in getting attention. Be sure to follow local sign-posting regulations.

Overall, as the seller you should oversee the use of all forms of advertising that may be effective for your auction.

Widen the Venue: Use a Live Internet Broadcast

Every auction seller today also has an option to discuss with the auctioneer whether they should conduct a live audio broadcast of the auction on the Internet, with live bidding accepted over the Internet.

The live broadcast widens your venue from only your local region to the whole world. It is a venue issue, not just a technology issue. Suddenly, your auction is not just a local event, but a global event with global bidders. It costs money to provide this service, so you must discuss these options with your auctioneer.

> **SOLD!**
>
> Many auction company managers routinely reject items of low quality that are unlikely to sell. Not everything a seller offers to an auctioneer is accepted for sale.

What types of auctions justify the cost of adding Internet bidding? Auctions with any items likely to be of interest to people worldwide, meaning the unusual, rare, and collectible. What can bidders not find at a local auction? Rare artworks by a certain artist, collectible toys and dolls, rare coins, to name a few. Think of eBay as an example. People look on there primarily to find what they can't find at a local store or auction.

As a seller, consider these questions when deciding if you want to add a live Internet broadcast and bidding:

> Do you want to use the Internet bidding interactively during the floor auction, which may upset the regular loyal attendees, or do you want to use the Internet to only accept bids prior to the floor auction and then the auctioneer will executive the bids in the same manner as any left bid?

> Do you want to keep the bidder information confidential?

> Do you want access to all the auction bidding information, including under-bidders (such as the second highest bidder)?

So when you think of auction venue, think not only of the local location, but how wide a reach you want. Also think of the different auction formats you want at your venue. There are the traditional onsite live floor auctions, *absentee auctions*, reverse auctions, and others.

The Internet can be used to collect bids for any of these auction methods. Let's discuss the differences between the live floor auction and an absentee auction and how the Internet can support both these auctions.

def•i•ni•tion

Absentee auction is an auction that is conducted remotely, without a bidding room where people participate in the bidding.

To gather your own information about live Internet auction broadcasts, do an Internet search using that exact phrase, or others such as "broadcast auctions" or "online auction service providers." Then read their information and discuss it with your auctioneer.

Also, as an unusual venue, consider the absentee auction. This is an auction that is conducted remotely, without a bidding room where people participate in the bidding. Instead these auctions take place in a room with phones, fax machines, and computers. This is still a live auction, with a location (but not a public one) and can be considered by the seller.

In the old days before the Internet there would be a bid board on the wall where the bids (and up to bids) would be posted so that each person handling a phone would have access to the current bid information. To allow everyone the opportunity to bid, these auctions would usually remain open until the phone did not ring for a period of time, usually 10 to 30 minutes. By adding real-time bidding via the Internet to absentee auctions, most sellers can watch the action on their computer and do not need to call in every few minutes to check the status of their bids.

This has allowed auctioneers more flexibility in the way they choose to close auctions. For example, they can now have each lot close when that lot has been inactive for 10 minutes, keeping only the active lots open.

Real-time Internet bidding for absentee auctions has many other advantages as well. One of the best advantages is that the bidders can examine the bid status on all the lots and look for bargains, what is classically called *bottom fishing*. This will increase the sell price of many of the lots that would otherwise not sell or would sell for the opening bid. A good Internet auction service will allow you to e-mail the invoices at the end of the auction, so that you will get your money from the buyer sooner. An Internet package should offer a variety of other e-mail options as well: an e-mail to all bidders who have not bid, an e-mail to all bidders who are not the high bidder on any lots, and invoice reminders to late payers and all bidders on a specific lot, and more.

Live floor auctions need a set of functions similar to absentee auctions, with additional features. The primary feature they need is an interactive page that displays the lot that is currently on the floor. The display must include the description, the current bid, and whether the remote bidder is the high bidder or not. Also the amount that the remote bidder will be bidding when the Bid button is clicked must be clearly displayed. A picture on the page clarifies which lot is currently on the floor. This page should also offer the bidder the option of bumping the bid by entering any dollar amount higher than the next minimum bid. Space for a message from the auctioneer allows the auctioneer to contact the remote bidders with important information.

Internet bidding packages that are available in the current market offer two distinct methods of accepting remote bids. One method is to have the remote bidder's bid immediately accepted by the computer, the other is to require the clerk to click the Accept button before the bid is accepted. The difference between the two methods can have a major impact on how the bidding proceeds.

In the first case, where the computer immediately accepts the bid, the clerk will offer the bid to the auctioneer. Remember just because the computer has accepted the bid does not mean that the auctioneer has accepted it. The auctioneer can accept the bid from the clerk, or can accept the bid from the floor. When the auctioneer accepts the bid from the floor, the clerk must notify the remote bidder that the bid is on the floor and that their bid has not been accepted.

A robust Internet bidding system will provide a "one-click" solution: the clerk clicks this button and the remote bidder is notified that they do not have the high bid. The major advantage to having the computer accept the remote bid is that other remote bidders are immediately notified that the bid has increased and that they must increase their bid to win the lot. In other words this method allows the remote bidders to raise the bid several times in a few seconds.

The alternative method is where the clerk accepts the bid from the remote bidder only when the auctioneer recognizes the clerk as the high bid. The problem with this system is that other remote bidders cannot bid until the clerk accepts or rejects the bid that is currently being offered. This can cause a backlog of bids and can create a confusion among the remote bidders as to how much they are actually bidding or whether their bid is being handled at all.

The bidder's interactive page should not include a place for the bidder to ask the auctioneer a question. When the lot is open for bidding, it is too late for the bidder to ask a question. The question will interrupt the pace of the auction, and remote bidders just as with attendees have ample time to ask questions prior to the start of the auction and should not be encouraged to interrupt the auction.

The live floor auction will always close one lot at a time, usually in sequence. The software package you select must have the flexibility to allow the auctioneer to skip lots and easily return to them so that when there is a delay in bringing a lot to the floor, the auction can proceed without causing a problem.

When a bidder is ready to leave a floor auction, the Internet package must be ready to print the auction invoice. Remote bidder's invoices should be available to mail immediately upon ending the auction. Similarly consignor payment information should be available at the end of the auction.

Another popular option today is to use the absentee auction Internet package to display the online catalog and to accept bids prior to the auction. Some systems allow remote bidders to actively bid against other bidders during this pre-bidding period, while other systems only allow blind bids (that are not competitively bid). Any good package will allow leaving an "up to" bid. Just before the floor auction starts, the auctioneer has the option to close the Internet bidding and print out a report that is used to bid against the floor on behalf of Internet bidders. Several auctioneers prefer this because they feel it gives them more control then just allowing remote bidders to place bids.

As you can see, there are similarities between the absentee auction and the live floor auction models. The best Internet software packages merge the features of both into one package, providing the auctioneer with the ability to gather bids before the auction, control bidding during the auction, invoice immediately at the end of the auction, and obtain detailed information about all the active Internet bidders.

The Least You Need to Know

- Indoor auctions are usually the best for comfort, safety, and effectiveness in an auction process.

- The auctioneer will recommend the best location to you and tell you why that venue is the best for your type of auction. But the final decision is up to you, as the seller who hires the auctioneer.

- It's important to include your auction location in all advertising.

- Using a live Internet broadcast is like widening your venue from a local to a global stage to reach more bidders.

Seller's Roles at Auction

In This Chapter

◆ Steps to prepare and display your items

◆ Your duties at the auction

◆ When to expect your check

Did you consider that, as the seller, you have roles and duties before, during, and after the auction? A wise businessperson does not just turn over all responsibility to another (be it an auctioneer, banker, attorney, or other) without providing oversight and direction.

This chapter gives you an overview on some of the most important duties and roles you have in the three phases of auction, including duties to protect yourself.

Preparation and Display of Items

In preparing to consign an item or hire an auctioneer, consider these actions as part of your role and duties.

Get Your Item Appraised

Part of your preparation is to get a professional appraisal or do your own research to determine a price value. This is your responsibility to pursue to protect your own interest.

Some auction firms, such as art auction house Bonhams & Butterfields, will evaluate your special items at no charge and in complete confidence. At that firm, for example, you can attend one of their auction appraisal events held regularly at their galleries in San Francisco and Los Angeles and in other major metropolitan areas. You may bring up to five items with you for appraisers to evaluate.

Or you can have the company's specialists conduct insurance and fair market value appraisals. Insurance appraisals, used for insurance purposes, reflect the cost of replacing property in today's retail market. Fair market value appraisals are used for estate, tax, and family division purposes and reflect prices paid by a willing buyer to a willing seller.

Provide Full Item Description

You must provide as full and honest an item description to the auctioneer as possible for posting in the auction catalog and for the auctioneer to describe from the podium on auction day.

Do you know a lot of factual information about your item, or do you know only what grandma told you? Of course, a professional appraisal to determine value will also give you item description details that can be used for the catalog, but if you are not getting a professional appraisal, here are some tips on finding descriptive information yourself.

A catalog entry with description.

6007	1998 Mercedes Benz S320 101,241 miles 3.2L L6 FI Condition 3 Kansas Highway Patrol impound yard Topeka, KS	8500.00	14605
4476	1977 Davis 30+4 trencher Approx. 1900hrs Broken hydraulic hose See disclosure form for details Condition 3 Wichita State University Wichita, KS	7100.00	13252
5181	Ford 8700 tractor with dual rear tires and front weights Condition 3 KSU Animal Sciences and Industry Manhattan, KS	6700.00	12932
1002	1984 Kenworth Construct W900 449,799 miles New batteries See disclosure form for more information Condition 3 Syracuse, KS	6600.00	14635

Let's take artwork, for example. Basic information to provide about a work of art includes its value, the artist who created it, its ownership history, any repairs done to it, and its condition.

> **From the Podium**
>
> Remember that you, as seller, are the boss of your auction and have important roles and duties to all parties.

To do research on the Internet, make a list of keywords that accurately describe your art. These should include the name of the artist; the city, state, region, and country where the art was created; and the type of art, the date, the subject matter, and other pertinent details. Type your keywords into an online auction search engine, such as artbusiness.com, as recommended by eBay.

At this early stage, typing more than one word at a time greatly reduces the number of search matches. Use more than one keyword only when you get hundreds or thousands of matches on a single keyword search. Add keywords one by one until the search narrows and the results pretty accurately match your art.

See how many and what types of items come up on each *keyword search* and compare them to the art you have for sale. Note those keywords that bring up items most similar to your art. Search completed items as well as those currently up for sale. Completed sales give you the most accurate idea of what your art is worth, but may lack pictures (many sellers quickly remove pictures when their auctions end). Sales in progress aren't that good for price research, but they show how active bidding is on particular items and, most important, show images which are essential for comparison with your art.

See what sells for how much. You should have some idea of what art similar to yours sells for online and how common it is when the time comes to set your minimum bid and asking price. When a search yields more than 50 results, arrange and study them in order of selling price, from highest to lowest (eBay has this display option). This shows not only what items get the highest prices, but also what types of title lines, descriptions, and quality of images help fetch those prices.

def•i•ni•tion

> A **keyword search** is done by entering keywords in an Internet search website, such as Google.com, to find the most specific information possible.

When describing your item in a catalog or online, avoid use of words such as "rare," "fantastic," "important," or "famous," recommends artbusiness.com. They may look great and make your art seem special, but they're space wasters that buyers hardly ever type into search engines when looking for items to bid on. Every single title line word you use should give specific information about your art.

Photos for the Catalog

Don't forget how important the online and printed catalogs are for people who can't get to the online auction to bid there. They may be bidding on the Internet, by phone, or by placing an advance bid with the auctioneer.

To help them, use good clear images to show your art. Bidders want to see details. Show the front, back, and other important areas of your art. Show close-ups of signatures, areas of damage, areas that are particularly well done, and other strong points. Good-quality images help sell your art and net you higher prices.

Keep image sizes less than 100K or so to speed downloads for potential bidders. Avoid blurry pictures or ones that are too small. People who cannot clearly see what they're bidding on tend either to bid low or to not bid at all.

The auction firm will likely take the photos of your items for the catalog, but you should check the quality and text descriptions to be sure your items are presented as well as possible.

Also research what specific elements help sell items in your category, such as art. For example, here are some general tips about art auctions from ezine.com. There are exceptions to every rule, but here are a few guidelines to consider when buying/ selling items at an auction:

- Horizontal pictures are better-liked than vertical ones.

- Works featuring girls are more popular than those featuring boys.

- Landscapes prove to be more interesting than seascapes.

- Pictures depicting images of life are more appreciated than death scenes.

- Domestic animals or those in a docile setting are more desirable than wild animals.

- An artist's experimental pieces are not as valuable as those from his/her main body of work.

Set Your Opening Bid and Prices

An important decision you have is to recommend to, or at least agree with, the auctioneer on your item's opening bid, acceptable bid increments, reserve price (if you want one), and the final desired target price. Earlier chapters discuss what these are, but you will want to clarify with the auctioneer how the bidding on your item will proceed.

The more of a bargain an item looks like, often the more bids it attracts. High minimum opening bids and reserves can discourage bidding. Experienced auctioneers know just how to set these amounts, and he or she should tell you how they expect the bidding to proceed from opening bid through the increments to the reserve and beyond. But remember there should be no guarantees on final price, and you likely agreed to that when you signed the auctioneer's contract.

Determine the Auction Company's Services

Do you need to clean and store your item or items before auction, or will the auction staff do that?

To know what things you must do before the auction, and what services the auction firm will provide, ask the auctioneer and check for that information on the company's website.

For example, Absolute Auctions and Realty of New York says on its website that it earns its percentage fee (or commission) by providing the following services:

◆ Storage prior to auction.

◆ Cleaning/polishing/minor repair if required.

◆ Creation and cataloging of each lot (a lot is one item or a group of items sold as one unit).

◆ Photographing of each lot and creation of a professional slideshow presentation and digital catalogs.

◆ Advance auction marketing in print ads via direct mail notices and on website.

◆ Setup of Preview display.

◆ Informing of prospective buyers about your merchandise during Preview.

◆ Auctioning of each lot to floor bidders, absentee bidders, phone bidders, and/or Internet bidders.

◆ State-of-the-art integrated clerking and invoicing system for tracking your sold items.

◆ Complete printout of consigned items, with lot-by-lot breakdown of commission earned and balance due to you, sent with your check 30 days from the date of the auction.

That's a good checklist! With that firm, you do not need to clean and store your item before auction day. With others, you may.

Also find out if your items will be sold individually, in pairs or sets, or in tray lots or box lots. Lesser-valued household items and similar merchandise may be sold in table lots.

Many auction firms sell approximately 80 to 90 lots an hour. All items are cataloged in numerical order, and your consignment code is on the tag of every item. The auction firm can print out a list of your lot numbers so you will be able to estimate the time your items will sell. Find out all this information as part of your preparation.

Do you need to deliver your item to the auction house? Most auction firms will provide trucking services at a competitive fee charged to you. Find out what the fee is. Maybe you can do better with our own transportation arrangements.

Displaying Your Items

Displaying items at auction is an art that has been developed throughout the years to be most efficient for sellers and buyers, and to be efficient on preview day and auction day. The auction staff is usually skilled in this art and will tell you where and how they want to display your items. Listen to them, but also make your own suggestions as to how your items may be displayed for best viewing.

> **From the Podium**
>
> The auction firm will decide how to display your items, but feel free to also make your own suggestions.

Displaying refers to where the items are placed (on tables or a floor), lighting applied (soft or bright), if they are locked for safety (in a gun cabinet or china cabinet), if they are placed low or high, and many other factors.

Items displayed at auction.

Common sense principles include not blocking access for potential buyers to see all surfaces of the item, providing clear light to see any defects, and so on.

You want bidders to stop and see your items during a preview period and during the auction. Customers who stop and look are often the customers who buy. The challenge is to create displays that give them a reason to stop, look, and buy.

Yes, an auction site is not the same as a retail store, but why not think outside the box? Maybe use signage, tastefully, if the auction company allows it. Think how retail stores such as Wal-Mart do product displays and signage.

Also think of safety to your items and to bidders. Don't set glass items where they can easily be knocked off a table. Place trigger locks on guns and put gun racks where you and the auction staff can watch them.

Place tables in a manner that will leave room for customers to browse without feeling crowded. Make sure the tables, items, and areas are all clean, free of sharp edges, and well lighted.

Should You Attend Your Own Auction?

Should the seller attend his or her own auction where his property is sold? Yes! For many reasons you should, unless you anticipate serious problems. We'll discuss the pros and cons here.

You do not have to attend your auction. If you've consigned just one or a few inexpensive items to an auction, typically the seller just gets a check in the mail later. But if you're selling your estate, or you are the legal representative for your parents' estate, for example, you face a decision as to whether to attend the auction.

For an elderly person who has accumulated a lifetime of items, and is now selling them, it may be too hard emotionally to watch his life's collection being sold to strangers. Sellers such as this have broken down crying at auctions. Auctioneers sometimes recommend that these sellers not attend the auction.

> **From the Podium**
>
> It's important for you to physically be at the live auction of your property, unless there is a compelling reason not to be.

But if you can attend, you should. It's important you be there to assist the auctioneer when needed, answer questions from bidders, and watch over your property. This applies to the preview time, also.

The preview is a free public showing of property to be auctioned. The preview is an opportunity for buyers to closely examine individual items prior to the auction. Previews are typically held a day before the auction, or even hours before. For a Saturday night auction, a preview may be held on Friday from 3 P.M. to 9 P.M.

Many auction firms strongly recommended that all buyers preview items prior to bidding because all auction sales are final. So, you want to be there to answer bidders' questions and help the auction staff make sure bidders don't damage or steal your items.

Helping the Auctioneer

On auction day, stay close to the auctioneer so he or she can find you easily, but don't crowd the auctioneer. And, especially when your valuable items come up for auction, watch the auctioneer because he or she may signal you to come talk to him.

Why would he need to talk to you quickly? One example is that, during bidding, your reserve price may not be reached, but the final high bid may be very close to your reserve. If you are standing close by, the auctioneer will seek a quick okay from you to accept the lower price. If you are not present, he would not accept the high bid because he is under contract to sell your item only at the reserve price or higher.

You should also listen to the auctioneer closely when he or she describes the item at the beginning of the bidding. If the auctioneer makes a mistake, such as saying an item is Waterford crystal when it is not, you should correct the auctioneer immediately. The bidders will be relying on the auctioneer's description, and may claim later that they bid specifically because he said "Waterford." But if you help him correct such an error immediately, no dispute can then be made.

Also, make yourself known and available to the clerking staff. They may have questions for you and the auctioneer as the day progresses and buyers are paying and checking out.

Helping Bidders

In the previews, encourage potential bidders to ask as many questions as possible. You want them to be fully informed about what they are bidding on before they bid. This minimizes the chances of problems after an auction has ended.

Answer all bidder questions thoroughly, completely, and quickly. You may make a friend for your next auction item. Also, save all e-mail correspondences with bidders who contact you before, during, or after an auction.

One way for sellers to really anger bidders is to bid on your own items without having announced that openly to the crowd. As discussed in earlier chapters, seller bidding is legal if disclosed. If explained to them, bidders will understand that you can bid on your own items to get the price up to a reserve, but if not explained, they become suspicious and can disrupt an auction with protests. Avoid this problem by being open.

A Few Do's and Don'ts for Sellers

Here are a five do's and five don'ts the seller should follow on auction day:

Do the following:

- Stay close to the auctioneer.

- Meet the auction staff, including the ringmen, who are all working to get the best price for you. Tell them thanks for their help.

- Ask the auction staff if they have questions about your items.

- Watch for theft, concealment, and damage to your items.

- Help bidders by answering all their questions politely.

Do not do the following:

- Lie to any party, from auctioneer to bidders.

- Badger or micro-manage the auctioneer.

- Interrupt the bidding.

- Be overly visible or arrogant, projecting a public image that you are the boss of the event.

- Bid on your own items without announcing that to the audience.

After the Sale: Getting Paid

What is the seller's role after an auction? One duty is to secure and take home immediately any of your items that did not sell. Don't leave them. It's not the auctioneer's responsibility to store them.

Also if an item did not sell, a bidder may still approach you after the auction to make another offer. Keep your eyes open for this. You should also ask the auction company for the names of bidders on your item, if the company has the names, so you can contact them afterward to see if they are still interested. You may decide to drop your price to a level the bidder accepts.

It's also good manners and good business for you and the auction staff to help any buyers in need of loading their new purchases for transport home.

Of course, you're wondering when and how you'll get paid for the items you've sold:

A few auction firms are known to pay the seller at the end of the auction, when possible; but typically it takes 30 days for sellers to get payment because auctioneers must pay expenses from the auction proceeds and it takes time to get payment from absentee bidders, phone bidders and Internet bidders. Auctioneers must keep funds in separate accounts and pay multiple sellers, as occurs in large consignment auctions. It takes time to reconcile balances and verify payments are made correctly.

Here is an example of an auction seller payment and finalization procedure, a description from Absolute Auctions & Realty of New York: "You will receive a complete itemized printout of your items—including lot numbers, descriptions, individual prices, and the net total—and a check from Absolute Auctions & Realty 30 days after the date of the auction. In addition, we send you copies of advertising and any news stories regarding the auction. Last but not least, we provide you with an Auction Evaluation Form asking for your feedback. It will take just a few minutes to complete it and return it in the self-addressed stamped envelope, but it is an important tool for continually improving our services to clients like you."

The large art auction house Bonhams & Butterfields describes their payment procedure, on their website, in the following way: "Payment to consignors after the auction (is made) 35 days after the completion of the sale of any property. We will pay you the net proceeds received and collected from the sale of property after deducting our commission and any other expenses, fees, and charges due hereunder or required by law, provided that no claim has been made against any of the property or proceeds of sale and further provided that the buyer has not given notice of intent to rescind the sale."

Buyer Beware

Don't just walk away immediately when the auction is over. You may miss a post-auction offer.

Be sure to keep copies of all payment papers and other correspondence you receive from an auction company.

The Least You Need to Know

 ◆ The auction staff will decide how your items are displayed at the auction site.

 ◆ Check the auction catalog online and in print to be sure photos and descriptions are correct for your items.

 ◆ Stay close to the auctioneer when your items are being sold so you can answer any questions.

 ◆ Most auction companies pay the seller about 30 days after the auction is completed.

When Problems Arise

In This Chapter

◆ Solve disagreements with the auctioneer

◆ When bidders and buyers create conflict

◆ Top tips to prevent auction problems

Selling your property at live auction usually goes very smoothly. Good preparation, good procedures, and patience get you through this business event easily. But there are times when problems develop. As you will see in this chapter, problems fall into several categories and there are often easy solutions or, at least, good guidelines for solving problems.

Problems with the Auctioneer

Problems with your chosen auctioneer can crop up before, during, and after the auction. If you have chosen an auctioneer that is professional, and whom you seem to get along with easily, you likely will solve problems in short order.

It can be a problem from the start if you and the auctioneer disagree on the planning aspects of the auction, such as when and where the auction is to be held, the format (absolute or reserve), fees, and so on. To solve this problem, keep in mind that you are the boss with the final decisions (you are hiring him, not vice versa), but you are also well advised to take much of the experienced auctioneer's advice.

SOLD! _____

Who are auctioneers? Ninety-three percent of auctioneers are men. Of auctioneers, 35 percent are college graduates, and 35 percent have some college credits.

Present clearly to the auctioneer why you are taking the stand you are on each issue. Do research so you understand the auction formats. Get input from other business professionals, and you may get comparative fees from other local auctioneers when you negotiate with yours. However, be aware that those who cut their costs to the bone may also cut the quality of their services to you.

Solving disagreements can be done with compromise and trust. The relationship between seller and auctioneer should include these elements, also.

Unreasonable or Exact Price Expectations

An important problem to avoid is for the seller to have unreasonably high price expectations, or even an exact price expectation. Sellers sometimes expect a far higher price for their items than can be obtained at auction.

For example, an auction company will often publish in the auction catalog an expected price range for the item. This alerts bidders of the expected value range, but is no guarantee to any party. However, it can create an expectation that some sellers rely on. That is why auctioneers often have language in their contract that the published price range is not any promise of the price to be obtained.

From the Podium

You must accept that auction prices are unpredictable. Don't expect an exact price or range.

The auctioneer will try to get the highest price possible for the seller, but should not make price promises. A real-life example occurred when an auctioneer was contacted later by a client who said the auctioneer sold the client's furniture piece too low at $250. The client had agreed to sell with no reserve (no minimum price required) for the piece, but the auctioneer also had published the estimate in the catalog at $750 to $1,000, trying to get the interest level up. Which party was right?

Attorney Kurt Bachman says this issue depends on the language in their contract and the auctioneer's actions as the agent for the seller. Sellers commonly complain about the purchase price of items sold by absolute auction (no reserve). When items are sold at an absolute auction, there is always a risk that the item will be sold for less than the appraised or fair market value. When discussing the possible sale of property with the seller, an auctioneer should advise the seller on the benefits and risks of selling property without a reserve.

The seller should understand the risk and fully accept it. Don't gripe later if you agreed earlier! If you don't want to risk it, put a reserve price on your item. The auctioneer should also advise the seller on the appropriate amount for the reserve.

Auctioneers also try to be careful not to make estimates to the seller about what price they think the item will bring. This is hard because sellers ask that question. Naturally, you want to know, but don't fall prey to your own unreasonable expectations.

When an Auctioneer Refuses You

Sometimes an auctioneer will decline to do business with you for some reason. The auctioneer may find that your property is not suited to an auction, that he is not suited to best sell your property, that you cannot agree on terms, or many other reasons.

Solve this problem by getting a referral to another auctioneer. Sometimes one of you initially won't trust each other for some reason.

Sometimes sellers are just looking around for free appraisals and free advice on how to sell their property. Don't be one of those. Profitable business is based on strong and honest relationships between you both. Anybody who constantly questions your recommendations, nit-picks at your decisions or judgment, is not interested in developing a good business event with you.

Don't Lie

Sellers sometimes create problems with the auctioneer (and buyers) by telling lies or misleading them about the item being sold.

Don't mislead anyone about clear title to ownership or about the condition of an item.

Sometimes sellers who know items are stolen will try to sell them at auction before the authorities can catch up to the seller. But auctioneers are watching for clues to this, including a vague or unrealistic background story, little knowledge of the item, and an eager willingness to accept a price far below wholesale value.

Merchandise doesn't have to be stolen to present problems for seller and auctioneer. If ownership of the item is under dispute, you can get caught in the middle. Angry parties from legal dissolution and divorce cases, which are eager to dispose of merchandise before ownership can be contested, often offer merchandise to auctioneers.

Most auctioneers have a statement in their listing agreement that specifically says that the seller of the property represents and warrants that they have good and clear title to that property. If you don't truly have clear title, don't lie to anyone about it.

Auctioneers and savvy bidders now check the Internet for stolen items, because the web provides a host of national and worldwide resources for identifying almost any imaginable type of stolen property. Many state and local law enforcement agencies have websites such as the Los Angeles Police Department's at www.lapdonline.org, which includes an extensive section listing stolen art. All local police departments can be found online at www.usacops.com. They also check for stolen motorcycles and vehicles at www.tshooters.com/stolen/stolen.htm.

Problems with Buyers and Bidders

One of the problems you have with buyers is collecting money after the auction. This can be when they go to pay at the clerking desk, or if they stop payment on a check days later. Because the buyer is technically buying from you, the seller, it is up to you to collect, but the auctioneer will often help with that process.

Let's look at one situation. What happens if a bidder forgot his checkbook, and wanted to buy a large item such as a tractor, or even bid on a piece of real estate? Should the seller accept a promissory note to be redeemed with cash or certified funds later?

Buyer Beware

The seller, not the auction-eer, is generally responsible for collecting nonpayment from buyers.

The issues that arise from nonpayment of a promissory note are similar to those that arise with a check. One benefit to securing payment by a promissory note is that you can add specific provisions for the repayment.

For example, in the event of a default, a promissory note should permit the recovery of collection costs and expenses, including reasonable attorney fees. A check, however, will usually result in a faster payment. Nonpayment of a check is also a criminal violation in some jurisdictions. Promissory notes and checks are common forms of payment—which one is better for you will depend on your business and situation.

Bidders at auction.

The seller is generally responsible for collecting for nonpayment from a buyer. The auctioneer is the agent of the seller. His job is to bring a willing buyer and a willing seller together to complete the transaction. The resulting contract is between the buyer and seller. Therefore, when a buyer fails to pay for an item the seller should generally sue for breach of contract (even when the check or promissory note is made payable to the auctioneer). Because the auctioneer is not a party to the contract the auctioneer normally cannot bring a claim for breach of contract.

An auctioneer, however, may bring a claim against a debtor for a bad check or for failure to pay a promissory note if the check or note are made payable to the auctioneer. The costs and expenses involved in attempting to collect the debt may discourage auctioneers from seeking to recover payment. As a practical matter, however, an auctioneer may be willing to try collecting from the buyer to make sure he or she obtains his commission.

Preventing Theft by Attendees

As you walk around at your auction, you may see attendees trying to steal items, conceal items, or damage items, especially in a preview period. This is a problem the auctioneer and his staff should be watching for, and intervening when necessary. Many auctions also have a uniformed security guard that can take action for you.

Here's an example of concealment that you might see. An auctioneer says that "At an auction, one of our floor workers spotted two women hiding several pieces of nice glass in some box lots of small household items. These boxes would never bring more than a few dollars each. We planned to sell the pieces of glass individually, as we expected them to bring more than $50 apiece. It was obvious these women were attempting to 'buy' these pieces for nothing by purchasing the boxes for very little. Of course, this would hurt our consignors and us. When we confronted the women, they denied doing anything wrong and said they just wanted the items grouped."

What can you, the seller, or the auctioneer do? Attorney Steve Proffitt says that three things can be done:

First, the auctioneer has a legal right to deny admission to the auction to any person the auctioneer deems to be abusive, disorderly, intoxicated, or noncompliant with the rules and terms for the auction, or a potential threat to be such.

Second, the auctioneer announces that he has arranged the merchandise for the auction and directs that it not be altered, moved, or disturbed in any way by any person, other than normal inspection at the spot where the merchandise is located. The auction staff will assist anyone who has a question or request about a lot or item. In the event any person, other than a member of the auction staff, is detected altering, moving, or otherwise disturbing any merchandise, that person will be required to immediately leave the auction, not return, and, at the discretion of the auctioneer, may be barred from future auctions.

Third, the auctioneer can announce that any instance of theft or vandalism will be prosecuted to the fullest extent of the law. You want to convey a clear and bold message that leaves no room for misunderstanding the rules.

But, you and the auctioneer should never jump to conclusions. When an issue arises, try to learn as much as you can before you do anything. If action is necessary, try to handle the matter quietly. You never want to make a public spectacle and embarrass someone or publicly brand that person "a thief," even if you're right. Such is the fertile soil from which lawsuits sometimes sprout and then you would be on the defensive. Take the person off to the side and address the issue, with at least one witness.

Never try to physically eject someone from your auction. Never touch such a person in any way, lest you find yourself on the wrong end of a warrant for assault and battery and a visit by the police.

Bidders Dispute the Announcements

Sometimes a bidder will not hear the auction day announcement that the terms of the auction have been changed. They may say "You can't do that. You have to stick to the printed terms I read earlier."

Not true. Auction day announcements generally do take precedence over prior advertisements. Auctioneers can generally correct any errors or advise the audience of any issues that have come up.

However, an exception is that auctioneers should not attempt to convert an absolute auction to a reserve auction on the day of the sale. The fact an auction is advertised as absolute creates the expectation that the sale will be conducted as an absolute auction. An exception is that there can be extenuating circumstances. The auctioneer can cancel the absolute aspect and as a courtesy to bidders, and with their permission, open the bidding subject to seller confirmation. Bidders can travel from far away, incurring time and travel expenses, to attend the auction because the sale being advertised is absolute. That auction should be conducted in the manner specified in the advertisements.

Buyer Refuses to Complete Payment

There are times when a buyer will dispute the bid price he gave, soon after or at a later time, and do it through his credit card company. This is a collection problem. The auctioneer may or may not help you with this situation.

Here is a story about that from an auctioneer who sold a 1970s muscle car, and the story of how he dealt with the problem.

"The owner and I expected the car to bring $3,000 to $3,500," he said. "The whole auction fell into place wonderfully. The right buyers were there; we could tell by how well the parts and accessories were selling.

We had the car strategically placed in the auction to sell about 90 minutes to 2 hours into the auction. The crowd was in a good mood and having fun. The car went up on the block. As the auctioneer, I was optimistic. I asked for a bid of $8,000. The opening bid was $2,000, then bidding went to $3,000 and $4,000. The bidding was fast and aggressive.

The next bid was $5,000 and then continued in $500 increments right up to $9,000. We weren't done yet.

The bids kept coming in from three bidders and came to rest at $11,000 (more than three times what we had expected!). The seller was happy, while the whole crowd was buzzing. We had hit a home run! The rest of the auction was fun and aggressive, it went well.

At the end of the auction I asked the cashiers how the buyer paid for the car. We generally hold titles if a buyer pays by noncertified check. I thought this might be the case. I was told that the man paid by credit card and he received his signed title.

I was a little surprised that he put $11,000 on his card. That is when they told me he only paid $1,000 for the car. I told them they must have misread the clerk sheet. The cashier said 'no.'

The buyer asked us to double-check the clerk sheet, he wanted to be sure it was correct. I couldn't believe it. My clerk must have been hypnotized, and she missed it big time. I looked at his receipt and saw that the only other purchase he made was a box of radios for $110, so his bill came out to $1,110. It should have been $11,110.

As most people are honest I jumped to the conclusion that in the excitement of being the winning bidder he must have misread the receipt and would honor the difference to be put on his credit card. I called the phone number he provided and talked to a woman who claimed to be the buyer's wife. I told her that her husband left the site and had been charged an incorrect amount, and that I was going to put the difference on the same credit card he used earlier. I also told her to have him call me if there were any questions. She said he was not home yet but that would be fine. I ran the card using the numbers off his receipt and it went right through. I paid the seller, and we went on with life.

Two and a half months later I received a notice from my credit card service that I had been accused of a fraudulent charge and that they had removed $10,000 from my account.

I was given a chance to explain my position. I had provided the card service company with the chain of events, 10 pages of supporting information (from terms and conditions to flyers, and so on). The item that I was sure was my 'ace in the hole' was that I had used a digital voice recorder. I had a copy burned on CD and included that in my answer, but I found that MasterCard and Visa will not consider any recordings when settling disputes.

Because the buyer did not sign for the additional $10,000, the credit card company considered I was out of luck. I called the prosecuting attorney for that jurisdiction and he was not interested and gave me a runaround.

I called the police for their assistance. They said that they would try to help if I couldn't work it out on my own. I called the buyer; his memory was not so good. I told him I had a voice recording of the auction. He said if he could hear the bidding, he would be sure to make it right. What he was really saying was 'Prove you have a recording.' I sent him the recording and after several more phone call attempts, contacted the police. An officer convinced this guy that, with that recording and the amount of money involved he was going to lock him up on a felony conviction, so the guy finally paid me."

Problems with Outside Parties

In the preparation or sale of your property at live auction, you may have problems with outside parties. In other chapters we've already discussed how family members, especially siblings, can create problems in estate auctions. Let's look at a different type of situation.

A problem with real estate is that some sellers want their property at auction to be listed with their local *MLS (Multiple Listing Service)* board, which shows properties for sale in traditional listings. But, most MLS listing boards do not allow listings sold by auction.

A solution is to examine the listing service agency's written contract with the MLS board. The contract would state the terms and conditions for using the MLS service. The listing service agency should review the contract to make sure that the MLS board is in compliance with it. It may be that the contract does not prohibit using the word "auction" or other auction terms in the MLS listing. If necessary, you can contact a local attorney to help you review the contract.

def•i•ni•tion

The **MLS (Multiple Listing Service)** is a listing of properties for sale by real estate agents. Most in use today do not allow auction listings.

If the MLS board is violating the contract by refusing to allow the word "auction" and other auction terms in the MLS listing, the listing agency could threaten to sue for breach of contract. The threat of the lawsuit may be enough to get their attention and encourage the board to comply.

There also may be other issues involved. The MLS board could be engaging in unfair competition or in violation of state or federal anti-trust laws.

Repossession

You may be selling an item in an auction and find that an outside party tries to repossess it. Maybe you thought you had fully satisfied a previous debt on the item. What can you do?

An auctioneer had this situation when he took a consignment of a living room set that the owner recently purchased from a store that was liquidated. The manager of the store told the auctioneer that the furniture was, in his opinion, not fully paid for. But the consignor had showed the auctioneer a receipt for the furniture.

The answer is that, as with any auction, the answer will depend to a great extent on the contractual relationship of the parties. The general rule is that title to goods sold at auction passes at the fall of the hammer. However, as with any other sale, an auction may be subject to an express condition, such as payment in full, so that title does not pass to the buyer until that condition is satisfied.

So the terms of the sale between the consignor and the furniture store control the situation. A solution may be to sell the item at auction and the parties would agree, in writing, that the money is distributed so the store owner receives the outstanding amount due him and the consignor receives the balance.

Five Tips to Prevent Auction Problems

Be skeptical. Be skeptical of everybody in the auction transaction. They are not your relatives, spouses, or best friends. This is a buy-and-sell business deal. Prudence requires that you deal with them at arm's length. People lie, so it's incumbent that you be inquisitive and skeptical about all the factors that relate to your decisions, says auction attorney Steve Proffitt.

Question everything. Develop a detailed checklist of questions to ask your auctioneer at each stage. This can be a contract to take valuable asset to auction. Still, asking good questions is only half the formula to learning the truth. Be a good listener and understand the answers that people give to those questions. Then auctioneers should use their logic and experience to carefully weigh these answers. Take nothing for granted and nothing at face value. Instead, be objective and consider whether answers make sense.

Research public records. Research public records for judgments and liens that are recorded against your own property, if you have any question about it. The auctioneer will be doing this to protect himself, and find out about your credibility.

Remember the "reasonable care" standard. In all that sellers and auctioneers do they should be very careful! The reasonable standard under which most auctioneers work is "reasonable care." This is the degree of care that a reasonable person would have exercised under the same circumstances. Your employee, the auctioneer, must use reasonable care in their dealings with you and your assets.

Document everything. Anything important should be documented and you should do that as the seller. Letters, faxes, notes, e-mails, contracts, inventories, accountings, and telephone messages are all examples of important business records to organize and preserve in permanent files. Sure, it takes a few extra minutes to write down what you're doing and why you're doing it, but it doesn't take nearly as long as it would to defend a lawsuit over a matter that a written record might have squelched.

The Least You Need to Know

◆ Unreasonable or exact price expectations on an item create problems between the seller and auctioneer. Auction prices are unpredictable.

◆ The seller is generally responsible for collecting nonpayment from buyers.

◆ Never physically throw out a bidder from an auction yourself. Call the police.

◆ To solve disputes, document everything.

Glossary

absentee bid   A procedure which allows a bidder to participate in the bidding process without being physically present. Generally, a bidder submits an offer on an item prior to the auction. Absentee bids are usually handled under an established set of guidelines by the auctioneer or his representative. The particular rules and procedures of absentee bids are unique to each auction company.

absentee bidder   A person (or entity) who does not attend the sale but submits, in advance, a written or oral bid that is the top price he or she will pay for a given property.

absolute auction   An auction where the property is sold to the highest qualified bidder with no limiting conditions or amount. The seller may not bid personally or through an agent. Also known as an auction without reserve.

accounting of sale   A report issued to the seller by the auctioneer detailing the financial aspects of the auction.

Accredited Auctioneer Real Estate (AARE) Certified Estate Specialist (CES)   The professional designation indicating expertise in conducting auctions of real estate.

agent   A person who acts for or in the place of another individual or entity by authority from them.

appraisal   The act or process of estimating value.

apprentice auctioneer   An auctioneer who is in training, operating under the supervision of a licensed or experienced auctioneer.

as-is   Selling a property without warranties as to the condition and/or the fitness of the property for a particular use. Buyers are solely responsible for examining and judging a property for their own protection. Otherwise known as as-is, where is and in its present condition.

auction   A method of selling property in a public forum through open and competitive bidding. Also referred to as public auction, auction sale, or sale.

auction block   The podium or raised platform where the auctioneer stands while conducting the auction. "Placing (an item) on the auction block" means to sell something at auction.

auction listing agreement   A contract executed by the auctioneer and the seller which authorizes the auctioneer to conduct the auction and sets out the terms of the agreement and the rights and responsibilities of each party.

auction marketer   An individual who contracts with sellers for the auction method of marketing property. In the case of real property, he or she may not actually conduct the sale but is directly responsible for all aspects of marketing the property.

auction marketing   The method of marketing real property utilizing the auction method of sale.

auction plan   The plan for pre-auction, auction day, and post auction activities.

auction price   The price of a property obtained through the auction method of marketing.

auction subject to confirmation   *See* reserve auction.

Auction Technology Specialist (ATS)   The professional designation indicating expertise in auction technology.

auction value   The price which a particular property brings in open competitive bidding at public auction.

auction with reserve   An auction in which the seller or his agent reserves the right to accept or decline any and all bids. A minimum acceptable price may or may not be disclosed and the seller reserves the right to accept or decline any bid within a specified time.

auction without reserve   *See* absolute auction.

auctioneer   The person whom the seller engages to direct, conduct, or be responsible for a sale by auction. This person may or may not actually call or cry the auction.

auctioneer subcontractor   An auctioneer hired by the principal auctioneer.

ballroom auction   An auction of one or more properties conducted in a meeting room facility.

bank letter of credit   A letter from a bank certifying that a named person is worthy of a given level of credit. Often requested from prospective bidders or buyers who are not paying with currency at auctions.

Benefit Auction Specialist (BAS)   The professional designation by the National Auctioneers Association indicating expertise in the techniques of creating successful benefit auctions.

bid   A prospective buyer's indication or offer of a price he or she will pay to purchase property at auction. Bids are usually in standardized increments established by the auctioneer.

bid acknowledgment   A form executed by the high bidder confirming and acknowledging the bidder's identity, the bid price, and the description of the property. Also known as memorandum.

bid assistants   Individuals who are positioned throughout the attendees at the auction to assist the auctioneer, spot bidders, and assist prospective bidders with information to help them in their buying decision. Also known as ringmen, bid consultants, bid spotters, or groundsmen.

bid caller   The person who actually calls, cries, or auctions the property at an auction, recognizing bidders and acknowledging the highest bidder. Commonly known as an auctioneer.

bid rigging   The unlawful practice whereby two or more people agree not to bid against one another so as to deflate value.

bidder number   The number issued to each person who registers at an auction.

bidder package   The package of information and instructions pertaining to the property to be sold at an auction event obtained by prospective bidders at an auction. Sometimes called a bidder packet or due diligence package.

bidder's choice   A method of sale whereby the successful high bidder wins the right to choose a property or properties from a grouping of similar or like-kind properties. After the high bidder's selection, the property is deleted from the group. The second round of bidding then commences, with the high bidder in round two choosing a property, which is then deleted from the group and so on, until all properties are sold.

bookkeeper or clerk   The person who is responsible for the accounting and paperwork at an auction sale.

broker participation   An arrangement for third-party brokers to register potential bidders for properties being sold at auction for a commission paid by the owner of the property or the auction firm.

buyer's broker   A real estate broker who represents the buyer and, as the agent of the buyer, is normally paid for his or her services by the buyer.

buyer's premium   An advertised percentage of the high bid or flat fee added to the high bid to determine the total contract price to be paid by the buyer.

caravan auctions   A series of onsite auctions advertised through a common promotional campaign.

carrying charges   The costs involved in holding a property which is intended to produce income (either by sale or rent) but has not yet done so, for example, insurance, taxes, maintenance, management.

catalog or brochure   A publication advertising and describing the property(ies) available for sale at public auction, often including photographs, property descriptions, and the terms and conditions of the sale.

caveat emptor   A Latin term meaning "let the buyer beware." A legal maxim stating that the buyer takes the risk regarding quality or condition of the property purchased, unless protected by warranty.

Certified Auctioneers Institute (CAI)   The professional designation awarded to practicing auctioneers who meet the experiential, educational, and ethical standards set by the NAA Education Institute.

Certified Estate Specialist (CES)   The professional designation indicating expertise in marketing services to professionals who deal with estates.

clerk   The person employed by the principal auctioneer or auction firm to record what is sold and to whom and for what price.

collusion   The unlawful practice whereby two or more people agree not to bid against one another so as to deflate value or when the auctioneer accepts a fictitious bid on behalf of the seller so as to manipulate or inflate the price of the property.

commission   The fee charged to the seller by the auctioneer for providing services, usually a percentage of the gross selling price of the property established by contract (the listing agreement) prior to the auction.

conditions of sale   The legal terms that govern the conduct of an auction, including acceptable methods of payment, terms, buyer's premiums, possession, reserves, and any other limiting factors of an auction. Usually included in published advertisements or announced by the auctioneer prior to the start of the auction.

contract   An agreement between two or more persons or entities which creates or modifies a legal relationship.

cooperating broker   A real estate broker who registers a prospective buyer with the auction company, in accordance with the terms and conditions for that auction. The broker is paid a commission only if his prospect is the high bidder and successfully closes on the property. Also known as a participating broker.

critical path   Sequence of key tasks to be done by an auction contractor or other designated parties on specified dates, leading to desired goals.

dual agency   The representation of opposing principals (buyers and sellers) at the same time.

due diligence   The process of gathering information about the condition and legal status of assets to be sold.

estate sale   The sale of property left by a person at his or her death. An estate auction can involve the sale of personal and/or real property.

Graduate, Personal Property Appraiser (GPPA)   The professional designation awarded by the NAA Education Institute (formerly American Marketing Institute) to qualified property appraisers who meet the educational and experiential requirements of the Institute and who adhere to a strict code of ethics and standards of practice. GPPA-M indicates a master level of expertise with multiple years experience in personal property appraising.

groundsman   *See* bid assistants.

hammer price   Price established by the last bidder and acknowledged by the auctioneer before dropping the hammer or gavel.

listing agreement   *See* auction listing agreement.

listing broker   A real estate broker who has a listing on a property and cooperates with the auction company by allowing the auction agreement to supersede his or her listing agreement.

market value   The highest price in terms of money which a property will bring in a competitive and open market under all conditions requisite to a fair sale, the buyer and seller, each acting prudently, knowledgeably, and assuming the price is not affected by undue stimulus.

memorandum   Sometimes also referred to as a bidder acknowledgment, or broker acknowledgment, the memorandum is signed by those parties either on the auction floor or in the contract room.

minimum bid auction   An auction in which the auctioneer will accept bids at or above a disclosed price. The minimum price is always stated in the brochure and advertisements and is announced at the auctions.

multi-property auction   A group of properties offered through a common promotional campaign. The properties to be auctioned may be owned by one seller or multiple sellers.

multi-seller auction   Properties owned by many sellers, offered through a common promotional campaign, are auctioned in a single event.

National Auctioneers Association (NAA)   An association of individual auctioneers united to promote the professionalism of auctioneers and auctions through education and technology.

National Real Estate Auction Committee (NREAC)   A national committee developed by the National Association of Realtors in April, 1990 to provide education to members concerning real estate auctions, to identify issues, and monitor, review, and analyze trends affecting the real estate auction industry. It also is charged with formulating policies for consideration by other policy-making NAR committees, its executive committee, and board of directors.

no-sale fee   A charge paid by the owner of property offered at a reserve auction when the property does not sell.

onsite auction   An auction conducted on the premises of the property being sold.

opening bid   The first bid offered by a bidder at an auction.

participating broker   *See* cooperating broker.

preview   Specified date and time property is available for prospective buyer viewing and audits. Also known as an open house or inspection.

referring broker   A real estate broker who does not have a listing on a property, but refers the auction company to a potential seller for an auction. Usually earns a flat-fee commission for referring product to an auction company.

regroup   A process used in real estate auctions where a bidder has the opportunity to combine several parcels of land previously selected by other bidders, thereby creating one larger parcel out of several smaller parcels. This process is often used in conjunction with bidder's choice.

reserve   The minimum price that a seller is willing to accept for a property to be sold at auction. Also known as the reserve price.

reserve auction   An auction in which the seller reserves the right to establish a reserve price, to accept or decline any and all bids, or to withdraw the property at any time prior to the announcement of the completion of the sale by the auctioneer. *See* auction with reserve.

sales manager   The person designated by the auction company who is responsible for organizing the details of an auction. Also known as a project manager.

sealed bid   A method of sale utilized where confidential bids are submitted to be opened at a predetermined place and time. Not a true auction in that it does not allow for reaction from the competitive market place.

seller   Entity that has legal possession (ownership) of any interests, benefits, or rights inherent to the real or personal property.

subject to confirmation   *See* reserve auction.

tax sale   Public sale of property at auction by governmental authority, due to nonpayment of property taxes.

terms   The period of time that an agreement is in effect.

terms and conditions   The printed rules of the auction and certain aspects of the Purchase and Sale Agreement that are read and/or distributed to potential bidders prior to an auction sale.

tie bids   When two or more bidders bid exactly the same amount at the same time and must be resolved by the auctioneer.

trustee's sale   A sale at auction by a trustee.

upset price   Commonly known as the reserve price.

withdrawal   Failure to reach the reserve price or insufficient bidding.

Allied Organizations and Resources

The following organizations are allied with the live auction industry and can offer information.

National Auctioneer License Law Officials Association (NALLOA)

NALLOA provides a forum for states with auction license laws that are members of NALLOA to communicate and strive to endorse reciprocity (acceptance of each state's licensed auctioneers to practice in neighboring states).

President:

Robert A. Hamilton
602 Stellata Drive
Fuquay-Varina, NC 27526

919-567-2844

bob@ncalb.org

Executive Secretary:
Barbara Schoen
10524 Providence Drive
Louisville, KY 40291

502-239-6772

Shoenhors@aol.com

National Association of Realtors

NAR helps its members become more profitable and successful. It seeks to be the leading advocate of the right to own, use, and transfer real property. NAR provides professional development, research, and exchange of information among its members and to the public and government for the purpose of preserving the free enterprise system and the right to own, use, and transfer real property. NAR also has an auction committee and promotes the auction method for the sale of some properties.

www.realtor.org

Chicago (Headquarters)
National Association of REALTORS
430 North Michigan Avenue
Chicago, IL 60611-4087

Washington, D.C.
National Association of REALTORS
700 Eleventh Street NW
Washington, DC 20001-4507

American Bankruptcy Institute

ABI is dedicated to research and education on matters related to insolvency. ABI was founded in 1982 to provide Congress and the public with unbiased analysis of bankruptcy issues. ABI membership includes 7,500 attorneys, auctioneers, bankers, judges, lenders, professors, turnaround specialists, accountants, and other bankruptcy professionals providing a forum for the exchange of ideas and information. ABI is engaged in numerous educational and research activities, as well as the production of a number of publications both for the insolvency practitioner and the public.

www.abiworld.org

American Bankruptcy Institute
44 Canal Center Plaza, Suite 404
Alexandria, VA 22314

703-739-0800
703-739-1060 (fax)

Livestock Marketing Association

In 1947, the National Livestock Auction Association began as a grass roots organization dedicated to providing auction marketers with access to the latest industry information and a voice in federal and state government. In October 1978, punctuating 30 years of action in legislation, LMA successfully challenged the authority of the Packers and Stockyards Act to regulate tariffs and fees charged by independent auction markets. LMA's landmark legal victory freed auction markets to determine and post their own charges for service, independent of government intervention.

www.lmaweb.com

Livestock Marketing Association
10510 NW Ambassador Drive
Kansas City, MO 64153

1-800-821-2048
816-891-0502
816-891-7926 (fax)

lmainfo@lmaweb.com

Farm Credit Consulting Services, Inc.

Farm Credit Consulting Services helps organizations successfully navigate today's critical business and leadership challenges by reducing costs, improving efficiency and results, or attracting and retaining top talent, and developing them for the future. The company partners with clients to find business solutions and develop innovative strategies that will position them as market leaders.

www.fccservices.com

FCC Services, Inc.
PO Box 5130
Denver, CO 80217

720-747-4200
720-747-4202 (fax)
1-888-ASK-FCCS

St. Jude Children's Research Hospital

The mission of St. Jude Children's Research Hospital is to find cures for children with catastrophic illnesses through research and treatment.

www.stjude.org

American Society of Appraisers

The American Society of Appraisers is an organization of appraisal professionals and others interested in the appraisal profession.

www.appraisers.org

Books

The following books about the live auction business can all be found on Amazon. com, and other outlets for purchase. Their titles and date of publication are listed in the next section.

Nonfiction Titles

Bradley, Sandy. *Benefit Auctions: A Fresh Formula for Grassroots Fundraising.* Paperback, 2004.

Furr, James W. *How to Buy Cars & Trucks, Vans & SUVs At Wholesale Prices From Government Auctions.* Paperback, 2006.

Hildesley, C. Hugh. *The Complete Guide to Buying & Selling at Auction.* Hardcover, 1997.

Hindman, Leslie. *Adventures at the Auction: The Ultimate Guide to Buying and Selling at Auction In Person and Online*. Paperback, 2002.

Martin, Stephen J. and Thomas E. Battle III. *SOLD!: The Professional's Guide To Real Estate Auctions*. Paperback, 2005.

Mays, James. *The Savvy Guide To Buying Collector Cars at Auction*. Paperback, 2006.

Menezes, Flavio M. and Paulo K. Monteiro. *An Introduction to Auction Theory*. Hardcover, 2004.

O'Keef, Richard. *Shake the Money Tree: How to Produce a Winning Fundraising Event With a Live and Silent Auction*. Paperback, 2007.

Rogers, Barbara. *How to Make Boxes of Cash with Self-Storage Auctions*. Paperback, 2007.

Stefanick, Frank. *Inside The Auction Game*. Paperback, 1991.

Fiction Titles

Honness, Elizabeth. *Mystery of the Auction Trunk*. Hardcover, 1956.

Mcallister, Anne. *The Great Montana Cowboy Auction*. Paperback, 2002.

Vizurraga, Susan. *Miss Opal's Auction*. Hardcover, 2000.

Chapter

Sample Forms

The documents included in this appendix are the Buyer Registration form and the Absentee Bid form. Please review each carefully.

****

Buyer Registration   Date _____
Please Print

Name_____
            Last   First   MI

Home Address_____
              Street Address   City   State   Zip

Company Address_____
              Street Address   City   State   Zip

Phone_____   Phone_____

          Home #   Company #

E-mail Address_____
Drivers Lic. #_____

Would You Like to Be Added to Our Mailing List?: Yes / No
Method: Mail / E-mail/ Fax # _____

Method of Payment

1.____ Company check w/bank letter guaranteeing payment for this auction only

2.____ Personal check (any out-of-state check requires a Bank Letter of Guarantee)

3.____ Cashier's check or certified check

4.____ Cash

Terms of Auction

1. ALL BIDDERS and others attending this auction agree that they have read and fully understand these and all terms posted at auction office (cashier station) and agree to be bound thereby. This is a partial list of terms for the auction. A more detailed list of terms is posted at the cashier station. (Please read all terms.) The auctioneer also reserves the right to add or change terms by posting or oral announcement at the auction.

2. IDENTIFICATION: All purchasers are required to have a Bidder's Number to bid. Please provide accurately and completely, all information and signatures required.

3. PLEASE show your number to the clerk after each purchase to eliminate possible error.

4. DISPUTE BETWEEN BIDDERS: If any dispute arises between two or more bidders, the auctioneer may decide the same or may immediately put the lot up for sale again and re-sell to the highest bidder. The decision of the auctioneer shall be final and absolute.

5. AS IS: Each item is sold "As Is, Where Is." Make sure you have inspected the items before you purchase. All sales are final. The Auction Company assumes no liability for owners of guarantee.

6. RESPONSIBILITY: Purchaser assumes complete responsibility for item immediately upon the auctioneer saying "sold."

7. PAYMENT: Complete payment in full is required day of auction. Nothing is to be removed from premises before settlement.

8. CLAIMS: No claims will be allowed after goods are removed from premises.

9. RECORDS: The record of sale kept by the auctioneer and clerk will be taken as final in the event of any dispute.

10. PERSONAL AND PROPERTY RISKS: Persons attending during exhibition, auction, or removal of goods assume all risks of, damage of, or loss to person and/or personal property, and specifically release the auctioneer from liability; therefore, neither the auctioneer nor his principal shall be liable by reason of a defect in or condition of the premises on which the auction is held.

11. AGENCY: The auctioneer is acting as agent for seller only and is not responsible for the act of its principals.

12. LEGAL ACTION: Bidder agrees that any legal proceedings arising out of this auction, including any litigation, will be initiated against bidder in (this county) and (this state's) law will govern.

13. THANK YOU for attending today's auction.

****

BIDDER # _____

Absentee Bid

I wish to place the following bid(s) at the auction to be held on _____
_____ at the XYZ Auction Center. I understand the auction staff will
execute the bids as a convenience to me and will not be held responsible for any
errors or failure to execute bids. I understand that my bids are placed subject to the
Absentee Bid Terms of this company., and that I will be responsible for the purchase
price, which includes the buyer's premium, as well as all applicable taxes or shipping
costs. Shipment will not be made until payment has been received. **NOTE: The lot
is handwritten on tag in red. <u>Please print clearly.</u>**

Lot # ____	Bid $ ____	Lot # ____	Bid $ ____	Lot # ____	Bid $ ____
Lot # ____	Bid $ ____	Lot # ____	Bid $ ____	Lot # ____	Bid $ ____
Lot # ____	Bid $ ____	Lot # ____	Bid $ ____	Lot # ____	Bid $ ____
Lot # ____	Bid $ ____	Lot # ____	Bid $ ____	Lot # ____	Bid $ ____
Lot # ____	Bid $ ____	Lot # ____	Bid $ ____	Lot # ____	Bid $ ____
Lot # ____	Bid $ ____	Lot # ____	Bid $ ____	Lot # ____	Bid $ ____
Lot # ____	Bid $ ____	Lot # ____	Bid $ ____	Lot # ____	Bid $ ____
Lot # ____	Bid $ ____	Lot # ____	Bid $ ____	Lot # ____	Bid $ ____
Lot # ____	Bid $ ____	Lot # ____	Bid $ ____	Lot # ____	Bid $ ____
Lot # ____	Bid $ ____	Lot # ____	Bid $ ____	Lot # ____	Bid $ ____
Lot # ____	Bid $ ____	Lot # ____	Bid $ ____	Lot # ____	Bid $ ____
Lot # ____	Bid $ ____	Lot # ____	Bid $ ____	Lot # ____	Bid $ ____

****

Index

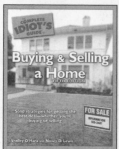

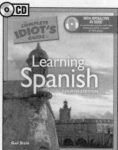

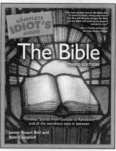